With The Prep's Centenary approaching, it seemed important to write a history of the school and to bring Peter Larcombe's history of the first 65 years up to date. We approached David Williams, an eminent local historian who had just finished co-authoring *Ightham: At the Crossroads*, a history of Ightham, to ask if he would write our book and we were all delighted when he agreed.

David has lived in the Sevenoaks district for most of his life and was a pupil at Sevenoaks School. He is also one of the authors of *Seal: The History of a Parish* and gives a variety of talks and tours around the area.

In the last three years David has immersed himself in all our memorabilia and records, as well as spending many hours in local libraries and at Sevenoaks School. He has also been editing and incorporating passages from Peter Larcombe's work. David has used reminiscences from a considerable number of old boys, girls, staff, and parents and the end result is a true reflection of life at The Prep over 100 years as seen by the people who have been involved with the school. We are incredibly grateful to David for this remarkable history.

On a personal note, we feel so privileged and proud to have led The Prep with such a fabulous team of personalities around us, both in and out of the classroom. It is very much this family of people, and this community that has developed over the years, that makes The Prep truly special.

Edward Oatley, Philip Oldroyd, and Luke Harrison

TO

THE BOYS AND GIRLS PAST AND PRESENT

OF

SEVENOAKS PREPARATORY SCHOOL

1919 – 2019

It is with old boys in mind that we have
written & it would seem appropriate to dedicate it

TO
THE BOYS PAST AND PRESENT
OF
SEVENOAKS PREPARATORY SCHOOL
1919 – 1984

The handwritten dedication in the original 1984 version
of *The Half & Half's* by Peter Larcombe and Jeremy Crang

TO

THE BOYS PAST AND PRESENT

OF

SEVENOAKS PREPARATORY SCHOOL

1921–1928.

The dedication in Rev. C.G. Holland's book *Perilous Seas, 1931*

Sevenoaks Preparatory School
The First Hundred Years

David Williams

Cover Fawke Cottage, Godden Green
Frontispiece Dedications
Back cover, from top Garden at Vine Court Road, 1922
Pre-Prep pagoda, Stake Farm, Godden Green, 2016
Sports day, Knole Paddock, 1965
Senior sports day, Godden Green, 2018

Published by
RED COURT PUBLISHING
Seal Kent

ISBN 978-0-9930828-3-2

Printed and bound by Short Run Press Limited, Bittern Road,
Sowton Industrial Estate, Exeter, EX2 7LW

Contents

Foreword

When Edward Oatley asked me if I would help with the writing of the history of Sevenoaks Preparatory School as part of the preparations for the celebration of its first 100 years in 2019, and then immediately told me that all the records of the school up to 1967 had been destroyed in a massive bonfire in December 1967, my heart sank. It was uplifted, however, by the discovery that in the 1980s, Peter Larcombe–a member of The Prep's staff and an alumnus–had, with help from a number of other staff members and alumni, especially Jeremy Crang, literally handwritten in beautiful script a history of the school up to 1984 entitled *The Half & Half's*.[1] This was some 40,000 words long and included several photographs and other images.

Between 2000 and 2009, this manuscript was typed up by some 400 pupils at The Prep under the supervision of Alan Chant with the addition of further material, especially by Angela Lucas. It now included some 120 images and the recollections of many past staff and alumni. Many of these had been recorded in a special edition of the school magazine *The Souvenir Post,* published in 2000 on the occasion of the Millennium 'Old and Present Families' reunion, and in a commemorative issue of *The Prep Post* published in 2005 to mark Edward Oatley's retirement. By 2013, the draft manuscript was some 60,000 words long, but it was never published.

For the early years, I have relied substantially on the draft of *The Half & Half's*. A lot of the content of the draft consists of verbatim quotes from staff and alumni and many of the later chapters were written in the first person. I removed many of the direct quotes which, word for word, are included on the 'Memories' CD which accompanies this book (and is also available on the school website) and rewrote the manuscript in the historic tense. Fortunately, most of the records since Edward took over the school in 1978 have been kept by him or by the school, and so researching and writing the history of the more recent years has been more straightforward. For these more recent years, I have relied largely on the school magazines and newsletters and the recollections of alumni, staff, parents and friends. I have attempted, not always successfully, to reconcile these when they have differed from each other. I apologise for any errors that have crept in and also for excluding those many achievements and adventures by pupils and staff over the first hundred years that I have not been able to record either because of space or because I haven't been told about them!

I have followed the conventions in *The Half & Half's* for names. Staff and parents are prefixed with Mr, Mrs, Miss etc. with given name(s) or initials (where

---

1 For an explanation of this title, see page 14. The reason for the apostrophe cannot be explained. My conclusion is that Peter Larcombe would have just thought it looked more elegant than 'The Half & Halves'.

known). Pupils and alumni are usually referred to with given names (where known) and surname. Well-known public figures usually have no title. In each chapter, the first reference to a person is in bold. Subsequent references are not in bold and, depending on context, given names may be dropped.

In addition to recollections from staff and alumni, the accompanying CD also contains a wonderful collection of quotes from pupils aged from 6 to 13 recorded in December 2017, in answer to the questions 'What do you like best about The Prep?' and 'What is your best memory of The Prep?' It also includes Edward Oatley's diaries from his charity bike rides.

As well as acknowledging my enormous debt to Peter Larcombe, Jeremy Crang, Angela Lucas and the many others who contributed to *The Half & Half's* for material included in the 2009 draft, I also received a lot of information on the early years of The Prep from Sally Robbins, the archivist at Sevenoaks School who produced a tremendous piece of research on this period. For the more recent period, Janet and Edward Oatley have been the source of an immense amount of information and I have received considerable help from Liz Reading and T.J. Richards in the school's Development Office. I am grateful for the many alumni and current and past members of staff who sent in their memories or were interviewed for the CD, especially Ian Culley, Tim Dickinson, Luke Harrison, Philip Oldroyd, Peter Ratcliffe, Marjorie Shea, Donald and Alison Smith, Penny Spencer-Allen, Lyn Witton and many, many others. Emily Smith and Janet Oatley did a wonderful job in proofreading the drafts. Sarah Harris has been responsible for selecting the images, with Janet Oatley's help, and for typesetting and arranging for the printing of the book. The quality of the end result is testament to her immense expertise. My thanks to all.

David Williams
Seal
April 2019

Prologue

The second half of the 19th century saw the beginning of the transformation of Sevenoaks from a market town with a population of about 5,000 in the middle of that century, into a thriving commuter town of over 18,000 at the beginning of the 21st century. The initial growth in population to nearly 11,000 at the outbreak of the First World War was directly linked to the coming of the railway in the 1860s, accompanied by the building for the first commuters, usually professional men, of substantial villas in some of the undeveloped roads near the two stations. With these new residents came a demand for day preparatory schools for both boys and girls. In the early 1900s the Head of Queen Elizabeth's Grammar School (as Sevenoaks School was then known), Mr George Heslop, annexed a local prep school, The Beacon, and maintained two preparatory classes for boys under 10 as part of his school. However, the experiment did not survive the First World War.

Sevenoaks was a quiet rural market town until the latter half of the 19th century, with a gradually increasing population rising from 2,640 in 1801 to 4,695 in 1861. The town, built on the top of the east-west Greensand Ridge, was the point where the road from Tonbridge divided with one branch, originally a turnpike road, going to Bromley and London and the other up the Darent Valley towards Dartford. It was just south of the main east-west highway, the turnpike (now the A25) from Godstone to Wrotham. The town was surrounded by a series of large country estates, with Knole to the east the largest and oldest. In a clockwise direction going south these included Riverhill, Ash Grove, Beechmont, Kippington House, Montreal, Chipstead Place, Chevening, Bradbourne, Greatness, and Wildernesse.

The first railway came to Bat & Ball station in north Sevenoaks in 1862. In 1868 a direct line was opened from Charing Cross and Cannon Street to Tubs Hill station (now Sevenoaks) and the next year the two Sevenoaks stations were linked. Soon bankers, stockbrokers, lawyers, accountants, and other professional men, realising that they could now commute from the countryside to their workplaces in London, began to move with their families to towns like Sevenoaks. They built substantial villas in the streets, some of them newly laid, near the two stations: in St John's Road, Bradbourne Road and Bradbourne Vale Road near Bat & Ball; in Granville Road and Hitchen Hatch Lane near Tubs Hill; and in Park Lane, Vine Court Road and Avenue Road in the area north of the Vine cricket ground roughly equidistant from the two stations.

Wealthier commuters built a ring of larger mansions slightly further from the stations, on the slopes of Mount Harry, in Bayham Road, on the old Kippington estate, and to the south near the Common or on the Tonbridge Road. Later, in the 20th century, many of these became schools, old people's homes, or were sub-divided into flats.

This influx of families created a demand for preparatory education for both boys and girls. Since the late 18th century, there had been schools in Sevenoaks which prepared boys for entry to the major boarding schools at ages between 10 and 13. These included The Sevenoaks Academy in The Red House in the High Street founded in 1796 by **Mr John Baptiste Anquetil**, a former Sevenoaks School teacher; Scottiswoode House School, opened by **Rev. John Jackson** with his wife **Laura** in 1867; and **Mr Christopher Town**'s Lonsbury College, both in the St John's area of Sevenoaks. However, these and others like them were small-scale operations which came and went, often because they were established by an individual who ran the school with his or her spouse and one or two junior teachers, but then closed or was passed on to family on his or her retirement or death. The Sevenoaks Academy closed in 1885 and Scottiswoode House was a day school for girls by 1891 and closed shortly afterwards. The Avenue House School on Avenue Road moved from Braintree to Sevenoaks in 1886 and was a typical example of a small school. According to the 1891 census return, the principal **Mr John Thornton** and his wife ran the school with their daughter, a music teacher, their son – who later took over the school – possibly one or two non-resident teachers, and three resident domestic staff. The return shows 24 boarders (all boys) aged between 9 and 15.

In 1882, **Col. J.S. Norman** acquired a small prep school at 18 St John's Road called The Beacon, which had been founded around 1863 by **Mr Arthur Lockwood** in a large four-storey house with extensive grounds. Although it had been very successful initially, by 1881 it was struggling to attract pupils; there were only 12, and they soon left. Col. Norman revived the school's fortunes, numbers increased, and there was a demand for more boarding places. By the mid-1890s, larger premises were needed. His response was to divide The Beacon by building a new boarding school to be called The New Beacon on land acquired from the Montreal Estate near Cross Keys, where it remains to this day. It opened in early 1900 with the capacity for 60 boarders and was soon advertising itself as a preparatory school 'for boys for Eton, Harrow and other public schools'. The original school remained in St John's Road and was, according to various Sevenoaks directories of the early 1900s, one of a number of schools in the St John's area of Sevenoaks providing preparatory education for boys. It advertised itself specifically as a preparatory school for Sevenoaks School. Other preparatory schools for boys in Sevenoaks included Beechmont ('for gentlemen's sons for Eton and other public schools') and St Aldates in St John's Road ('for gentlemen's sons') while The High School for Boys in Vine Court Road and Bradbourne College, a high school for girls at 16 Bayham Road, both had preparatory classes for boys. With two exceptions, none of these schools from the period before the First World War survived beyond the 1930s. The exceptions were Bradbourne College, which closed in the late 1960s having changed its name to Bradbourne House School, and The New Beacon, which not only survived but still flourishes in the 21st century.

At the end of the First World War, Sevenoaks School was suffering from the deprivations of the war, a shortage of staff, and a falling roll. The Headmaster, **Mr George Heslop,** had been there since 1898 and had achieved something of a revival in the school's fortunes in the early years of the new century. When he had taken over there were just over 50 boys in the school; by 1905, he had increased the roll to 100. At that time in schools like Sevenoaks, 10 or even 9 was the usual age for boys to start their secondary education, while few stayed beyond 16.

The school's pre-First World War records mention 'preparatory' classes more than once. In 1902 and 1903, the school lists used the term preparatory to cover two forms of boys under 10, 'below' the other six forms, which took boys up to 16 or 17; in these two forms, there were 19 boys in 1902 and 23 in 1903. According to **Brian Scragg**'s *Sevenoaks School: A History,* the increase in the roll was helped by annexing The Beacon school in St John's Road and it is possible that the preparatory classes continued to use The Beacon's premises. However, by 1907, the house had been knocked down and replaced by eight smaller houses. The term preparatory was not used in the next extant list for Sevenoaks School in 1913 and **Mr Ernie Groves,** who taught there for over 40 years from the mid-1920s and was involved in the early years of The Prep, suggested that in the early 1900s there was some ad hoc provision made for younger brothers of older pupils should their parents be abroad. However, this practice seems to have lapsed quickly. In the 1911 census, Sevenoaks School had 32 boarders listed, ranging in age from 10 to 18, although there would have also been some day boys. A report of His Majesty's Inspector of Schools in 1920 (of which more later) makes it clear that in 1917 there was one boy admitted under the age of 10, and in 1918 eleven boys – but it is unclear whether they were simply on the cusp of 'proper' attendance at age 9 or much younger. Certainly, the case of the solitary 1917 pupil makes it clear that there was no regular intake of younger pupils who could have formed a specific preparatory class in the school.

Circumstances in Sevenoaks School during the First World War had not been conducive to any further innovation, as both the school and the Head struggled to cope with the tribulations caused by that conflict both in terms of the personal cost (Mr Heslop's only son was killed on the first day of the Battle of the Somme in 1916) and home front privations. By the end of the war, the school was in a sorry state. The first post-war issue of *The Sennockian* (the magazine for alumni) recorded that 'Its staff was depleted, its work and games disorganised'. In 1904, there had been 60 boarders and 40 day boys on the roll; by 1919, the numbers had dropped to 19 and 29 respectively.

1

When We Were Very Young (1919-28)

Mr Geoffrey Garrod, started classes for younger boys at Sevenoaks School. As a result of an official inspection in 1920, these classes were formalised as a preparatory school linked to Sevenoaks School and from these modest beginnings the first 100 years of the history of The Prep can be traced. In 1922, Rev. C.G. Holland – who had returned to teaching at Sevenoaks School the previous year – and his wife Mary bought 4 Vine Court Road, and moved in with 35 boys to establish The Prep's first independent home. For several years, the close connection with Sevenoaks School continued. Rev. Holland and other masters taught at both schools and details of The Prep were included in the senior school's 1925 prospectus. In 1925, the Garrods left Sevenoaks School and in 1928 the Hollands retired through ill-health and sold The Prep. Gradually, the direct links with Sevenoaks School weakened.

Origins

Mr Geoffrey Garrod was appointed Headmaster of Sevenoaks School in April 1919 and brought with him his wife **Margaret** and 4-year-old son. A former scholar of Winchester and New College, Oxford, he had qualified as a barrister before taking up teaching and came to Sevenoaks from the City of London School. Although he and his wife were at Sevenoaks for only six years, they revitalised the school, trebled the numbers and laid down many of the foundations for its subsequent growth.

It is entirely plausible that Mrs Garrod decided to form a preparatory class in order to teach her son. This theory is supported by both the statement in the 1920

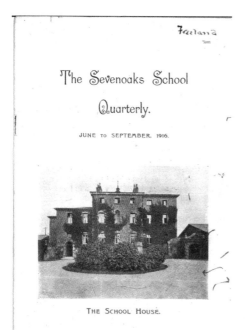

The Sevenoaks School
Quarterly.

JUNE TO SEPTEMBER. 1916.

THE SCHOOL HOUSE.

above A 1916 copy of a Sevenoaks School magazine showing the original view of School House from the road.

below The Prep's first home, 'The Cottage', is indicated in this photograph from 1993. This area of the school is still called 'The Cottage Block'.

inspection report that there was, by March of that year, a: 'Kindergarten class of 21 children, with an age range of 5–9 [...] conducted in the school buildings by a separate staff [...] run as a private venture' and also by the recollection of an Old Sennockian, **Frederick Pearce**, that when he joined the school in September 1920 it had its own preparatory school, housed in the then sanatorium building (known as The Cottage). The Cottage had been built in 1900 next to the new swimming bath as a sanatorium and a dormitory, and Mrs Garrod's original preparatory class was in two rooms on the ground floor; one room upstairs was also possibly used as a classroom although, according to the 1920 inspection report, the school porter and his wife lived in both of those. There was a cobbled area outside which could still be seen as late as 1984. This was the boys' playground and they took lunch in the main school house.

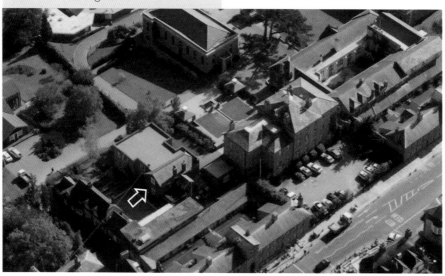

In their 1920 report, the Inspectors recommended that 'the matter [of the Kindergarten] should be regularised by the Governors assuming responsibilities for this department in accordance with Clause 45 of the [School's] Scheme'. According to the December 1921 *Sennockian*, it was this recommendation which had resulted a year later, in September 1921, with the Kindergarten class becoming formally known as a preparatory school and officially linked to Sevenoaks School. By the end of that first term, Mrs Garrod's prep school had 35 boys. **Brian Scragg**'s history failed to make the connection between this preparatory school and The Prep and erroneously thought that the Kindergarten class 'must have been closed or moved elsewhere shortly thereafter […] for no reference appears to it after 1920', even though *The Sennockian* of December 1921 mentioned the 'new' preparatory school.

For many years, the staff and alumni of The Prep also believed that it had not been founded until 1921 when **Rev. C.G. Holland,** who taught at Sevenoaks School, and **Mrs Mary Isabella Holland** bought 4 Vine Court Road from the Church of England Society for Waifs and Strays which had recently vacated the property, then known as St Michael's Orphanage for Girls, as their own residence to live in and start a prep school there. The belief in this date was so strong that the 50-year anniversary of The Prep was held in 1971.

However, when researching for the original *The Half & Half's* some ten years after that anniversary, **Mr Peter Larcombe**, with help from Sevenoaks School Registrar **Mr George Alcock** (whose wife **Rosemary** taught at The Prep in the 1960s and whose two boys are alumni) and the retired Bursar **Col. Jim Smart**, discovered the connection with Mrs Garrod's preparatory class from 1919. The traditional story was that she had started the class with just six boys. That is uncorroborated, but if it were true in spring or autumn 1919 then the huge leap to 21 pupils within a year is remarkable. It might simply reflect the very real need in the locality for such an establishment, or it could just be that the 'six' was a number plucked out of the air. Classes continued to be held in The Cottage at Sevenoaks School until April 1922; then, an advertisement in the local *Sussex Chronicle and Courier* announced that, owing to the growth of the school, from the following term (which started on 5 May 1922) The Prep would move to its own premises in Vine Court Road, Sevenoaks where the Hollands were living. The Hollands took 35 day boys onto the roll and, according to a neighbour, **Miss Vanda Salmon**, **Mr Ernie Groves** also lived in the house.

Head and staff

The text of *The Half & Half's* categorically states that Rev. Holland was the Headmaster of The Prep from 1921 to 1928 (he wrote a novel, *Perilous Seas*, published in 1931 and dedicated it to 'The boys past and present of Sevenoaks Preparatory School 1921-28') but other evidence points to his wife Mary being the Headmistress. She was not from France or Belgium as some alumni recalled,

A 1950's dust jacket from Rev. Holland's novel, which he had dedicated to the boys.

but Durham born and bred, although the couple had spent some time abroad in those countries and been married in Bordeaux, France before the First World War. A prospectus for The Prep dating from the early 1920s described Mrs Holland as the principal 'assisted by qualified staff of masters and mistresses' and some alumni have referred to her as the 'Headmistress'. The prospectus then says that 'the general discipline of the house is under the direct supervision of Rev. C.G. Holland, M.A., Hon C.F., assistant master at Sevenoaks School'. It would appear that the running of the school was a joint endeavour with perhaps Mrs Holland managing The Prep on a day-to-day basis while her husband, along with some of the other Sevenoaks School masters (Mr Groves, **Mr J. Moss** and **Mr Ronnie Marchant**), continued to teach part-time in both schools. One thing is clear from the recollections of alumni – that Mrs Holland had a very fiery temper and the boys were scared stiff of her.

Rev. Holland had taught at Sevenoaks School from 1911 to 1913 before carrying out parochial work and seeing service in the First World War as an army chaplain. He returned to Sevenoaks in September 1921 and was given 'a hearty welcome' on his return to teaching Latin and divinity, as a French expert and as an old friend of the school. In July 1923, the Holland's only child, **Peter**, was born. One Prep alumnus recalled that he used to wear a purple hat and he had very beautiful fair curls, masses of them, and that he could easily have been taken for a girl.

Other teachers, besides the fiery Mrs Holland, included two full-time teachers: **Mrs Evans,** a nice, kind, gentle lady who got much more work out of the boys in her quiet way, and **Miss Bassett,** an 18-year-old teaching the Kindergarten, a young and inexperienced teacher whom, of course, the boys played up a little. In the 1950s and 60s she taught at another prep school in Sevenoaks, Winchester House, where she was a colleague of a young master who was later to become Headmaster of The Prep, **Mr Edward Oatley**.

Most of the other members of staff of The Prep were part-timers who spent the rest of their time at Sevenoaks School – including the Rev. Holland. Another part-time teacher was **Mrs Edwards** and, for her sins, she was supposed to teach the boys music and singing. This was the last lesson on Thursday afternoon every week, perhaps so that the other teachers could get the early bus home out of earshot!

Mr Moss was the gym instructor, a great character and an ex-army Sergeant Major who used to have the boys marching, turning, and even country dancing! As he also taught at Sevenoaks School, this early discipline stayed with many of the boys who, when they went into the Services, were already well-practised in the art of drilling and discipline, thanks to 'dear old Mr Moss'.

In these early days, **Miss Swithinbank,** who was very tall and slim and a strict disciplinarian, managed, as well as teaching maths, to produce the annual school play, which always took place on the lawn in the open air during the 'long hot summers of the twenties, when the sun always shone', as one alumnus remembers. As a result of Miss Swithinbank's coaching, many of the boys took leading roles in the annual school plays at Sevenoaks School in the days of **Mr James Higgs-Walker**, who had succeeded Mr Garrod as Headmaster. These productions were regarded as the highlight of the school year, and two free tickets were always given by the Rev. Holland to the two boys that came top in Latin. **Hubert Loughlin,** who received these tickets once, became a professional actor with Sir Laurence Olivier at the Old Vic but never fulfilled his potential, being killed in 1944 at the Anzio Landings in Italy during the Second World War at the age of 25.

Fabric

The house consisted of a basement and three storeys, in the top one of which Rev. Holland and his family lived. The boys entered the drive and went down some stone steps on the left of the building (the steps up to the front door were for staff only) to the basement, where there were allocated pegs for their clothes and a cloth bag in which were their plimsolls. They were required to change into these plimsolls immediately after they arrived and if they were caught anywhere else but in the basement hall without them on, they were given at least 50 lines!

One of the rooms which stayed in the memories of boys who were at The Prep in the 1920s was the conservatory, leading off a classroom on the first floor. In this room were held all the important gatherings such as the daily prayers or the Remembrance Day ceremony, although one alumnus remembered the day when one boy received a beating in front of the whole school for bullying.

The 'quad' or playground was at the back of the house – it was possible to reach it through the conservatory as well as out of the back door of the basement and up some steps. It was on two levels, a large lawn and a raised bank at the far end with a playground and a large hut, known respectively as the Upper and Lower Quad. On the left-hand side of the lawn was an enormous fig tree; proper balls were not allowed and the boys improvised with rolled up newspaper tied with string.

Second Floor

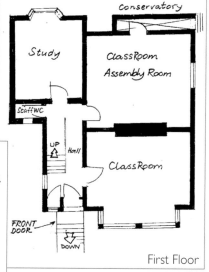

Conservatory

Study

Class Room
Assembly Room

Staff WC

UP   Hall

Class Room

FRONT
DOOR

DOWN

First Floor

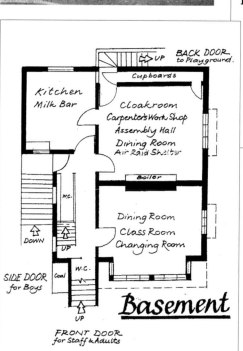

BACK DOOR
to Playground.

Cupboards

Kitchen
Milk Bar

Cloakroom
Carpenter's Work Shop
Assembly Hall
Dining Room
Air Raid Shelter

Boiler

W.C.

Dining Room
Class Room
Changing Room

DOWN   UP

SIDE DOOR
for Boys

Coal

W.C.

UP

Basement

FRONT DOOR
for Staff & Adults

top left Vine Court Road in 1920.

above and left Floorplans drawn by Mr Peter Larcombe for *The Half & Half's.*

The multi-purpose rooms suggest changes over time but also illustrate how limited space was. By 1938 102 boys were on the roll in this one building. Eventually other classrooms were added but at the expense of an already small playground.

Academic

The boys received basic instruction in arithmetic, English, spelling, writing, history, geography, French, and occasionally Latin along with divinity, some art and dramatics, and lots of sport. The prospectus referred to the Kindergarten conducting teaching by the Froebel method, which emphasised the importance of play-based, child-centred teaching, and **Mme Fagge** teaching French by the 'Direct Method'. There was little or no science teaching. German and regular Latin came later when the boys went on to Sevenoaks School (known as the 'big' school) or other grammar or public schools. To most boys, it seemed a foregone conclusion that they would automatically progress into the 'big' school if they passed the necessary exams in arithmetic, English, and French and The Prep was considered to be a good training centre for boys wanting to go to Sevenoaks School.

It is interesting to note that the 1920s prospectus concluded with the statement that the 'boys are taught to learn and *think*, not merely to acquire a certain number of facts, while it is recognised that the true aim of education during these important years of a boy's life is the development of moral character.' These are objectives which still apply nearly 100 years later and would be endorsed by staff and parents in the early 21st century.

School life

The 1920s prospectus described The Prep as a home school for little boys where 'ample accommodation is provided for 40 day-boys and 10 boarders', although none of the recollections of the alumni of the time refer to there being boarders at the school. Most of the boys walked to school every day from home, while a few came to Sevenoaks by train and finished their journey by walking from Tubs Hill up St Botolph's Road to the Vine. The occasional boy did come by bike but virtually no-one came by car – there were not many to speak of anyway. There was one chore for the senior boys who had to fetch and take home the very small boys for the first few weeks of their first term. Where possible, the boys went home for lunch. For those that stayed, leading off from the basement hall was a kitchen and farther along was one of the classrooms, which doubled up as the dining room for those who stayed to lunch.

Fees were eight guineas[2] (£8.40) a term with a discount for boys who were born (or possibly lived) within ten miles of the school. The uniform consisted of a grey flannel suit with short trousers, a grey flannel shirt, a black and red striped tie, and grey stockings with a black and red ring around the top. The cap, which was half red and half black, had a white badge with seven acorns and was known as a 'half & half'. The Prep boys were always the butt of jokes by

---

2 A guinea was 21 shillings in pre-decimal currency (£1.05 today) and was used mainly for professional fees, auction prices, especially for horses, and horse race winnings.

Back garden of 4 Vine Court Road in 1922, the year in which The Prep moved there. *from left* H. Renwick, A. Staines, G. Anckorn, G. Anderson, Nixon, Sillis, J. Daws, Neve, Wrigley and Flaxman.   *Photo: Gordon Anckorn collection*

Another outdoor class photo from Vine Court Road, which also shows the Lower Quad marked out for tennis. This is dated more specfically, 4 July 1922.
Photo: Staines family, Staines II is seated in the middle of the central table.

the local errand boys and school children due to these caps, but they were worn as a badge of honour and defended in many sore contests (and hence the title of Mr Larcombe's original manuscript).

Sport and recreation

One of the great disadvantages of Vine Court Road was that it had no playing fields of its own. Because of this, journeys of varying distances were made to grounds belonging to other organisations, each with its own distinctive character. Perhaps the most charismatic of sporting venues was the historic Vine cricket ground almost on the school's doorstep, one of the oldest in England. The first cricket match to be reported in full in the newspapers took place on the Vine in 1734, but the ground had been used for several decades before then. During the summer months, The Prep boys had the privilege of using the northern edge of the outfield for cricket. The journey from the school to the Vine was no more than a stone's throw: along the pavement only as far as the Baptist Church and then simply a bound up the grassy bank, either to hurdle or duck the chunky wooden fence that still encircles the famous turf.

The public recreation grounds in Holly Bush Lane, then the home of the bowls club and the town's tennis courts, provided further sporting facilities. A slightly longer walk along the pavement in the opposite direction to the Vine, 'The Rec', as it was always known, afforded cricket pitches for the overspill from the Vine during the summer. During the winter months, the boys changed into their football kit at the school and clattered and scraped their way down the pavement to play football at 'The Rec'. The pitches most frequently used were at the far end, and few boys could resist a spin on the roundabout which stood beside the pavilion. Certain boys will also never forget the delicious cherries, nor the skill they acquired in knocking them down, from the branches that overhung the field from a neighbour's garden. Also in Holly Bush Lane was Vine Lodge School, a girls' primary school. When the girls' playing field was made available to The Prep as an extra football pitch, there were extraordinary complications as the girls' break time coincided with the middle of games and frequently they would gather round and spectate, creating excitement and not a little embarrassment.

Knole Paddock also accommodated sporting activity and provided the longest and most difficult journey, largely because of crossing Seal Hollow Road with so many boys. For that reason, boys walked two by two in a strict 'crocodile' formation down the hill to the playing fields at the bottom. Some cricket in later years was played there, and to one side, where today Lady Boswell's School stands, lay the 1st XI football pitch. There was one pitch that no one who played on it could ever forget, as it incorporated such a slope that the art of football became not so much goal-scoring as simply keeping the ball in play on the field. Time after time the whistle blew and players were forced to scramble down the bank and through the thorn bushes in an ill-fated attempt to rescue the ball before it reached the roadway beneath. More often than not, more time was spent rescuing the ball than playing the game. In the later years, Knole Paddock became the scene of many memorable sports days.

From the very start, football and cricket had been the traditional games played at The Prep. Rev. Holland was a football fanatic, coaching the boys and refereeing matches himself on Wednesday and Friday afternoons. With only 35 boys in the early 1920s, it was not possible to field more than one school team. However, this team did play matches against other local prep schools, Knole School (which was associated with Bradbourne College in Bayham Road), Nayland House (also in Bayham Road), The New Beacon, and Yardley Court in Tonbridge. The New

Beacon was rather out of their league as the boys there stayed to U14 and U15 levels; in any case, they regarded themselves as 'too exclusive' to mix with the locals, as their boys were all boarders and most went on to the larger public schools.

For generations of the boys, cricket at The Prep was synonymous with Mr Marchant. This greatly loved character was for many years between the two world wars the professional groundsman at the Vine, a first-class player and an excellent coach. The members of The Prep cricket 1st XI received special coaching from Mr Marchant, for which there was a charge. His tutelage continued at Sevenoaks School. Fenton, the traditional house for Prep boys, supplied most of the school XI at cricket and many of the Vine teams after they had left the school. Although few fixtures were played in these early days, if a boy was good enough (and lucky enough?) to score 50 runs in a match against other schools, they would win a bat—two of the boys who did this were remembered, **Ronald Martin** and **Alan Stains**. When playing cricket for the 1st XI, the boys wore a white shirt with the school badge sewn on the left breast; white shorts with the school belt (an elastic red and black one, the clasp being in the shape of a snake); grey socks, and white plimsolls.

From the early days at The Prep, boxing was a popular sport with the boys. Introduced by the Rev. Holland, Mr Groves instructed a few pupils at an 'extra cost' during the 1920s.

Sevenoaks School

Despite moving to the new premises in 1922, The Prep maintained links with Sevenoaks School for some years. The December 1923 *Sennockian* reported that in his speech day address, Mr Garrod mentioned the steady but excellent progress made in The Prep and advised parents to send their young sons to this school, where the groundwork was thoroughly taught, while the 1920s prospectus for The Prep said that preference was given by Sevenoaks to boys from there. The Prep continued to expand and, according to the *Sennockian* of April 1924, numbers had risen to 50 boys. The 1925 Sevenoaks School prospectus made reference to the fact that 'in connexion [sic] with the Grammar School there is also a Preparatory School in Vine Court Road for boys aged 5-10 under the charge of Rev. C.G. and Mrs Holland…'. Applications were 'to be made to Mrs Garrod at Sevenoaks School, as usual'. Boys from The Prep took part in the annual Sevenoaks School drama productions and the two schools continued to share staff.

In 1925, the Garrods left Sevenoaks for Belfast where Mr Garrod became principal of the Royal Academical Institution; the Hollands continued to run The Prep for another three years until in 1928 they retired due to Mr Holland's poor health, although he lived until 1952. With the arrival of the new Headmaster, **Mr Miles Jukes**, the direct links with Sevenoaks School ended.

2

Manners Maketh Man
(1928 - 39)

The Hollands sold The Prep to Mr Miles Jukes, a war veteran who came from a family of churchmen. He inherited 30 boys and, over the next ten years, increased the roll to over 100. A library was started, sport became more formalised, a school magazine was published and a house system was put in place. Mr Jukes' wife died in 1933; they had no children, but Mr Jukes took in a few boarders who lived with him. In Sevenoaks, the break-up of the large estates and the consequent building of houses continued. Families who moved into the large houses on the old Wildernesse and Kippington estates were attracted to the town by the availability and variety of schools. The electrification of the railway from London, completed in 1934, make the area even more attractive for London commuters. The period saw mixed fortunes for preparatory schools in Sevenoaks as some closed down, although others prospered as The Prep did and one new one for day boys, Winchester House, was established in 1936.

Head and staff

In 1928, **Mr Miles Norman Jukes**, MA, a 41-year-old wounded veteran of the First World War, bought the school. Mr Jukes only had one lung; the other was shot out in the Dardanelles during the disastrous Gallipoli campaign in 1915. His father, his grandfather, and his other forefathers for generations had been churchmen, latterly in Essex and Devon. His family expected him to follow in their footsteps and go into the Church. He was educated at Haileybury College, then the theological college at Wells in Somerset where he found digs in the ancient town of Glastonbury. In history lessons, he used to tell the boys the famous Glastonbury legend of how Joseph of Arimathea, the wealthy merchant, had brought his teenage nephew, Jesus, to trade in Somerset, and how, after the Crucifixion and Resurrection of Jesus, he had returned to Glastonbury and planted his staff there. It sprouted and grew into a thorn bush which can still be seen today and is supposed to bloom every Christmas. Mr Jukes would cap this unlikely tale by saying 'My landlady had a cutting of the Glastonbury Thorn in our front garden, and sure enough, it used to blossom at Christmastime. It was a moth-eaten little bloom, but it did actually bloom, all the same'!

In 1908, four years after Mr Jukes left Haileybury, he went to Oxford University. He never did go into the Church for, while he was training, the First World War broke out and he joined up. After the war, with an MA from Pembroke College, Oxford, he went into teaching and became Headmaster of Ghyll Royd Preparatory School in Yorkshire. In 1928, he and his wife **Nancy** came to Sevenoaks, buying the house in Vine Court Road (together with a smaller plot next to it) and the goodwill of The Prep from **Rev. C.G. Holland** and **Mrs Holland**. The Jukes themselves had no children but inherited 30 boys. By 1931, there were 72 pupils and by 1938, 102. In that year, Mr Jukes was joined as a partner and Joint Headmaster by Cambridge University educated 37-year-old **Mr Frank Grahame Morgan,** the son of a clergyman, who lived in Amherst Road with his wife and parents.

In May 1933, Mrs Jukes died after a long illness at the young age of 54 and Mr Jukes then looked after himself in the flat at the top of the school for many years. It was known as the *Crow's Nest* by the boys, as Mr Jukes would supervise play time from a window. Out of his concern for the boys, Mr Jukes took in occasional boarders. There were two brothers **Paul** and **Barry Churton**, who were without a father; Mr Jukes had them living in the flat and cared for them like sons. It is possible that Mr Jukes never really recovered from the blow of losing his wife so young. In November 1938, he was summoned before magistrates at Basingstoke for driving dangerously and failing to stop after an accident. His solicitor said that Mr Jukes was suffering from a nervous breakdown and would be indisposed for another three months or so. He was fined £20 and had his licence suspended for a year.

Many alumni remember Mr Jukes with affection, describing him as a wonderful man whose firm gentleness added a dimension of security to their lives, and a neighbour from Vine Court Road, **Miss Vanda Salmon**, described him as a charmer. One alumnus did, however, remember him rather differently and put this down to his war experiences. Many men returning from the First World War bore the indelible traces of that terrible experience and this affected their behaviour in civilian life. Mr Jukes' experiences in the Gallipoli campaign could have accounted for a strangeness in him which some pupils noticed.

Mr Jukes inherited several of the Hollands' staff including the senior mistress **Miss Swithinbank,** the young **Miss Bassett**, the physical training instructor

Mr and Mrs Jukes pictured at their first school, Ghyll Royd Preparatory School in Yorkshire.

Staff circa 1930: *(l-r)* Miss Creese, Mrs Jukes, Mr Jukes, Mr Cauley and Miss Brunton, whose father was the photographer as evidenced by the stamp on the mount.

Photograph submitted to *The Half & Half's* by John Breething, an alumnus from 1932-38, with the note 'I am enclosing an old photograph which may be of interest, together with most of the surnames. Christian names were not used in those days!' His three stepsons and three grandsons later attended The Prep.

Mr J. Moss, and **Mme Fagge**, who taught French – a very short little lady with little sense of humour and an inability to keep good order. Because of this, she was subjected to a great deal of good-natured ragging. She usually wore a black dress and a black straw hat which remained firmly planted on her head. At the time, cigarette cards were very popular with the boys, who always had a plentiful supply of 'swaps'. They were usually pictures of animals, fish, and birds and had sticky backs. One alumnus recalled that the younger **Booker** boy crept up behind Mademoiselle and stuck a cigarette card with a fish illustration on her hat. At the end of the lesson, she put on her coat and left the school, cigarette card still in place. This was fortunate for young Booker, because if the Headmaster had seen the card, Booker would have found sitting down rather painful for a few days! A new teacher was **Miss Gentry.**

None of these teachers appear in a school photograph of 1930 or 1931, so perhaps they had moved on. There were 72 boys on the photograph along with the original teachers and three new teachers, in addition to Mr and Mrs Jukes. One is **Miss Brunton** – young Miss Brunton – who had taken over the teaching of Form 1, the Kindergarten. Her father took the picture and the name 'Brunton' is embossed in the right-hand corner of the mount. One alumnus recalled that, aged about 6, he was in love with Miss Brunton and he once brought her a box of chocolates to let her know it! **Mrs Creese** was the teacher of Form 2 while **Mr Cauley** took the top class, Form 3. Mr Jukes taught Latin and scripture. Mr Cauley divided opinion amongst the alumni. When **John Ellis**, who left in 1938, was shown the school photograph, he looked away quickly when he caught sight of Mr Cauley, a good-looking man but with a mouth that could make him look rather cruel. Ellis said that the boys were terrified of him; he used to throw the board rubber at them and clip their ears. Some said he had a short fuse.

Fabric

The Jukes, like other Heads' families, lived in the flat on the top floor, but they had a modern two-storey house built on the plot of land next door. However, when his wife died, very soon after they moved in, Mr Jukes sold the new house and retreated back to the upstairs flat in the school. Also living in the house in 1939 was a 64-year-old caretaker, **Mrs Maria Francis**, and her husband **Arthur**. Two of the rooms in the basement were being used as cloakrooms, and the other was the caretaker's day room. The only playground was still at the back, a very dusty plain terminating in a steep and equally dusty bank. The obvious and very satisfying game for the boys was for a certain number to occupy the bank and for the rest to try and take possession of it. They all found this enthralling and fortunately nobody was ever really hurt in the battles that ensued. Although there would be the inevitable fight now and then, none of the alumni remember much in the way of bullying. Another favourite occupation was making tracks down the bank so that Dinky toys could run down and the great challenge of whose would go furthest – without pushing, of course. There were the usual games of marbles and conkers in season; conkers were collected from the trees in St Botolph's Road and Woodside Road, the lower part of which was unmade in those days. Yo-yos were also a great craze.

Academic

Kenneth Kevis said that he owed the school a great debt, not least for an invaluable pointer to the intellectual world provided by Mr Cauley – a man who he said possessed a fairly wide culture and who would quite often pass on to the boys information, not strictly speaking in the curriculum, but sometimes of greater value. Two examples were remembered. One day Mr Cauley told the boys in considerable detail about The Schlieffen Plan, the German military manoeuvre at the start of the First World War that came within an ace of defeating the French and British armies. For some reason, this excited Kevis' historical imagination and led him, as years went on, into many fascinating historical paths. The other was a story by Robert Louis Stevenson, *Thrawn Janet*. By the very reiteration of the word 'thrawn' (a Scottish dialect word), Kevis suddenly became conscious of the power of language and what lay to be discovered in literature. He remembered fondly Mr Cauley's gifts of arousing interest and curiosity. **Patrick Leneve Foster,** who left in 1937, was another who praised Mr Cauley's maths teaching, saying that he must have had a great deal of patience as the age range of the boys in the class was wide and they were not all doing the same problem as they worked through their exercises.

Mr Cauley did other things of value too. In the Headmaster's study he built up and administered a library. Even John Ellis admitted that this is where his horizons began to expand through reading. He was also responsible for a single-issue school magazine in 1938, *The ECHO*, being helped by the fact that his father was a printer. Mr Cauley wrote an amusing letter addressed to 'Snooks', apparently because that surname is a corruption of Sevenoaks.

'Dear Snooks,

'You tell me that you are disappointed to find that there is no School Ghost on the premises. I share your distress, but not your surprise. After all, the school is not the right shape for one; it contains no deepest dungeon, though I believe that rumours concerning such a place are current in the Fourth Form Room.

'A ghost, you know, my dear Snooks, requires a gloomy building of great age, or at least some picturesque ruin, for its home. Our school is not old and it contains no ruins except for certain copies of Durell and Fawdry, Book 1, and these are haunted only by those industrious spirits A, B and C, who perform such prodigies of digging, cycling and climbing. For which they are, as you know, rewarded by remarkably unfair divisions of unlikely sums of money.

'There seems no doubt, however, that the school is inhabited by bad fairies

whose chief delight is to cause the disappearance of caps and football boots,
and worst still, chalk. I am frequently called upon to discover missing articles,
or to solve the problem of how Snodbury Minor is to play football in three left
boots, two shirts (both too large for him) and no shorts.

'A little strategy (i.e. the detaining of Snodbury) can easily solve the
problem temporarily and a short search usually reveals any missing articles
and shows that the fairies are mischievous rather than destructive. What does
baffle us is a request to find something that has not even been brought to school
at all. When this happens, as it does frequently, we give up the struggle.

'After all it is quite easy to mislay an egg, as any hen will tell you; but it
passes the ingenuity of man to unscramble one.

'Yours sincerely
'A.H.C.'

School life

There was a system of penalties and rewards to help discipline, whereby 'stars' were awarded for good work or conduct and 'stripes' for bad work, talking, or eating sweets in class. If a boy was given a stripe, he would fill in a green docket and take it to the Headmaster. After being told off, he would be taken to a large board in the entrance hall by the Head, who stuck a little green dot against the boy's name. On the other hand, a good piece of work or conduct was awarded a quarter of a star. When the boy had four quarters, a red dot would be placed beside his name and two stars would cancel one stripe.

If the net total got to ten stripes, there was a visit to the Head's study, where the miscreant was given six strokes of the cane. At the end of term, prizes were awarded for those gaining the most stars, and punishment was meted out to those who had overdrawn the stripes account. It was something of a grievance that whereas whole stripes were awarded straight away, one could only earn a quarter of a star at a time, and the path of virtue was (as usual) a tedious one. The odds were against an individual, as he had to get eight good points to cancel one bad point. As a system, however, it worked very well.

In the 1930s, most boys walked or rode bikes to school, for the roads were much safer then with far fewer cars about and still some horses and carts in use. If the boy lived nearby, he might go home for lunch and back again in the afternoon. The boys who didn't go home to lunch were called the 'Dinner Boys' and Mr Cauley used to take them into the town to eat at Parises, a delightful café in the High Street. In Dartford Road, there was a newsagent-tobacconist run by **Sam Winter**'s father. It served as the school tuck shop, and before the war sold fireworks to the pupils and their families. The boys would spend their few pennies on aniseed balls, gobstoppers, etc. and a small wafer cup filled with a gooey mallow substance which sounds revolting. They were also introduced to the exotic fizzy drink *Tizer*.

Every autumn, Mr Jukes – being anxious for the boys' safety, whether on foot or on bikes – reminded them to be very careful how they used St Botolph's Road when the leaves were falling from the conker trees and the rain made them dangerously slippery. One unfortunate did crash his bike into one of the trees and broke his spine, confining him to a wheelchair for life. Some from further afield like Westerham used a special bus. There was another, less serious, accident when a pupil was looking through a doorway, which he should not have been doing. The door, which had glass panels in the upper part, was pushed shut, and unfortunately closed over his head, which was then sticking through the glass. There was a lot of blood, and his face was quite badly cut, but no lasting damage was done.

The school was none too warm in the winter, so the boys went well wrapped up. In the classroom, there was a coke fire that didn't seem capable of giving out much heat, and if Mr Jukes was taking the class he would ask if the boys wanted warming up. He would then take the boys outside to do exercises, which warmed them for a short time, but the effect soon wore off.

One of their chief pastimes at school was swapping. The boys would go to each other's homes to indulge in this delightful exercise, but as they had no idea of the value of anything, the most unequal exchanges took place, and a really expensive toy would be exchanged for some trashy object that happened to take their fancy. The mothers would have to intervene to prevent or reverse some of the more outrageous transactions.

Sport and recreation

As the school grew, sport became more formalised. For football, the boys went to the recreation ground in Holly Bush Lane and changed into their heavy leather boots with large studs on the soles. The ball was also heavy leather and when wet it was not a good idea to try heading. In the early 30s, the coach was Mr Cauley followed by **Mr Forshaw**. Games were on Tuesday and Thursday afternoons. **John Breething** remembered playing a 3-3 draw with the parents; both the Breethings, father and son, scored goals. Fixtures were also played against Ravenswood in Tonbridge, St Michael's in Otford, and a school at Halstead.

During Mr Jukes' time, formal house matches became established, which served to supplement their rather threadbare fixture list. *The ECHO* of 1938 revealed that that year was quite a rewarding football season for Scott house: 'This term, I am glad to say, we have been quite successful in football. In the first round we drew with Dickens 1-1. **Smith** pulled off some good saves in goal, and **Dewar** did well at centre-forward. We beat Kipling in the second round 5-0. Dewar beautifully headed in a goal from a good corner by Foster. In the third round we again were victorious, this time against Shakespeare. We won 2-0, although **Jackson** (Shakespeare) time and again turned back the Scott attack'.

Cricket was played on the Vine and coached by **Mr Ronnie Marchant.** Through his efforts, many boys had an excellent grounding in the sport. Fixtures

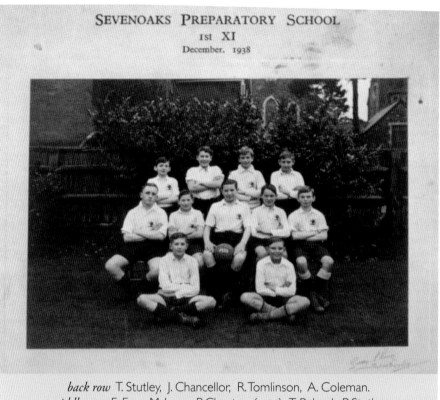

SEVENOAKS PREPARATORY SCHOOL
1st XI
December, 1938

back row T. Stutley, J. Chancellor, R. Tomlinson, A. Coleman.
middle row E. Fox, M. Lang, P. Churton *(capt)*, T. Ryland, P. Stutley.
front row J. Breething, J. Lark.
Paul Churton and his brother were two of the boys looked after by Mr Jukes.

reported in *The ECHO* of 1938 were against St Michael's, Ravenswood, and Sevenoaks School. Although there appear to have been few fixtures, these offered an interesting insight into the disciplined and regimented approach to the training of young cricketers during this era.

There were also boxing lessons in the basement or out in the open from Mr Moss and later **Mr Eric Tozer**. Boxing lessons were charged at 10s 6d per term (53p). However, after Mr Jukes left, boxing was no longer offered as a sporting option for the boys.

Compulsory physical torture, or physical training as it was officially known, was by tradition a highly regimented and military

Evidence of Sports Day in 1939 when M.G. Lang came first in a 100 yards race.

operation. The boys, in shorts and plimsolls, responded in unison to commands from their instructor to put their hands above their heads, or to lie down, or to march around in circles. This was considered to be the way to guarantee mass physical fitness. Three regular venues were used: the playground, the Vine Baptist Church hall, and the outskirts of the Vine Cricket Ground.

Swimming and lifesaving classes were started by Mr Jukes at the public baths in Eardley Road. They were held in the summer term under the personal supervision of the Head, a one-time President of the Sevenoaks Swimming Club, during the school's allotted periods. According to the school prospectus of the time, parents wishing their boys to take part were expected to provide them with a season ticket costing 15s (75p).

Mr Jukes divided the school into houses named from the literary world: Kipling, Scott, Shakespeare, and Dickens. *The ECHO* of 1938 recorded that for Kipling house, it had been a mixed term: 'This term has not, I fear, been very successful. Our exploits on the football field have not been encouraging, although some have played well. In school work, **Dunmore** major, **Carter** and **Lang** minor have attained places in the first three positions'. A more optimistic note was struck in the Dickens house report: '…the spring term was extremely successful in both work and games. **Jessup** worked very well during the term and scored two stars for the House. There were a few disappointments but thankfully very few stripes. Referring to football, there was a definite improvement all round. One outstanding boy was **Tomlinson,** who very nearly won his position as the school goal-keeper. All last term Dickens house never lost a house match, an extremely good record'.

Other schools

While The Prep, under Mr Jukes' stewardship, prospered, not all the local competition was so fortunate. Avenue House School, which advertised itself as 'The High School for Boys' and which was situated close to The Prep, between Dartford Road and Vine Court Road, closed and the building was demolished in 1934. Kippington House School for Girls, which had taken small boys, closed in 1938.

The New Beacon, which continued to be run by the Norman family, had been an all-boarding school but began to take day pupils in the 1930s. Oak School in Hitchen Hatch Lane, although mixed, was a direct competitor to The Prep, advertising itself in 1930 as a Preparatory School for Girls and Boys 'near the station and bus routes', and in 1936 further competition emerged when **Mr Percy Wilson** started Winchester House, a day preparatory school for boys in Granville Road.

St Michael's School in Otford was full-time boarding (which it remained until the 1970s), so not really in competition with The Prep, except for sporting fixtures. Founded in 1872 it was intended for sons of the Clergy, officers of the

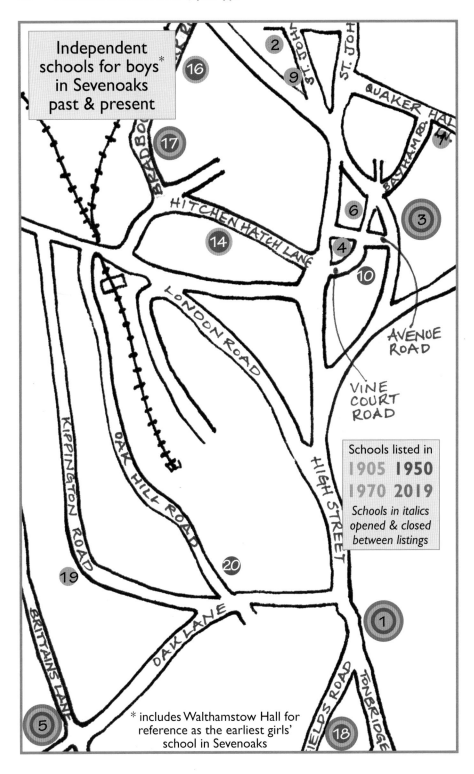

Independent schools for boys* in Sevenoaks past & present

Schools listed in
1905 **1950**
1970 **2019**
Schools in italics opened & closed between listings

* includes Walthamstow Hall for reference as the earliest girls' school in Sevenoaks

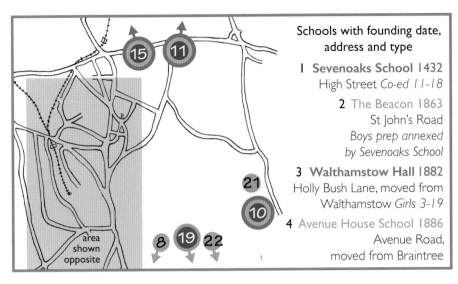

Schools with founding date, address and type

1 **Sevenoaks School** 1432
High Street *Co-ed 11-18*

2 The Beacon 1863
St John's Road
*Boys prep annexed
by Sevenoaks School*

3 **Walthamstow Hall** 1882
Holly Bush Lane, moved from
Walthamstow *Girls 3-19*

4 Avenue House School 1886
Avenue Road,
moved from Braintree

5	**The New Beacon** 1900	Brittains Lane	*Boys 4-14*
6	High School by 1901	Vine Court Road	*Boys prep and senior*
7	Bradbourne College by 1903	Stoneville Park (corner of Quaker's Hall & Bayham Rd.)	*Girls prep, senior & boys prep (Knole School)*
8	Beechmont by 1905	Gracious Lane	*Boys prep*
9	St Aldates by 1905	St John's Road	*Boys prep*
10	**Sevenoaks Prep** 1919	Park Lane, Godden Green. Originally in 'The Cottage' at Sevenoaks School, then moved to Vine Court Rd.	
11	**St Michael's** 1925	Rowdow, Otford (moved from Hackney, all boys)	*Co-ed 2-13*
12	**Oak School** by 1930	Hitchen Hatch Lane	*Co-ed prep*
13	*Kippington House by 1935*	Kippington	*Girls, few pre-prep boys*
14	**Winchester House** 1936	Hitchen Hatch Lane Orginally Granville Road.	*Boys prep*
15	**Russell House** 1938	Station Road, Otford (moved from Kemsing)	*Co-ed 2-11*
16	St Hilary's 1942	Bradbourne Park Road	*Merged W. Hall 1997*
17	**The Granville School** 1945	Bradbourne Park Road. Originally in Granville Road	*Mostly girls 2-11*
18	**Solefield School** 1948	Solefields Road	*Boys 4-13*
19	Foxbush 1949	Hildenborough (moved from Tonbridge)	*Boys*
20	*Freston Lodge by 1955*	Oakhill Road	*Boys prep*
21	Stake Farm Cottage 1962	Park Lane, Godden Green	*Girls, finishing/crammer*
22	**Sackville** 1987	Hildenborough	*Boys, co-ed 11-18 (2016)*

Army and Navy, and of professional men whose families had been marred by bereavement or by some form of domestic unhappiness. In 1925, it moved from Hackney to Beechy Lees in Otford, which had previously been owned by the wealthy Barclay Field family. In these years it had between 25 and 50 boarders, with only one holiday during the year.

3

A Shorter Way of Eating Prime Beef (1939-45)

War was declared in September 1939, and the staff and boys had to adapt to the very different restraints and conditions of war-time. At that time, there were 95 boys and eight staff. For some it was a time of excitement, for many a source of worry. Mr Jukes and Mr Morgan continued running the school while staff came and went according to the needs of the war effort. In 1942, a notable new member of staff was Mrs Agnes Lang, who was Headmistress from 1948-57 and continued teaching at The Prep until 1960.

The war

Any new boy who arrived at The Prep for the first time during the war and stood in the hallway outside the Headmaster's study would have immediately been conscious of eyes staring down at him from the wall beside the door. The eyes were set in the bulldog-like face of the Prime Minister, Winston Churchill, and his portrait hung there from the time he came to office until the end of the war. This was not just a picture; it was a symbol of the atmosphere of the nation, determined not to be defeated by Hitler.

For many boys, their fathers were away in the forces and they lived with their mothers and siblings. But for the mother to appear at the school was the most terrible disgrace that could befall a boy, the most embarrassing of his life. If your mother walked you to school, she had to be turned back before they came in sight of the building, for fear someone might see them. If a mother did actually come to school, then her son would be forced not to own her, the shame was so great. The school was their world, a boys' world, and it was quite separate from home.

True, there were a few adults in their world, but as far as the boys were concerned, these two worlds had to be kept apart.

By necessity, the boys had to be much more independent than children are, probably, now—and one of the things contributing to that was the very way they reached school and went home. No one came by car. For one thing, hardly anyone in the district actually possessed a car. Those who did, except people like doctors, for whom they were essential for the good of the community, had to lay them up in their garage so that every drop of fuel could be saved for the war effort. The bicycle was popular. The **Larcombes** used to cycle to school, home for lunch, and back again in time for afternoon lessons. Bus services were then frequent and cheap. **David** and **Paul Clark** caught the bus each morning at 8:40 am from the Riverhead end of Bradbourne Vale Road, paying 1d fare (2½d became 1p in 1971). Without fail, if they were sitting down and an adult got on for whom there was no seat, one of the boys would have given up his seat to them. That was just a natural courtesy of life. The Clarks walked home in the afternoon via Woodside Road, then very undeveloped and rural, and by Bradbourne Lakes. This took 20 minutes. Later on, they also used bikes. This was the era when the cycle shed really came into its own.

The cavernous basement also came into its own for another, grimmer reason. It was used as a cloakroom for hanging coats and as an air-raid shelter. Whenever the air-raid siren sounded, the whole school went into the basement. They were grouped together into classes, crammed onto a few benches, and continued as best they could with lessons. Sometimes most of the day was spent in the basement.

All windows in wartime were criss-crossed with strips of brown paper stuck to the glass. This was to reduce the risk of injury from glass splinters if a bomb exploded nearby. It also reduced the light. After dark, windows had to be 'blacked out' to prevent light helping enemy bombers, although the boys usually went home before dark, especially as the daylight-saving provisions of British summer time were extended during the winter and doubled in the summer.

4 Vine Court Road escaped being hit during what was called 'the bombing', though a landmine fell in the recreation ground off Holly Bush Lane, next to Walthamstow Hall, where the boys played football. It didn't explode, but was defused during the day while all the school children nearby were kept in the shelters. The Club Hall, on the other side of the Vine pavilion, was demolished one night so completely that it was never rebuilt, but turned into the Vine Gardens, opposite the entrance to Knole Paddock. In 1940, an unexploded bomb landed just round the corner on Dartford Road opposite **Mr Winter**'s shop and the school was shut for two days, and the staff and pupils evacuated to the Cornwall Hall, where normal school work was resumed for a time.

There was one exciting incident that occurred during the Battle of Britain, which for most people in Sevenoaks was their introduction to the war. It was fought above their heads in the clear blue skies of August and September 1940.

Most boys watched regular aerial daylight combat, observing planes on fire and air crew parachuting. Biggin Hill, the famous fighter station, was of course close by. During this time, the school was an unofficial home guard post and the Headmaster, **Mr Miles Jukes**, was an air-raid warden. The alarming moment that called for his greatest feat of courage came when a parachutist, who had baled out of his crashing plane, floated down into the playground right by the conservatory. Mr Jukes hadn't seen the plane and he had no idea whether his gate-crasher was British or German. He was left in no doubt, however, as he hurried to help the pilot disentangle himself. 'Quick, get a taxi to Biggin Hill,' the pilot said. 'It's the second time the buggers have had me down today!'

Although it may seem in retrospect that the war was an exciting time, that is, of course only true of a small number of incidents. In fact, the overriding long-term effects were simply deprivation, uncertainty and, of course, fear. Almost everything any child asked for—toys, sweets, sports apparatus—was simply unobtainable. Life was very grey. Most boys had fathers in the services and feared hearing of their deaths—as occasionally happened. Incidentally, many fathers in the services were less well paid than in their peacetime occupations, so that many families were financially hard up. Fatigue was a perpetual problem, as nights were often disrupted by air-raids when families went to their shelter. Early in the war, most people had an Anderson shelter dug into a hole in the garden, normally cold and wet. Later, Morrison shelters were made available within the house, which avoided disturbance—although, of course, people were still often woken by gunfire and bombing.

Everybody was provided at the outbreak of war with a gas mask, which had to be carried everywhere. The container was a box about 7in by 5in by 5in, carried by a shoulder strap. This had to be taken to school and out to the playground and was a perpetual appendage. The boys were all terrified of leaving them behind and being caught without them in an enemy gas attack; however, for the record, they never had to be used.

There were practice drills for putting on the rubbery smelling gas masks, and for taking them off. Both operations were difficult because the front of the face was covered by what looked something like a snorkel mask, but with a heavy metal tin on it resembling a nose. This was held to the face by stiff straps going over and around the head. The boys felt as if they would either suffocate or die of the smell.

Health and nutrition were a problem for everyone during the war. The authorities provided every schoolchild with, at first, ½ pint and later ⅓ pint of milk during morning break. The milk was delivered every morning in crates which were left near the front steps. The distribution of it in the right numbers to the right classes, and then the washing up of the empty bottles and the re-loading of the crates ready for the milkman, was carried out by a small team of boys whose base was the 'Milk Bar' in the kitchen. The operation was the highlight of their day. There were other important routines for the sake of the war, such as the 'coughs and sneezes spread diseases' ritual that began with every boy displaying his handkerchief and then coughing into it as a reminder of correct behaviour.

The boys also, about twice a term, had their vital statistics taken. This was called 'weights and measures'. The school had no restaurant for midday meals. Some went home, a few brought sandwiches, and many went to a British Restaurant. These were a wartime institution set up by the Ministry of Food and run by local government or voluntary agencies on a non-profit basis, selling simple, cheap meals. There were two in Sevenoaks to which the boys were taken by **Mrs Agnes Lang**, that outstanding and motherly teacher who was one day to become Headmistress of The Prep, or **Mr A. Handley**, the maths master. One was in the Cornwall Hall, and the other halfway down St. John's Hill. For two courses, the price was 6d (2½p) for children and 9d (nearly 4p) for adults. The Government issued recipes to help improve the variety of meals, largely based on potatoes and vegetables as protein such as meat, eggs, cheese, and fish were very scarce. **Ian Carmichael** recalled that the food was awful and called by the boys the PMH, which for the uninitiated stood for 'Pig's Muck Hole', although that wasn't enough to put him off sending his son, **James**, to The Prep in later years. These restaurants were run by volunteers and one reason for their popularity was that they provided meals over and above the food ration.

Mrs Lang remembered that when they paid, the boys were given tokens for the meat and sweet courses, and if they didn't like the pudding on the menu on a certain day, they would save up their tokens until there was a pudding to their taste and then they would have two or three helpings, one after the other. On their return to school, if they had been to the Cornwall Hall, the boys passed Turners Nurseries and if they had enough money, they would buy ½lb cherries for 9d (nearly 4p, very expensive).

Most boys managed well on this wartime fare and many parents deprived themselves to give the better food to their children. There was, occasionally, even an advantage in having a father overseas. The thrill when a small wooden crate

School photograph 1943, taken in the garden at Vine Court Road.

would arrive from Africa or elsewhere full of those fruits they could just remember from before the war – tangerines, grapefruit, lemons! Food rationing didn't end until 1951, six years after the war.

Heads and staff

During the war period the staff, who always taught in their black gowns, were headed by joint principals, Mr Jukes and **Mr Frank Morgan,** Mr Jukes having gone into partnership with Mr Morgan shortly before the war began. Mr Jukes, the elder principal (as he had only one lung, the boys in their ghoulish fashion expected him to die any day), was by 1945 in his late 50s – a widower, large, burly, and genial. He customarily wore a hairy Harris tweed suit of gingery hue. The Morgans now lived two doors away from the school in a semi-detached house, having moved from Amherst Road. **Mrs Betty Morgan** helped out in certain emergencies, such as when **Graham Larcombe** started school in the Kindergarten; he hated it so much and screamed so much that Mrs Morgan decided to take him out shopping with her to Dartford Road.

Miss Cardinal, the Kindergarten teacher, had owned her own school and was a formidable lady, clad in a tweed suit, burly and very tough, with short hair and with a brisk, no-nonsense view of life. She was an exacting disciplinarian, but well liked. She sounded as if she could be rather a dragon, with the occasional eccentricity – indeed, it was said that she kept a cow in her kitchen. It is certain the principals kept out of her way as much as possible. However, she had a heart of gold and a shrewd perception.

Her reports were as outspoken as she was. Of **Tony Larcombe,** she wrote: 'So dreadfully noisy, always talking. Never ceases at all, from the time he arrives at school until the time he leaves. He would make much better progress, if he only would stop shouting at the top of his voice and listen to the lesson being given. A most intelligent boy.' That her pupil was an advisor to Kent's teachers later in his career obviously would not have surprised her. Her students had a thorough grounding in the '3Rs'.

In 1939, Miss Cardinal was assisted by young, pretty **Miss Gwen Bewsher** who also taught art. Her sets for the Sevenoaks Players delighted many; later, she taught at St Hilary's, the girls' school in Bradbourne Park Road. Amongst the other staff at different times were **Mr Herbert Small**, whose speciality was music, and his step-son, **Mr Cyril Small**, who taught maths. **Mrs Gray** and **Mrs Sterry** both had boys at the school and bald **Colonel Brigstock** with a great white moustache took those boys who were not first division quality for football. **Mr Ronnie Marchant** continued to teach football and cricket throughout the war. Mr and **Mrs Handley** both taught during the war. Mr Handley taught maths and had a reputation with the boys of enjoying lunch in the nearby Vine Tavern. They even sang a little ditty about him.[3] Mrs Lang came in 1942 and taught geography and English; she was remembered by her boys with affection. Most teachers wore gowns although **Mr Eric Tozer**, who organised sport, wore the best part of his old RAF battle-dress much of the time.

Fabric

4 Vine Court Road was plainly decorated in functional style. Woodwork was dark; most walls were painted dark green up to the height of about 5ft, where a thin black line was drawn; above that, the walls were cream. The floorboards were uncovered, and in each class two boys stayed on each afternoon to sweep the floors. The furniture was mainly two-seater desks, each section having a lift-up lid; books were kept within. A wooden bench with a back-rest was fixed to the iron chassis. Each desk had an ink well and the boys used dip pens and much blotting paper. Fountain pens were rare and ballpoints not invented. Penknives, however, did exist, although they were not intended to be used on the desks. However, they certainly were. When **Peter Larcombe** returned to The Prep as a master, he found the names of many of his contemporaries, and even relations, incised in the woodwork of these everlasting desks. Their longevity was such that for years in the 1980s and 1990s **Mme Jacqueline Homer**, the French teacher, had one in the corner of her classroom for her books.

One alumnus described the prevailing theme of the school as one of cheerful, robust dignity. There was little bullying, although **Ted Prangnell** recalled shamefully that during the war there was an Italian boy who got badly bullied by some older boys. The bullies nick-named him Tomato, because his name sounded a bit like that. The teachers were liked; the boys liked each other, their work, and their play – they were happy. There was an atmosphere of steady decorum about the place, and this encouraged self-confidence that had a formative long-lasting effect on many of them.

But it would be wrong to suggest that the school was peopled by youthful plaster saints (not even older plaster saints – seeing one member of staff was sent

3 *There's a tavern on the Vine, on the Vine.*
There old Handley gets his wine, gets his wine.

to prison and two dismissed during this period!). On a couple of occasions epic fights occurred in the playground but it was recorded that the victor in both cases later apologised. In all schools then it was customary to behave in a respectful and formal manner towards teachers. Nevertheless, punishment occasionally became necessary. Sometimes, the boys were kept in for half an hour after school ended and given additional studies. On rarer occasions, a miscreant was caned in the study and those boys privileged to be in the adjoining fifth form room glued their ears to the wall to get the full sound effects. Such occasions, however, were rare.

Because the school was small in numbers and compact in area, and because the boys were sent home as soon as lessons ended to avoid the risk of air raids, there was little need for a disciplinary force. Accordingly, the prefectorial system was not much developed. Each form elected two monitors but their duties were minimal, largely limited to organizing floor-sweeping and grate-clearing work.

Heating was by open coal fires; there was no central heating. Coal fires, though cheerful, are inefficient and so the school was cold, especially as almost every boy then wore short trousers – longs being usually enjoyed by those over 13. School photos show a number of boys who could well be taken for young men. For various reasons, certain boys did remain at The Prep beyond the age of 13. **John Lark** was one such boy. At the end of his Prep days he had to move away for a year or so, having gained a place at Sevenoaks School. However, as for some reason on his return the place could not be taken up, he came back to The Prep for the time being and when Peter Larcombe joined the school in 1942, John Lark was the head boy, aged 15.

There was one ceremony in the life of the school, which must have been started by the boys, and it was graciously condoned by the staff. On the last morning of term, each form had a feast in the form rooms. By necessity, it was frugal – just little bits of this and that done up in a tin – but shared out. There were no packets of crisps or lollies, just ordinary food, but it was exciting to share titbits with friends, with holidays the following day and no staff supervising! A moving highlight of the last day of the school year was when boys who were leaving went round to say goodbye to every member of staff and to thank them for all they had done.

Academic

Mr Morgan taught French – there was one particular boy who was better at French than most of the others, whose name was **Olley**, and Mr Morgan always referred to him as Professor Olley. The boys were given a good grounding in what were then the usual school subjects, according to age. In the Kindergarten, they were mostly concerned with learning their multiplication tables by rote and spelling by repetition. Later they moved up through English, geography, history, scripture, arithmetic, geometry, and algebra. At fifth form level (today's equivalent is Form 7) they began French and Latin. The French text book was published by

Longmans and Mr Morgan liked to permit himself the frequent witticism, 'Now get out your Long Men'.

Writing paper and textbooks were in short supply because of the war. It is perhaps difficult, today, to grasp the implications of simply not having enough books or paper. The school's success in maintaining its teaching standards was all the more remarkable in the light of such shortages. The Latin primers, for instance, inherited from the 1930s, were already defaced in ink with steel-tip nibs. Every copy read:

A SHORTER WAY OF
EATING PRIME BEEF

Whereas it had begun, when the books were new, as:

A SHORTER
LATIN PRIMER

Whatever subject Mr Jukes was teaching (and he taught history from a book without pictures, scripture straight from the King James Bible of 1611, and Latin) every time the boys came across a word they didn't know, he took them back to its Latin derivation. Like this they learnt how to understand the meaning of words they had never seen before. A number of alumni have paid tribute to the effectiveness of Mr Juke's scripture teaching, which he linked in with a daily reading from the Gospels, which he read himself at Assembly – for which the school gathered, pressed into the fifth form room, with its attached conservatory.

From this wartime period a number of boys entered the Christian ministry, just as a group had in the early twenties. However, until the 1980s when **James Stephen** and **Phil Groves** studied at theological college, there seem to have been many years when no boys followed this career.

Science and art were both absent from the timetable. Education had always been classics-centred in the past and science was not yet thought important, although occasionally a member of staff might read the boys something scientific. Paul Clark remembered one spellbinding lesson that left the boys rather depressed because it 'proved' that in the future they would have to live only on pills instead of food.

There were no official school plays in the war years, but the boys organised their own little concerts and plays in the basement. The standard wasn't very high but they were enjoyed. There were no school clubs or societies, with the exception of the Young Farmers Club, which was part of the war effort. A visit with Mr Jukes and a few boys to the Fyfe family's farm at Heverham (the **Fyfe boys** were at The Prep) was recalled as a highlight. Mr Jukes started to keep ducks, and to keep them happy he built a little pond for them. The water in his pond got very dirty and had to be changed regularly, so Mr Jukes would put a hosepipe in the water and siphon it out. This meant he had to start off by sucking hard on the hosepipe and the boys all hoped that he would get a mouthful of muddy water – and one day, according to **John London**, later mayor of Sevenoaks, he did!

One activity (a useful one as well) that was laid on by the school was the opportunity for carpentry lessons. This took place in the basement that was turned into a carpenters' workshop by having a row of benches there with vices on them. It was **Mr William Cook**, a builder from St. John's Hill, who came in to give lessons. The boys were not allowed to make anything until they had mastered a joint. There was another skill a number of boys picked up from none other than the Head himself, and that was knitting! It was wartime and soldiers needed knitted socks and other things. Tony Larcombe became an expert at knitting gloves on four needles, while Peter Larcombe's main line was Fair Isle hot water bottle covers!

One particular afternoon, Peter Larcombe had a story that he had written read on the wireless (as the radio was then called). He had written this story as a composition for Mrs Lang and she was so pleased with it that it was sent in to Children's Hour – that daily programme which probably contributed more to the boys' education, for those who were daily listeners, than all that was done in school! **Andrew McDowall** stood at the top of the basement steps and read out the letter that had arrived that morning to the tiers of boys below him listening agog. 'We would like to broadcast your story'. Signed (and really signed, in ink!) by Aunt Elizabeth (Elizabeth Jenkin).

1939 autumn term report for Andrew McDowall including some vital statistics!

Many boys, in the days before TV, read a lot. Popular books were Richmal Crompton's 'William' books and W.E. Johns 'Biggles' books, which Mrs Lang was always reading to them. *Coral Island* and other classics were popular. Comics were read as avidly and were swopped. Younger boys liked *The Dandy, The Beano*, and *Rainbow*, while older boys favoured *The Champion, Hotspur,* and *The Wizard.*

School life
School was very formal. The boys addressed each other by their surname and, indeed, generally did not know each other's Christian names. One or two nicknames, however, became acceptable. This produced the bizarre result that parents often had no option but to address their son's friends as simply 'Thornton' or 'Carmichael' across the tea table. In the case of brothers, the form of address was to add 'major' to the elder, or 'minor' to the name of the younger. For more than two there were numbers. Because there were two other Clarks at one time in the school, Paul was Clark 3, his younger brother David being Clark 4, but he gradually worked his way up to being Clark major.

The school uniform had not changed over the years. The cap the boys wore in the 1940s was still the same maroon and black, the half and half. The uniform was obtained from Horncastles in Sevenoaks who still supply school blazers. **Christopher Horncastle**, grandson of the tailor who had served the Hollands' school from the start, was to be a boy at The Prep in the 1960s.

Michael Busselle, a relation of Mrs Lang, was at The Prep during the war. After going on to Sevenoaks School, he took up photography and became one of Britain's leading landscape photographers as well as running a successful studio in London. He had over 50 books published, some covering his works, some on technical advice on photography, and a few on a favourite subject, wine. His best-known books were his first, *Master Photography*, which sold more than a million copies, and *The Wine Lover's Guide to France.*

Sport and recreation
For recreation, the boys played football and cricket and in the summer went swimming, which Mr Jukes was very keen on, but that was all. In their spare time, the boys roved the countryside, especially in Knole Park and at Bradbourne Lakes. Some went coarse fishing or collected birds' eggs or butterflies. Many were in the Scouts, some in Crusaders. Indoors, the wireless was the main entertainment.

The boys played marbles, both indoors and out; they made moving tanks out of a cotton reel, cut notches in the edges of the top and bottom, cut a piece of candle wax, made a hole through the piece for a washer, then took a piece of elastic or a rubber band, slipped it down the hole and stuck used matchsticks through the top and bottom ends of it. When the rubber band was wound up and the tank put on the floor and let go, it would crawl about–if you were lucky.

Many boys in those days went to Church or Sunday School. The cinema was at the height of its popularity, there being three in Sevenoaks, often with queues outside them all. The entrance price for boys was 6d (2½p). On Saturday mornings, a cinema club for children was held in the London Road cinema, then called The Majestic, later The Odeon and now The Stag Theatre. The other cinemas were The Granada on the High Street, demolished in 1960 when Suffolk Way was built, and The Carlton on the west side of St. John's Hill, which became an electrical factory.

Most boys probably didn't go away on holiday at any time during the war. Indeed, unnecessary travelling was officially discouraged by posters bearing slogans such as, IS YOUR JOURNEY REALLY NECESSARY? It is likely that, except for short bus rides, most boys never went very far from Sevenoaks during the whole of the war.

The end of the war

The approaching end of the war was heralded by the allied landing in Normandy on 6 June 1944. On that day, Mr Jukes announced to the whole school what he had just heard on the wireless news and thereafter he regularly showed the boys maps illustrating the Allies' progress. The boys' elation at this was, however, cooled by the first flying bombs. Mr Jukes called together the whole school one afternoon, probably in late June 1944, and told them that a terrible new weapon had just been officially disclosed and sent them home early. All were terrified at first of this low flying, pilotless aircraft propelled by a rocket and launched in the direction of London. As soon as the staccato engine was heard to stop they knew that the dreaded silence as it glided down would soon result in a shuddering explosion – and wondered where. Many landed in the Sevenoaks area.

The war finally ended when the Japanese surrendered in August 1945. The school had never been hit but could not help being shaken during the bombing and the doodlebugs. During a history lesson in the classroom beside the front door that looked out onto the road, Mr Jukes had just folded up his glasses and put them on the staff table. He stood up and walked over to the fireplace; as he did so there was a terrible crash and through a cloud of dust, which might well be mistaken for smoke, the pupils saw that the ceiling above the table had fallen down all over it and over the chair, where the Head had been sitting a moment before. In the 1980s, that area that had had to be replaced could still be seen clearly.

A new school magazine appeared at the end of the war – its red cover was the first colour printing in Sevenoaks!

To celebrate victory, Sevenoaks Urban District Council decided to plant seven more oak trees near the Vine war memorial to add to the two existing sets near *The White Hart* and around the northern boundary of the Vine, the latter having been planted to commemorate the coronation of Edward VII. **Mr Dyson Laurie**, (brother of a Lord Mayor of London, **Sir John Laurie**, whose home was

Rockdale) performed the ceremony and the boys all filed out across the road onto the triangle of grass outside the Vine Tavern and watched him tip the soil around the roots of the seven little saplings. Unfortunately, they didn't survive.

---------- 4 ----------

Men May Come and Men May Go (1945-58)

The post-wars years were difficult for the country as the slow recovery from the war effort began under a new Labour government. Initially, The Prep continued under its joint principals, Mr Jukes and Mr Morgan, but in 1946 Mr Morgan left. At that time there was a total of 143 boys and 10 staff. In 1947, Mr Jukes had a road accident and was greatly incapacitated. The role of Head was taken over by Mrs Agnes Lang and she continued, supported by Mr Jukes and a number of dedicated teachers, to develop the school over the next decade. In 1946, the population of Sevenoaks had been just under 14,000 and by 1958 was approaching 17,000. Most of the large estates around Sevenoaks had sold off some of their land or had been broken up, and the housing developments on land so released continued to bring more commuters to live in Sevenoaks, attracted by, amongst other things, the variety and number of private preparatory schools for both boys and girls in the area. For boys, The New Beacon and Winchester House, which was started just before the war, were joined by Solefield School, established by Mr Jim Ridler in 1948 in a large house near Sevenoaks School, as rivals to The Prep, while Bradbourne College still offered preparatory classes for boys. For girls, The Granville School started in 1945 (and also took one or two brothers of girls in their Forms 1 and 2) and Farnaby Girls Preparatory School opened in 1949, while the two private senior girls' schools in Sevenoaks, Walthamstow Hall (which had moved to Sevenoaks in 1882) and St Hilary's (founded in 1942) had preparatory departments. In 1957 Mr Jukes died and the school was purchased by Mr Kenneth Ely and his wife. Mr Ely took over from Mrs Lang as Head in September 1958.

Heads and staff

In 1946, for the sake of their daughter's health, the **Morgans** decided to leave Sevenoaks and bought a school on the Hampshire coast, leaving **Mr Miles Jukes** as the sole Headmaster. However, the next year Mr Jukes had a bad road accident which had very serious consequences. He was run over by a local doctor and he was never able to take a really active part in the school afterwards. Two women of character came to the rescue. Mr Jukes' sister **Mrs Mimi Grieves** moved to Sevenoaks to look after him and in 1948, **Mrs Agnes Lang** became Headmistress. She had joined the staff in 1942 with two sons and two nephews already being educated at The Prep and was a popular teacher. She taught the boys to enjoy poetry; **Paul Clark** recalled one she taught them was called *The Brook* and had the memorable lines:

> *Men may come and men may go*
> *But I go on for ever.*

These very words could have been applied to Mrs Lang over the long period she taught at The Prep, especially in her early years when the male teachers came and went as they served in the armed forces. She ran the school with the help of a very dedicated staff of men and women until it was sold in 1957 after Mr Jukes' death. Mrs Grieves was to become the chief guide at Knole where she emerged as one of its outstanding personalities, once broadcasting from the house with Richard Dimbleby.

Mr Jukes continued to teach; small groups of boys climbed to the top of the school, to the Head's bedroom at the back of his flat, overlooking the playground, where they would gather round his bed for a lesson. He had a great cradle over his legs, under the sheets, to protect them. Mr Jukes was, by now, a very heavy man and alumni remembered the squeaks from the stairs from the flat as the Head, with all his weight, would heave himself into each form room to announce some important news – like that of 1952: 'The King is dead. We now have a Queen'.

Among the staff was **Mr Streatfeild**, brother of **Noel Streatfeild**, the authoress, a **Mrs Wilson**, wife of the British Ambassador to Peking, **Miss Doris Charles** and **Mr A. Handley**. **Miss Cardinal** was still in charge of the youngest class. To the boys, she always seemed very ancient! The music teacher was **Miss Snipp**, and you can imagine the fun the boys had with a name like that. Another form was called The Remove, and it was taken by Miss Charles, a sweet little lady. The physical training instructor was ex-Millwall footballer **Mr Eric Tozer**, who was to move on from The Prep to Sevenoaks School, and then return years later.

In 1956, **Mr John MacIldowie** joined the staff and had a strange story to tell about how that came about. He was working for the fire brigade as a Home Office lecturer on civilian detachment when he had a vivid dream that he was to become a preparatory schoolmaster. He resigned from his job the following day and advertised himself by writing to all the prep schools in the area. They all replied, but the only one to offer a place straight away was The Prep. He

June 1946 staff: Mr H. Small, Mr E. Tozer, Miss Cardinal, Mr C. Small, Mrs A. Lang, Mr M. Jukes, Mr Eichorn, Miss D. Charles, Mr R. Marchant and Col. Brigstock.

May 1948 staff additions: Miss Snipp, Mr and Mrs Hanley.

Summer 1954: One of two photographs recently donated by Michael Wakefield who is pictured in the middle row, fourth from the right., aged 11½.

was interviewed by Mr Jukes and Mrs Lang and started in the 1956 autumn term. He taught history, religious instruction, English, some maths and physical education plus helping with football and cricket. He recalled that most of the classrooms were very cramped and one seemed to be breathing down the boys' necks! School lunches were brought in by outside contractors and served at tables in the basement of the big house, which was even more cramped and gave little elbow-room. There was a washing-up rota for the boys. PE took place in the tiny playground without any equipment of any sort.

Inspectors' reports

Reports by H.M. Inspectors on The Prep in the 1950s expressed some concerns about the school. One, in 1950, had commented 'The present premises are only just tolerable; they will need continuing attention to maintenance and it is above all desirable that the best possible use should be made of all the available space' and, with reference to the fact that some boys stayed at the school until they were 15, 'A preparatory school course does not normally set out to provide an education which is complete in itself …'.

A report in 1957 made the same point, that boys stayed at The Prep until they reached the then school leaving age. Although this report highlighted many problems, it also revealed two gems. The Inspectors couldn't speak highly enough of the Headmistress, Mrs Lang: 'Running the school with effectiveness and serenity', she had 'done much to inspire the pupils.' The other gem was Miss Charles, another veteran teacher with very high standards. In that year, at the age of 70, Mr Jukes died and the school was acquired by **Mr Kenneth Ely** and the two star teachers remained on the staff under the new Head. A new era was to begin, which would culminate in the most significant episode in the history of The Prep up to that time, the move over December 1968 and January 1969 to Godden Green.

Academic

Mrs Lang was very proud of the successes of the boys. **William Hamilton** became head boy of Tonbridge School and a member of the scientific team that studied the jungles of Brazil; he was given a professorship by the Royal Society at New College, Oxford. **Patrick Lang** became a civil engineer, while **Peter Lang** went on to Loughborough College and became a physical education and games master at Truro School. **Andrew Lang**, of Trinity, Oxford, was a classics master at Kings College School, Wimbledon. **Tony Gould** won a music scholarship to Trinity College, Cambridge, and then became music master at Harrow and subsequently at the City of London School. A good number of boys in the slightly younger generation followed their fathers into crafts and businesses, like **Michael Meldon** in the family upholstery business at Greatness Mill, and **Nicholas Quinnell** into the family removals business that had been going since the 1700s. Indeed, some of these boys, for various reasons, never went to any other school but The Prep.

THE SEVENOAKS PREPARATORY SCHOOL.

REPORT.

Name *Anthony Larcombe* Form *Junior* *Winter* Term, 19 *48*

	Terms percentage	Exams. percentage		Conduct
Scripture				*not too good.*
Latin				
French			*So dreadfully noisy,*	Height
History			*always talking never*	
Geography			*ceases at all, from the time he arrived at school*	Weight
English			*until the time he leaves.*	Chest
Spelling			*He would make much better progress, if he only*	Left Biceps
Reading			*would stop shouting at the top of his voice*	
Writing			*and listen to the lesson*	REMARKS
Arithmetic			*being given.*	
Algebra			*A most intelligent boy*	
Geometry			*LRC.*	
Science				
Woodwork				
Games				

Height: 4 1 5
Weight: 3 1 13
Chest: Deflated / Inflated
Left Biceps: Down / Up

Next Term begins at 10 a.m. on *January 19th*

Next Term ends on *April 6th*

Half Term Holiday on *Feb. 28th*

O E Lang *Headmaster*

An intelligent boy whose conduct is wanting and too young for bicep measuring!

School life

Gangs had always been an exciting part of school life. **Peter Larcombe** was in a gang called *The Leather Mask* and his brother **Tony** in what was named *Gray's Gang*, led by a boy called **Bernard Gray**. 'Wars' between the various gangs went on continually. Bernard lived in a house at Godden Green called Fawke Cottage which was later to become the school house when The Prep moved from Vine Court Road some 20 years later. At that time (1949-52), his mother was the housekeeper there and they lived in a part of the house near the kitchens. Tony Larcombe often visited the house but remembered more of the garden. There were endless potting sheds, little pig sties, greenhouses, and stores. Around these a gardener used to do his work whilst the boys hid from him, crept up on him, set traps for him, etc. It was a fantastic place to play! The gardener, **Mr Arthur Searle**, was still working at Fawke Cottage when The Prep moved there in 1968 and was interviewed before he retired by Mr Peter Larcombe, who was then on the staff, and some of the boys about the history of the house.[4]

In the 1950s, afternoon lessons started at 2.15 pm after a lunch break of 1¾ hours. This was to allow some boys to go home for lunch but for others food was brought in from Williamsons restaurant in the High Street (on the site now

4 See page 76. He was still working at The Prep in summer 1978, despite having officially retired after 40 years working at Fawke Cottage in December 1977.

occupied by Brewers) and served in the basement of 4 Vine Court Road. As an alternative to the set lunch at school the boys could spend their lunch money at Williamsons where there was choice. The long break meant that the boys had opportunities to visit Sportscraft–a toy shop in London Road, the Carnegie Library in The Drive next to the Methodist Church, and even Knole Park.

Sport and recreation

It was in the immediate post-war era that The Prep's football strip was modified. In the 1920s, the boys had worn a white stockinette shirt, with a Griffin badge on the breast if colours had been awarded, navy blue shorts, grey socks, and football boots covering the ankles, with steel toecaps. By the late 1940s, the socks had become maroon with white feet, and the white shirts were relegated to practice games. The colour of the shirt that signified The Prep was maroon, like its blazer and cap.

Alumni's impressions of the war and post-war years are generally of the austerity under which they lived. Sports kit was often worn out and dilapidated. The cricket bag always seemed to have a hole in it and when carried dropped stumps along the path; after each game there seemed to be more stuffing from pads in the bag than before. The lack of equipment, however, did not alter the enthusiasm for cricket. Boys, in all their spare moments, whether at home, in transit, or at school, were to be found constantly playing imaginary strokes or bowling imaginary overs and yearning for the real thing. It was pretty basic, no-frills sport and batsmen rarely had the luxury of two pads! But the cricket was enjoyed under the coaching of Mr Marchant. As one alumnus recalled, 'he taught a very high standard. He had just got that technique'.

Life-saving medallions and certificates were awarded each year. These swimming and lifesaving classes produced contrasting memories. One alumnus shivered at the recollection of lying on the side of the pool, cold against his back, whilst being used for resuscitation demonstrations. On the other hand, Mr Jukes inspired many boys in their swimming and none more than the **McDowall** brothers, **Andrew** and **John**. In 1946, their father presented the McDowall Challenge Shield to the school and John was the first to win it, although his prowess might have had something to do with the fact that a lake in their garden helped the brothers to become such good swimmers. Andrew had been one of the school's wartime head boys; his sons **Dudley** and **Richard** were to be Prep boys in years to come, as were his grandsons, **Andrew** and **Joshua**, whose mother **Mrs Christine McDowall** taught at the Pre-Prep until the family emigrated to New Zealand in 2008. Despite ill-health and an awareness of his advancing years that prevented him from undertaking any regular teaching, as late as the year of his death – 1957 – Mr Jukes was still responsible for instruction at the baths.

— 5 —

The JP and the Pickpockets (1958-68)

The first ten years of Mr Ely's headship saw The Prep develop to meet the increasing demands of education. The roll increased from between 110 and 120 (the school photo of 1960 has 113 boys and 12 staff) to 138 in 1968. The Carey Hall next door was hired to provide further space. Plays were produced regularly, school societies were established, sports day and services at a local church were begun. Outings to London and foreign holidays became a regular feature. The school magazine, The Acorn, became an annual publication. The Elys moved out of the flat at the top of the school house, which released space for a library and more classrooms. But more space was still needed and in 1967 Mr Ely began to look for alternative premises. Autumn term 1968 was to be the last time The Prep occupied 4 Vine Court Road. By then there were 138 pupils and 15 staff, while fees ranged from £40 to £50 per term.

Heads and staff

Mr Kenneth Crawford Ely, a 49-year-old R.A.F. veteran with experience of teaching, purchased 4 Vine Court Road and the school in 1958 following **Mr Miles Jukes**' death. He moved into the flat at the top of the house with his second wife **Betty**. **Mr Ronald Webb** and his wife **Connie** joined the school at the same time. Mr Webb was the Bursar throughout Mr Ely's years, while Mrs Webb taught music for 12 years until she died after a short illness in 1970. The Elys and the Webbs ran the school as a limited company of which they were the shareholders. In 1961, the Elys had a daughter, **Jane**, who from an early age took part in the school's activities, especially the plays. By this time, the Elys had moved into a flat in neighbouring Park Lane.

In 1959, **Mr Peter Larcombe**, an alumnus from the 1940s, joined the staff after teacher training at Loughborough College and was soon to become a major factor in the school. When **Mrs Angela Lucas**, who was later to teach at The Prep, first came in 1964 as a prospective parent to meet Mr Ely, she was impressed by the way in which the classroom walls were used to stimulate the boys' interests. In the Form 4 room, one wall was covered with mounted reproductions of famous paintings, another with the boys' paintings. Mr Larcombe, Mr Ely explained, taught art throughout the school, and the huge flats stored in the conservatory adjacent to the form room were part of the scenery he designed and painted each year for the school play. In the Form 5 room, the walls were hidden by hand-done history charts. They were told that Mr Larcombe taught history throughout the school as well as being an expert on local history, taking the boys to places of historical interest. He made his own slide lectures, with his own photographs and scripts. In Form 6, the top form at the time, were Mr Larcombe's scripture maps, charts, and coloured illustrations, because he also taught scripture throughout the school.

Meanwhile, **Mrs Agnes Lang** felt it was time to move on and in 1960 she retired to Eastbourne. Mr Larcombe, who was not only a colleague but had also been taught by Mrs Lang, gave the school's farewell presentation to her. He said, '…during the war days, when the male staff came and went, the boys used to have a saying, "Men may come and men may go, but Mrs Lang goes on forever". Today we can't say that at The Prep anymore'. That day, Mrs Lang presented a cup for Kindness, Courtesy and Consideration. A courtesy cup is still presented annually to the most deserving pupil.

In 1961, the other 'gem' from the Jukes years, **Miss Doris Charles,** retired. She lived scarcely three years more. Mr Larcombe was now the only link between the Jukes and Ely eras until **Mr David Clark**, another war-time pupil, came back to teach. He had left The Prep in 1947, went to Sevenoaks School, qualified as a chartered accountant, served his compulsory two years' National Service in the army and returned to the City, where he became a partner in a firm of chartered accountants. One day in the office his eyes misted over and he could not see a letter he was trying to read. His eyes cleared, but when it happened again a few weeks later he sought medical advice. After a lot of tests he was told that he would be totally blind within two years. He was 28 years old, married with two small children and a mortgage.

He was in and out of hospital, lost the sight of one eye completely, had to give up his work as an accountant and was at home doing nothing. In 1965, out of the blue, Mr Ely rang him. Although they didn't know each other, Mr Ely had been told that Mr Clark was doing nothing and he asked him if he would teach maths at the school. Although Mr Clark confessed that he could go totally blind within half an hour Mr Ely took the risk and Mr Clark began teaching at The Prep in September 1965.

At The Prep, the boys loved him and he gained much from their friendship. But suddenly, at the end of the spring term of 1966, Mr Clark became completely blind. He went away to Birmingham University to learn to teach the blind and, following his training, came back to Dorton House in Seal where he taught for nine years. He returned to The Prep to teach in 1983 and his story will be picked up in a later chapter.

Mr Colin Pugh taught history at The Prep for two years to gain experience to become the Headmaster of a prep school near Manchester. **Max Findlay** remembered him as an inspirational history teacher who brought out a love of learning (and of history) that has never left him. **Mr I.D. York**, who had two sons at the school, took over the English teaching. **Mrs Mary Duddy** taught French, always conscious that her accent was really French-Canadian. She seemed distinctly glamorous to the boys. A school photo from 1963, a copy of which unfortunately cannot be traced, also showed **Mrs Elizabeth Talbot** (whose husband **Harry** taught maths for years at Sevenoaks School), **Mrs Joyce Nixon, Mr Michael Barker**, a mathematician, and then **Miss Gertrude Daniels** and **Miss Gertrude Quillin**.

Miss Daniels had been Headmistress of Cobden Road School and then Vine Lodge. Always smartly dressed in a dark-coloured double-breasted suit, with her grey hair in an Eton crop, she had an aura of dignity and perfect discipline; she taught English and her brisk tones disguised how good she was at doing that. Only once was she ruffled. There was a boy called **Jonathan Skinner**, the son of a local butcher, who always seemed to get into trouble. What he can have done this day is unimaginable because Miss Daniels came into the staff room saying, 'I didn't know how not to murder Skinner'. Her wish was nearly carried out at the end of the afternoon by schoolboy **Paul Waite**. Paul had an Etch-a-Sketch Doodle Master—a thing like a grey television screen, on which it was possible to draw pictures by twiddling knobs. Even when lessons had finished, Skinner wouldn't stop playing with it. Paul gave him plenty of warnings but in the end he lost his temper and smashed the Doodle Master down over Jonathan's head.

At that moment, Mr Larcombe entered the form room to see Skinner's head rapidly going not exactly grey, but silver—and then watched as his face became exactly like that of the Tin Man from *The Wizard of Oz*. As the silver flowed down over his blazer collar and shoulders, Mr Larcombe hurried forward to brush it off, only to find his hands turning to silver too! Silver indeed it was; the secret formula that produced the pictures was mercury. Quicksilver! No one discovered how his mother coped, but the next day he returned, just his usual self.

Miss Daniels especially remembered the high standard of the singing at The Prep, how good the boys were acting as girls, the fire-drills—with a bucket of burning material put in different places to represent the fire—and the support parents gave to the school, even to the extent of a mother who acted as a 'lollipop' lady to help the boys over Dartford Road.

Miss Quillin taught geography–particularly a detailed course on her native land, the Isle of Man, so the boys always said. She and Miss Daniels lived in Sevenoaks Weald, yet when it snowed, Miss Quillin, in her 70s, thought nothing of walking to school up Hubbard's Hill! Another teacher in that photo is **Miss Mary Waters**, who did wonders for the small children of the first form, and she was greatly loved and respected by her pupils right into their adult life. She was, in her private life, something of an artist. Miss Daniels and Miss Quillin retired to Deal in 1969.

In the 1963 photo, too, was an alumnus, **Andy Sampson**, son of the Head of Halstead Place School for boys with learning difficulties, against whom The Prep had begun to have sports fixtures. Andy was the first of a generally fine succession of alumni or other young men waiting to go to college or university, who would come to help on the staff, usually for a year.

The 1967 photo included new faces that would become very well known. Mrs Lucas (with an English degree, which had included two papers in Anglo Saxon!) specialised in English. With her illustrator husband, **Derek**, she was beginning to write books of her own. Their son **David** was a pupil at the school. **Mrs Jean Davidson** taught the youngest children, **Mrs Kathleen Johns** was a talented mathematician, and among the men was **Mr Harold Templeman**, whose son **Michael** had been at the school. With his arrival, science, once of little or no importance in a prep school curriculum, had arrived.

That year, the young **Tim Dickinson** started at The Prep and it was to be the beginning of over 50 years' association of the Dickinson family with the school. In the autumn term of 1967, Tim's mother **Mrs Madeleine Dickinson** joined the staff to help her friend Mrs Davidson with the Kindergarten, then taking Form 1 for handwork and poetry, and eventually teaching in the junior school for almost 20 years. Her younger son, **Simon**, soon joined the Kindergarten. Tim went right through the school and sent two of his children there. His daughter **Alice** was there for Years 7 and 8, and his son **Will**, like his father, went all the

1967, the last official school photo at Vine Court Road with Mrs A. Lucas, Mrs J.

way through from Nursery to Year 8. When he left in 2014, Will was asked if he liked his school, to which he responded, 'I love my school and my school loves me', saying that he wasn't going to leave the school – instead, he was going to re-join **Mrs Sue Binnie**'s Nursery and go through again! The Dickinson connection continues, as Tim is now a current (2018) Governor of the school and his wife, **Eileen**, teaches art in the Pre-Prep and supervised the Little Oaks Club.

Inspectors' reports

That Mr Ely took all the criticisms of the 1957 Inspectors' report very seriously can be seen by the report of the three Inspectors who carried out a blitz lasting three days in 1961. Introducing the new Head, they noted that he had experience of preparatory school work, the R.A.F. – where he was a navigator – and, for a short period, the joint headship of a school for children with learning difficulties. However, it was the forward look the school was beginning to take that pleased the Inspectors. In 1950, there had only been 80 boys in the school; now, there were 119 on the roll. The fees in 1957 for seniors were 17 guineas (£17.85) per term, plus two guineas (£2.10) for stationery and games. Daily lunch cost 2s 3d (11¼p). By 1961, there had been an increase. For boys of five and six the cost was 18 guineas (£18.90) per term, 22 guineas (£23.10) for boys of seven and eight, and 25 guineas (£26.25) for boys of nine and over. Lunch showed the least increase, rising by 3d to 2s 6d (12½p) per day.

The great improvements made in the supply of books for the classroom and the library (these being financed in part from fines, including those levied for leaving things lying about), wall charts, and maps were commended, as was the work of particular staff, together with the out-of-school activities, like the societies that had played, in their opinion, a valuable part in the school's recovery. The report concluded that the school seemed a happy and stable community, which had won back its self-respect. Not all the school's problems had been solved, but its progress since 1958 was a remarkable achievement.

Davidson *(2nd and 4th on left)*, Mrs Johns and Mr H. Templeman *(3rd and 4th on right)*.

left A classroom on the quad. Photo was probably submitted to *The Half & Half*'s by Jeremy Henson. His brother Nigel, with Peter Barley, were assistant editors on the new school magazine, *The Acorn. (first edition cover, opposite)*
below Classes were also held in the Carey Hall. Jeremy Crang, who collaborated with Mr Larcombe on *The Half & Half's*, is fourth from the right (furthest back in the sunlight).

In 1984 the History Option Group visited Vine Court Road. They saw how little space the boys had had for recreation there – and by 1968 it had housed classrooms as well.

Fabric

One of the things the Inspectors pressed for in their reports before Mr Ely took over was a proper school library. Gradually this was built up and when in 1964 the Ely family, including Jane, moved into a flat in a house nearer the Vine Cricket Ground, they vacated the flat on the top floor of the school in which they had lived. The front room, with its lovely view of the North Downs, became the library.

In 1967, *The Acorn* reported that at the beginning of the autumn term over 40 new books were donated to the library, many of these as 'thank you' presents from boys who were leaving. There was a fair attendance of library users throughout the year. The double bedroom of the flat became the art room, but Mr Larcombe was always uneasy having a full class of boys there because he remembered so well Mr Juke's insistence, when he had been a pupil, that the floor was unsafe. In the 1980s, Mr Larcombe spoke to the then owner of 4 Vine Court Road, who told him that the first owner after The Prep had left had wanted to put a huge wooden chalet-type roof on the building. The architect had told them that the top storey could not take the weight. Perhaps the staff and boys of the late 1960s had a lucky escape in the art room!

For ten years, Mr Ely had developed the school to meet the increasing demands of education. Averaging between 140 and 150 boys between the ages of 5 and 14 on the register, he hired the Carey Hall of the Vine Baptist Church. It became a classroom, an assembly hall for morning prayers, parents' meetings, prize-giving, and a theatre for school plays. The school magazine, *The Acorn*, became an annual publication. The first issue covered the academic year 1963-64 and was edited by Mrs Betty Ely. The first 14 issues up to 1976-77 were on A5 paper and ranged from 28 to 40 pages. Mrs Ely was the editor up to issue 13, when Mrs Lucas took over. Apart from a photograph of Fawke Cottage after the move to Godden Green and the occasional cartoons, there were no images. The content usually had a short Headmaster's report or one from a senior member of staff, reports on drama, music, sport and outings and examples of prose and poetry from the whole school. It is clear that, right from the start, the boys were encouraged to write copy and most of the reports on activities were written by the boys.

But with all these activities and the increasing number of boys, the school remained confined to the house and hall and a new science lab and classroom, which took up too much of the old quads. It was still without its own sports facilities. Mr Ely had always been conscious of the limitations of the site in Vine Court Road and the comments of the Inspectors about lack of space. Mrs Ely

top left Leaving for the last assembly in the Carey Hall with Miss Daniels, Mrs Nunn, Miss Quillin and Mrs Lucas.   *top right* 'Old Boys Wall' in the conservatory. *bottom left* Mr Templeman and Mr Brunton follow Mr Ely to the last assembly. (*right*)

edited *The Acorn* and in the editorial for 1967-68 she broke some sensational news. She noted that the year had been eventful one way and another. School life, as is life in general, was marked by periods of change and the school was going through such a period. The year had started with the inauguration of the science laboratory built on some of the spare space of the playground, and ended with the possibility of a move of the whole school to a site two miles out of town. Even if this didn't take place, she went on to say, there were bound to be fundamental changes at intervals which, whether liked or not, would help to prevent stagnation and keep minds fresh to meet new challenges – 1968-69 could be a very exciting year, and so it proved to be.

During 1967, Mr Ely began to look around for an alternative site that would give the school its own games fields into the bargain. One of the properties that came up for sale was the historic Emmetts near Ide Hill but finally he settled on a house in idyllic gardens, woods, and fields at Godden Green and took up the tenancy of Fawke Cottage together with one adjoining field, both part of the Knole Estate. The grounds gave the school all it needed for sport and play, although the house not only had much lower ceilings but also rather smaller rooms than Vine Avenue! There weren't very many rooms they could use, either, so the (by now two) wooden classrooms on the playground at the Vine were transported to the new grounds and two more were added to accommodate all the boys.

Moving a school is like a nightmare! Would everything be taken or would some items be thrown away? Would all the furniture fit into the classrooms or did the school have to buy new, or second hand? Quinnells of Sevenoaks were enlisted to actually move the school and in charge of the operation was **Nicholas Quinnell**, who had been at The Prep at the end of the Second World War.

At the end of the autumn term of 1968, Mr Ely conducted the last assembly in the Carey Hall. The last assembly was a solemn occasion, especially for people like Mr Larcombe, who was an alumnus as well as a long-serving member of staff, and **Mrs Jo Nunn**, who had been the principal bell-ringer. Out in the playground she rang the bell for the last time and the boys filed into their form lines. One by one the classes made their way from the playground, past the conservatory where, throughout the years, leavers had chalked their names and school dates on the wall. They went out of the front gate to the Baptist Hall, the youngest boys first. Then came the staff, down the steps from the front door, and finally the Head in an old tweed sports jacket, laden with cups to be awarded for the last time at the Vine.

Academic

When Mr Larcombe was first employed at the school in 1959, part of his contract was to teach 'general science'–and general it was! But Mr Templeman came as a science specialist in 1967 and began 'Nuffield Science'. A wooden classroom was erected beyond the conservatory, in the playground, the gas laid on, and the science lab was born. Tim Dickinson remembers the total lack of heating in any of the early outdoor classrooms or, as they called them, 'the sheds'. Mr Templeman's popularity increased as winter settled in, for one simple reason: Bunsen burners. The boys pleaded with him to do any scientific test that incorporated them and they learnt to love this wonderful accessory. In his house in Vine Court Road, Mr Templeman had a collection of old wirelesses and other obsolete technical equipment. He and **Mrs Templeman** made the sixth-form boys welcome in their house and encouraged them to dismantle and study the parts of these relics while enjoying tea and cakes. They also hosted French

Mr Templeman and an Upper 6 cast for the annual French sketch at prize giving.

exchange students from Sevenoaks School, encouraging Prep boys to come and speak French with them.

Mr Templeman also taught French and as Mr Larcombe had taught it himself for a year, one of the fun things they did was for the Upper 6 to act a sketch in French at prize-giving in the Carey Hall. Prize-giving was an occasion for the choir to sing and an important guest addressed the boys and parents, and then presented prizes. One of the first speakers was **Mr Ernie Groves**, the senior master from Sevenoaks School who had taught at The Prep, part time, in the 1920s.

The Carey Hall was the scene, too, of highly successful parents' meetings. After a speaker of relevance had talked to the parents, they moved from their seats to talk personally to members of staff who stood at intervals round the walls. Perhaps the most notable speaker at the time was **Mr Kim Taylor**, the new Headmaster of Sevenoaks School, who decided to make endless and far-reaching experiments in education (and publicity) which had been neither tried, nor proved.

Under Mr Ely, assemblies took a new look. At first they were held in the basement, where the staff sat lined up in front of a huge old boiler, facing the boys. Later, they were held next door in the Carey Hall. Hymns from *Ancient and Modern* were sung, and boys took it in turn to read the day's lesson from the Bible and each day a different member of staff led the prayers.

At about this time the old hobbies society became redundant but, under the guidance of Mrs Lucas, periods for non-curriculum activities were established on Thursday afternoons. This helped boys who liked making things with their hands do something they really enjoyed. The principal project was producing drawings of old Sevenoaks, and making models of the buildings of ancient London.

Drama and music

Mr Ely's favourite pastime was the production of a school play. The first, in 1960, was *Toad of Toad Hall* with Water Rat superbly played by **Robin Graham-Brown**, who completely stole the show. From his first entrance he found a way straight to the hearts of the audience, and his solo was extremely well sung. **R.G. Campbell** proved a very popular Mole; his performance was a gem. In the title role of Toad, **S.C. Duddy** 'at first seemed nervous, but as he progressed he gained confidence and in disguise as a washerwoman had the audience continually laughing', as a reporter on the now obsolete *Sevenoaks News* wrote, adding that Badger was played by **Alexander Hamilton**, a robust character 'who must be commended for his acting'. There was one awkward moment which he overcame admirably. Having sat on a box rather heavily, there was a sound of splintering wood. It was most unfortunate that his next line should be 'Alas! What have I done?'. Sadly, this member of the Hamilton family, a number of whom were at The Prep, lost his life in a climbing accident in the Alps in the autumn of 1967 soon after going to Aberdeen University. The story about the splintering wood rings true to the insecure nature of Mr Larcombe's scenery construction. He began with Mr Ely's first production in 1960 and continued constructing and painting for many, many years. Boys and teachers used to hike the ten-foot high flats into the room by the conservatory with its 10ft 6in ceiling and paint them during one games afternoon a week for most of the spring term every year. The *Sevenoaks News*, however, praised Mr Larcombe's efforts and reported that each new scene produced gasps of admiration from the audience, especially the wild wood.

When *Midsummer Night's Dream* was produced in 1961, the audience gasped when the stylised tree standing in front of a beautiful reproduction of an orange grove from a medieval French tapestry began to wobble and Puck, played by **C.A. Parnell**, stepped onto the stage. The tree fell flat onto the stage, revealing the tea chest to which it was attached and which was intended to keep it standing. With great presence of mind, Puck picked it up and went on with his speech.

In 1962, there was an outbreak of petty larceny in the school. Mr Larcombe had a sense of humour failure as his handkerchief, car keys or wallet routinely vanished from his pockets only to be proffered to him by a small boy. Quite half the boys at The Prep were becoming proficient pickpockets, and it was official – that is to say they were being trained in their craft by a Justice of the Peace who was none other than their Head, Mr Ely! The J.P. and his pickpockets were rehearsing for their production of a musical that had recently opened in the West End – *Oliver*. Normally it would have been impossible to perform the play so soon after its opening but the composer, **Lionel Bart** himself, gave them permission. He was a friend of the father of the head boy, **Peter Arnold** (who played Charley Bates in the production). **Mr John Arnold**, co-director of the film *Genevieve*, acquired for The Prep a sky backcloth from a film studio and the set of flats that was used for many years afterwards. **Nigel Henson** starred as Oliver and Robin Graham-Brown played a spine-chilling Fagin.

In a later play, the constructional weakness of the set was demonstrated when a rather chubby boy had to enter the stage through a trapdoor in the wall. His head appeared through the trap and after a vigorous struggle he walked on, wearing the trap door like a life-belt!

Through the years there were many memorable performances, as a result of Mr Ely's skill as a producer—and always Mrs Webb was at the piano. *Oliver* was followed by *Hans Christian Anderson* in 1963. The next year saw the first attempt at *Where the Rainbows Ends* and then, in 1965, *Eliza Dolittle*, adapted by Mr Ely with music from *My Fair Lady*. In this, **Jeremy Henson** gave a glittering performance as Eliza and **James Graham-Brown** (Robin's younger brother) balanced him as Henry Higgins. Paul Waite had all the earthiness of Alfred Doolittle.

Jeremy Henson came of a family line of actors and actresses. His grandmother, the famous comedienne **Binnie Hale**, used to attend school functions; his father, **Basil Henson**, was on television sets all the time in those days and Jeremy later established himself as an actor in Canada. James Graham-Brown is known for his cricketing success and Paul Waite was one of those alumni who later came back to help on the staff. As art was his line, he relieved Mr Larcombe of scene-painting for a couple of shows.

In 1966, The Prep went to town on exotic oriental golden domes for *The King and I* with Jeremy Henson again—as Anna this time—and **Martin Sinha** as the King of Siam. *The Rebel Maid* in 1967 was a light opera about the Bloodless Revolution of 1688. **Christian Dodd** played the title role, and on the cast list for the second time appeared the name of **Douglas Reith**. In *The King and I* he had played Sir Edward Ramsay and now he was Sir Stephen Crespigny. He became an established actor and later an announcer on Radio 3. He was a capable horseman and this helped him obtain a part in the film *International Velvet*. Mrs Lucas remembers him, then aged 12, giving a speech of welcome in Latin to the guest of honour at speech day in the Carey Hall. In about 1983, he visited the school and Mrs Lucas was struck by the clarity and dignity of his spoken English.

By now a team was building up behind the scenes—Mrs Nunn with the properties, **Mrs Barbara Clements** doing the make-up, and **David Hawthorn** hotting things up a little on the drums.

The second *Oliver* in 1968 starred **Graham Fosh**, with **'Boysie' A.C. Waite**, Paul's younger brother, as Fagin. The second version was written up in the school magazine, *The Acorn*.

'This year's production, *Oliver*, went very well, with Graham Fosh as Oliver, **T.J. Hartley** as the Artful Dodger, A.C. Waite as Fagin, **I.D. Perry** as Mr Bumble, and **S.T. Barley** as Mr Brownlow really making the play with their excellent acting. The songs were brought to life by David Hawthorn playing the drums and Mrs Webb the piano. The fine scenery, made by Messrs Larcombe, **Salmon** and

1963 Hans Christian Anderson with Nigel Henson and Matthew Ridout.
1965 Eliza Doolittle with James Graham-Brown as Higgins and Jeremy Henson as Eliza.
1964 Where the Rainbow Ends. Ralph Lancaster-Gaye, David Hawthorn, David Prattent,
Nigel *and* Jeremy Henson, Nigel Ashcroft, Paul Waite, Maxwell Findlay and Peter Barley.
1966 The King and I. Martin Sinha as the King and Jeremy Henson as Anna.

Hynard, along with the torn, ragged costumes of the paupers and pickpockets, lent a sympathetic atmosphere to the production. The play was well received by the audience, raising money for the Science Fund.' For this production **Mr Derek Lucas** (Mrs Lucas' husband) produced a number of fake green £1 notes which were scattered liberally over the stage as the cast took its bow. As the curtains closed, there was a stampede. The entire cast broke loose in a mad rush to line their pockets! This was to be the last show to be staged in the Carey Hall at the Vine.

If drama was really a tradition at The Prep and Mr Ely had merely re-introduced it after a long interval, he very quickly started all kinds of activities that had not gone on before, including the introduction of notable societies which met each week after lunch. One was the musical society, started by **Mr Patrick le Marchant**, a young master who was only at The Prep for the first year of Mr Ely's headship, and then taken over by Mr Larcombe. Using records in the Elys' sitting room in the flat, the boys were introduced to concertos, symphonies, overtures and suites, with different instruments of the orchestra and particular works by famous composers. Every so often Mr Ely acquired a new Rogers and Hammerstein record, like *The Sound of Music*, and so they listened to something more modern. Of course, both *The King and I* and *Oklahoma!* were produced on stage by the school but as far as *The Sound of Music* was concerned, the consensus was that the boys wouldn't make very good nuns for long!

School life

One person who remembers the school in Vine Court Road under Mr Ely is **Mrs Penny Spencer-Allen**. When her family moved to Sevenoaks next door to the school in 1957 she was a tiny girl and little did she know that The Prep would become much involved in her life, one way or another. Mrs Spencer-Allen's three boys all went to the school in the 1980s and 90s and she taught in the Pre-Prep[5] in the 1990s. Having had a wonderful time exploring her new home from bottom to top, it was on reaching the top of the house that she discovered a room with a most interesting view. The attic window that pointed west looked way down onto a garden where she could see several boys in school uniform playing. They all wore grey shorts and jumpers and were being supervised by a teacher. She could hear a bell ring and they all ran and lined up to go into class. Their new next-door neighbours' son went to this school and they were told that the school was called Sevenoaks Prep and at that time was headed by a Mr Ely. Quite unknown to the neighbours' son, young Penny and his sisters used to have a huge amount of fun spying on him and his friends from the 'secret' attic window.

---

5 Up to 1992, Forms 1-3 and the Kindergarten were referred to as 'the Junior School'. From 1992, when Mrs Marjorie Shea took over, it was called the Pre-Prep, which was the generally accepted name for schools or departments which catered for 3 to 7-year-old infants. Although 'Junior School' was still used on many occasions internally and in writing, the term 'Pre-Prep' has been used for the rest of this book when referring to events from 1992 to 2018.

Her two brothers were sent to Winchester House, a school a short walk away in Hitchin Hatch Lane. It was there that a young teacher called **Mr Edward Oatley** worked and was eventually to become its Deputy Headmaster. He taught Penny's brothers sport and some other subjects, with his name coming up constantly at home as he was definitely one of their favourite teachers. The family met him many times at sports days, school fêtes, etc. so knew who the boys were talking about.

Mr Ely re-introduced the hobbies society, which had been disbanded some years before. It was an eye-opener to those staff that attended the firmly disciplined meeting. Mr Ely was in the chair; each week a different boy spoke about his hobby. The variety of the hobbies and the vast knowledge of a boy in his particular field were always impressive, but there were occasions when the presentation was awe-inspiring. To some of the staff, these presentations revealed skills and knowledge beneath the surface of the boys they were teaching.

Regular services were introduced in the town's parish church, St. Nicholas, three times a year, at Christmas, Ash Wednesday and Ascension Day. The carol services were splendid. Mr Ely trained the choir while Mr Larcombe rehearsed the boys who had been chosen to read the lessons of the Christmas story that fell between the first reading – that always belonged to the Headmaster or a member of staff – and the last lesson, which was always read by an alumnus. Since his name was never announced beforehand, it was an exciting guessing game to see who it would be. The most memorable of all such lessons was when **Peter Barley** returned from Westminster School to read. The rector of Sevenoaks, the **Rev. Eric M.T. McLelland**, conducted the services and **Mr G.A. Tester** was always at the organ.

At the other services, sometimes the rector preached, sometimes one of his curates. The journey with the boys from The Vine to the church and back was quite straightforward in theory but often didn't turn out that way in practice. There were around 150 boys, including the Kindergarten, to be walked most of the time in single file because the pavements full of shoppers were narrow, across the road from the Club Hall to the old police station. Done like that, the route had fewer little entrances to negotiate than on the other side of the High Street. The entire school, however, had to cross both the High Street and London Road where they met by the fountain. There was a pedestrian crossing across each road but only a short piece of pavement in the middle. In order to keep the school together so that it didn't break up into little groups of trotting boys trying to close the gaps and keep up with each other, it was important that the crossings were firmly manned by staff so that the school crossed both roads at once, holding up two flows of traffic. This inconvenience to the public always got the better of one young master, who regularly carried an umbrella. With extravagant gestures he would hold up the boys in the middle of a crossing and vigorously wave the traffic on with his umbrella. The result was always irreparable chaos as isolated trios of boys trotted unattended through the crowds of shoppers.

Over the years a great deal of money was collected at these services and various charities have benefited by it, especially, in the earlier days, The Royal London Society for the Blind (Dorton House School) in Seal.

A feature that a visitor to the school in those days would have noticed was that many of the boys were wearing a green badge, with a golden lamp on it, in their blazer lapel. This was the emblem of the Scripture Union, an interdenominational organisation to help young people read the Bible regularly. Every year an S.U. rally was held at the Cornwall Hall. Boys and girls from many local schools converged on it. In 1960, Mr Larcombe took two boys, **Jeremy Crang** and **Christopher Shields**, to the rally. Enthused, on their return the boys talked-up the S.U. at school and the following year, between 60 and 70 boys marched to the rally and two mothers came along to help!

The S.U. became an established part of The Prep. For many years quite two thirds of the boys had daily Bible-reading notes (and badges). One year they made their own banner, which they carried through the streets and displayed at the rally. Another year, the school choir, conducted by Mr Ely, sang in the rally. Perhaps the most memorable rally was when the guest speaker was **Mr George Cansdale**; he was the superintendent of the London Zoo and a children's television presenter. He persuaded **Tim Hartley** to stand by the exit with a boa constrictor over his shoulders on top of his blazer. To the astonishment of all the children who plucked up the courage to stroke it, the snake was as hot as the perspiring Tim!

It was in a more affluent age that the S.U died out at The Prep. For one thing, the rallies were discontinued, and for the other so many boys would order material which they were not prepared to pay for, that it became financially impossible to continue.

For many alumni, one of the most upsetting events was Mr Ely's decision to change the design of the cap. It now became maroon all over except for a black peak and a small streak of black at the side of the peak. The passing of the 'half & half' was mourned by one person in particular, and one no one might have suspected of having a strong attachment to this old symbol of honour. As a girl, **Betty Vintner** was often in the home of her cousins, **Kenneth** and **David Kevis**. It was the 1930s and the brothers went to The Prep. When they came home they always hung their 'half & half' caps on the hat stand in the hall, side by side. That memory was impressed on her mind. Little did she dream that she would ever have any closer connection with The Prep. By the 1960s when the cap design was changed she had become Mrs Ely, the wife of the Head!

In those days, each child had free school milk at break time, which was distributed outside the main school building. When the boys had drunk the milk they used to play 'British Bulldog' or marbles in the playground. Lunch was served in the basement of the main school building, which was very dark and dingy. The lunches were brought into the school kitchen in metal containers from a local café called *The Nell Gwynne* and heated by the indomitable and diminutive **Miss Jeffries.** Before lunch, the boys would have to queue up and have their hands inspected to make sure they had washed them; if they weren't up to standard, Miss Jeffries would tap them with her famous wooden spoon and send them off to wash them properly. Friday was the best day as there was a choice. Miss Jeffries would go round the tables brandishing her wooden spoon and inquiring, fish or rissoles? If a boy couldn't stomach the greens or left a slug from the salad at the side his plate, he received a tap on the head from the wooden spoon. Miss Jeffries not only cleaned the brass name-plate on the gate post outside the school and kept it dazzling but also was said to be the only person on earth the Headmaster was afraid of. Certainly, everybody else was! Appointed servers brought the plates of lunch to the silently waiting boys seated at the tables. Staff topped and tailed the tables and the boys sat in house groups. The houses had been reorganised by Mr Ely and bore the local names Weald and Vine.

With the lunch on the table, the head boy would say grace, and permission would be given both to eat and to talk – quietly. There was one memorable lunchtime. **Tim Barker** had left The Prep and the following year he won a scholarship to Gordonstoun. On this particular day, he had asked to come back and see the school. What was so special was that he had entered Gordonstoun at the same time as Prince Charles.

When Tim entered the dining room with a dignified Mr Ely, you would have thought from the awed but electric atmosphere that Prince Charles himself had come to lunch! There was no talking that day. All ears were strained to catch any titbit of gossip about the heir to the throne, as the Head and Tim, suddenly the school's greatest celebrity, conversed in annoyingly confidential tones.

One bizarre aspect of school life was the dreaded tartan shorts. These were kept in a cupboard in the Vine Court Road dining room in case your trousers were rendered useless by an emergency evacuation of solid waste. It was immediately obvious to all what anyone wearing them had done, and consequently the rest of the day was spent in misery by the offender.

One of Mrs Dickinson's responsibilities was to supervise afternoon rest in the Carey Hall next door to the school. Every boy in the junior part of the school had his own rug, and one of her earliest memories was trying to stuff all these dusty rugs into an incredibly small cupboard and shutting the door before they all fell out again. She also remembered the time when one of the little boys hid behind the heavy classroom door when the rest went to break. He wasn't missed until lessons were resumed and then the search was on. The police were called and they sped around town in their Panda cars. Half an hour later, the boy was found asleep on the edge of the Vine and remarked, 'I were sleeping under a tree!' It was a never-to-be-forgotten moment.

left A crocodile of boys on Knole Paddock Hill (now Plynouth Drive). *above & below* Cricket match on The Vine ground with Prep spectators and batsmen – some yet to bat and some not!

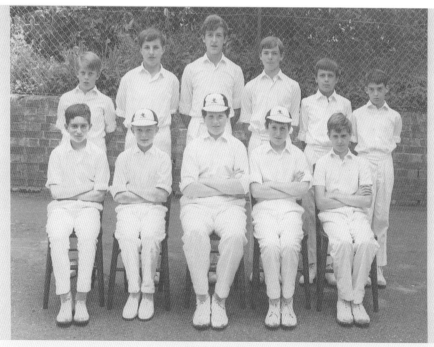

1968 First XI

back row T. Dickinson, P. McCracken, A. Dennison, T. Edwards, T. Hartley, A. Gist.
front row J. Brotherton, P. Downton, S. Barley (*capt*) G. Prout, C. Horsburgh.

Sport and recreation

With Mr Ely's arrival, The Prep's sporting life flourished as never before. A brisk and efficient administrator, he soon built up a full sports fixture list with football and cricket matches played against The New Beacon, Winchester House, Solefield, Hilden Grange, Streete Court School in Godstone, Sevenoaks School under 14s, and Halstead Place. Rugby was introduced by Mr Webb, the Bursar, with the first recorded match taking place on 8 March 1960, a 12-a-side game resulting in a 13-22 defeat at the hands of Hilden Grange.

In the winter, the boys trooped down to Knole Paddock or the Hollybush Recreation Ground for football in the first term, under the eagle eye of Mr Ely, while in the second term they played rugby. This was followed by the trek back to Vine Court Road with chapped thighs and blue toes. Cricket was played in the summer at the Hollybush Recreation Ground and on the Vine. Throughout the year, mothers were organised to drive boys to away matches. James Graham-Brown, who went on to Sevenoaks School and then played professional cricket for Kent and Derbyshire before going into teaching, remarked that, although the school had to borrow facilities, they showed again and again how much could be made of so little with dedicated and enthusiastic coaches.

Results inevitably varied over the years. In the autumn term of 1963 football started well with a 5-3 victory away to Halstead Place, but then there were six consecutive defeats with a goal tally of nil scored and 27 conceded. The 1967 side was far better with eight wins, including a 16-0 and 9-1 double against Solefield, one draw and just one loss 1-3 against The New Beacon. The colts side was also successful. The team had a memorable victory in the Kemsing football six-a-side tournament. Fifteen schools entered, divided up into three groups with five teams in each one; each team played four matches. The Prep beat Kemsing, St Thomas's, and Riverhead and drew with Bayham Road. This, with a goal aggregate of 8-2, was sufficient to win the group. As winners, they received a Milky Bar each!

However, the rugby side of the same school year was described in *The Acorn* as '…abominable. The whole side lacked guts and determination' while the cricket XI '…had a moderate season', although the young **Paul Downton** took 14 wickets with his off-spin bowling at an average of 4.50 runs each, and was awarded his 1st XI cap at the young age of 9. Paul went on to have a stellar professional cricket career with Kent, Middlesex, and England but admits that he was nearly lost to football while at The Prep. It gave him his first taste of an organised team sport with **Mr Ronnie Marchant**, whose greatest gift was teaching the boys the importance of trying to pass the ball. Then (and maybe even now) junior school football generally resembled a swarm of bees chasing an elusive fly as both teams converged on the ball. Mr Marchant somehow managed to impose a hint of organisation in the boys' frantic wanderings, and football afternoons, with the familiar 'crocodile' trek down to the Holly Bush Lane pitches, quickly becoming the highlight of the week. Up to the age of 11, Paul was certainly going to be a professional footballer, preferably playing for World Cup star-studded West Ham. Paul remembers that they must have had a reasonable colts team as he remembered an emphatic 14-0 victory over arch-rivals Solefield and a 9-0 win against Halstead Place.

For generations of the boys, from the establishment of the school at Vine Court Road, cricket at The Prep was synonymous with the name of Mr Marchant. This greatly loved character was, for many years between the two world wars, the professional groundsman at the Vine Cricket Ground, a first-class player and an excellent coach. He was the gentlest of men, who taught the boys not only sporting skills but also a lot about graciousness and humility. The fact that a couple of his prodigies went on to play for Kent, and one for England – and more importantly, that numerous of his flock went on to play and enjoy club cricket – speaks volumes for the personality and guidance of the man. He was connected with The Prep for 50 years and finally retired in 1970.

Tim Dickinson has clear memories of cricket at The Prep in the late 1960s and early 1970s, having captained the 1st XI in 1969 and 1970. The school played their home mid-week matches at Sevenoaks Vine on a wicket that had been prepared off the main square down towards the school. His first memory was playing against Hilden Grange and catching out **Chris Cowdrey**, who went on to play for Kent and England, at square leg watched by **Colin Cowdrey**, then the Kent and England captain, and **George Downton**, Paul's father who had also played for Kent, applauding the catch with the latter saying, 'great catch'. Tim remembers it being a proud moment but also, for the record, it was hit so hard that he put his hands in front of his face for protection and this time the ball stuck. Another time he had been asked to keep wicket and within the first 10 minutes **Simon Barley** had fired a bouncer in at the batsman who didn't get anywhere near the ball, but Tim did, as it hit him on the bounce in his left eye. He had to wear an eye patch for a month which hid the many colours that come with a black eye – he never kept wicket again. The fathers versus sons cricket match in 1968 when the school was still at Vine Court Road was played at Knole Paddock, as the Vine was not available at a weekend. It was a competitive and amusing match with the fathers' team – including three cricketers who had all played for a very strong Vine first team in Messrs **Rodney Crang**, George Downton and **Derek Ellison**, and despite being handicapped by having to use size 3 bats which were suitable for 9-year olds – succeeding in defeating the boys.

Paul Downton wrote that, reflecting on his cricket career, he was struck by one basic similarity between prep school cricket and today's county and test cricket: fast bowlers dominate the game! Just as Marshall and Holding, Thompson and Lillee won test matches on their own, so too did the terrors of the prep school circuit! For Solefield there was the double-barrelled attack of **Durdant-Hollamby** and **Parnel-Smith**. In reply, The Prep had the fearsome duo of Simon Barley and **Alan Dennison**. The Vine hosted one historic game where, put into bat, The Prep mustered only 14 against the onslaught but won the game by bowling out Solefield for 9! It is certainly true that in prep school cricket, the game is never won or lost until the last ball is bowled.

Mr Ely was a great cricketing enthusiast. As a committee member and Treasurer of the Vine Cricket Club and head of its junior section, not only did he ensure that The Prep's relationship continued to flourish, but the school's cricketing life prospered as well. The Vine's and The Prep's wickets were tended by Messrs **George** and **Jim Burnett** and the fact that conditions were always excellent may have had something to do with the fact that Mr Ely, as Treasurer, was responsible for paying the aforementioned groundsmen. New fixtures were arranged and, to the excitement of the boys, a new cricket school was built at Knole Paddock, enabling The Prep to practise there after school on Fridays during the autumn and spring terms. A number of boys even had the honour of being selected to have coaching during the winter by Kent professionals.

For those that didn't profess to be cricketers there was the unashamed and unembarrassed obscurity of the 'third game'. Mr Larcombe, securely perched on his shooting stick in his red cord jacket, directed operations in his unassuming manner. For all the aberrations that were being perpetuated in the name of sport by the unwieldy and uncoordinated, there was an atmosphere of joy as the non-sporting fraternity participated with a lack of self-consciousness. Mr Ely and his happy band of coaches had got it about right.

One of these was **Mr Brian Melliard** who used to offer small cash incentives at catching practice. These used to operate on a knock-out basis at the end of a games session. If you dropped one you could go home but the sixpenny bit was well worth competing for. The eventual winners would have to catch an enormous skyer.

The swimming tradition established by Mr Jukes continued when Mr Webb took classes for non-swimmers on Thursday mornings during the summer term. The Prep also had some athletic tradition. In Mr Jukes' time there had been a

Long jump heats at Knole Paddock with Mr Marchant on his signature shooting stick.

Between heats on Sports Day at Knole Paddock.

lot of cross-country with **Mr Eric Tozer** in Knole Park, which the boys entered through the hole in the wall in Seal Hollow Road. Yet no sooner had Mr Ely arrived than new developments took place. An annual athletics match against Halstead Place School was arranged, the first of which took place in June 1958, resulting in a 63 to 59 points win for The Prep. Sports days were introduced at Knole Paddock; the inaugural sports day was held on Friday, 6 June 1958. The ground was immaculately prepared by the groundsman and there was great excitement among the boys over the new experience of spending the preceding days doing sports heats.

On the big day itself Mr Pugh started the races, Mr Webb acted as the official recorder and Mr Marchant supervised the field events. During the course of the afternoon boys participated in events as diverse as the 220 yards, the egg-and-spoon race, and the potato race. After the final house relay, the trophies and prizes were presented by **Mrs Mimi Grieves**, sister of the late Head, Mr Jukes, and an old friend of the school. **R. Mullet** of Weald house won the very first Victor Ludorum, with 17 points. A tradition had been established which was to continue at Vine Court Road for the next 10 years and was later transferred to the new premises at Godden Green.

Outings and holidays

There were regular school outings, usually arranged by Mrs Nunn. The Vine was so convenient for the station that in 1968 Mr Larcombe took a party of boys in their own reserved compartment to Charing Cross, and then on a river boat down the Thames to Greenwich to visit the Observatory, the Maritime Museum, and the *Cutty Sark*. He also, as art master, took the top form each year to the National Gallery. Mrs Ely regularly took boys on Saturdays to the Children's Concerts at the Royal Festival Hall, again easily accessible from Charing Cross. But Mrs Nunn had a big heart, a big voice (she trained as an opera singer), a big dog, and a big vision, and it was she who pioneered school holidays abroad. In those days, it was unlikely that many families could afford a foreign holiday together but they could pay for one or two children to go. The first adventurous party set out from the school by coach in April 1966 – in a driving blizzard! The channel crossing – the party was on the last ferry allowed

Viewing the Prime Meridian marker at the Royal Observatory in Greenwich, 1968.

to go – was so frightful ('ghastly' was the boys' word) that Mr Larcombe vowed if they ever went again they'd go by air!

Despite this nightmarish start they had a delightful time in the Austrian Alps at a place called St Joann in the Tyrol, not very far from Salzburg, that fairy-tale city, the birth place of Mozart and the setting for *The Sound of Music*. Fortunately they had the pension, where they were staying, to themselves as (although many more uplifting and formal activities were arranged) fighting and playing in the stream at the back of the chalet were undoubtedly the boys' favourite pastimes. One of the legacies of the trip was a saying heard in the staffroom for a long time, which was coined by a farmer's son when on a coach trip through the majestic, snow covered Alps: 'Mount'ns, bloomin' ol' mount'ns. What do we want to see bloomin' ol' mount'ns for?'

The mountains the boys saw the next year were more spectacular than ever, probably the most beautiful sight in the world. They flew to Basle and took the train through Switzerland to Interlaken – a place the boys were convinced was named after Mr Larcombe – and would keep pronouncing it as if it were! In the hotel this time they had a juke box and a bowling alley, which passed many hours.

They sailed across Lake Thun, went up the cable car above Murren to Schilthorn to admire the Mönch, the Eiger, and the Jungfrau. This visit produced one or two unexpected results. As they gained height, suddenly **Nugent**'s nose produced a flow of blood which was finally stemmed only when presented with a can of Coca-Cola at the top. **Gordon Prout**, leaning

Lake Thun, Switzerland in 1967.

on the railings of the viewing platform, inadvertently dropped his unpeeled, hard-boiled egg over the side. As it descended towards Murren the boys speculated on the velocity of its fall and whether, if it hit somebody in the town, it would have gained the destructive power of a golf ball, a cricket ball, or some more deadly missile.

The weather was unpredictable. Following a very warm, sunny day there was a heavy snowstorm. With Alan Dennison as leader the boys rolled a gigantic snowball in the steep field behind the hotel. Finally, the whole group gave it a tremendous shove. It went rolling down the hill gathering speed and even greater size, coming to a halt, thankfully, on the level ground at the bottom; potentially it was a much more lethal weapon than Prout's egg had been.

Then they discovered that **Nigel Bears** had mumps. They could not find 'mumps' in the German dictionary and quite expected to be expelled from the hotel when the manager found out, but he was very kind and unperturbed. Mrs Lucas was with the party as well, this time with David and her daughter **Helen**, who–as the only girl–was very popular.

When they arrived home in England after each visit, the boys made an audio/visual presentation to show their parents. Many of the boys contributed photos; they brought back records of local music, made up their own sound effects with every person who was in the party speaking some part of the commentary. When the boys heard the sound tracks years later, they noted with alarm, 'Didn't we talk posh!'

Other schools

It was from this time that the Headmaster and staff tried to get parents to evaluate a wider range of schools that their boys might profitably go to, rather than the traditional local idea that every boy must go to Sevenoaks. In the following years, the range did widen with success. The magazines list the schools that boys happily settled into. They included: Westminster School, Dulwich College, Cannock School, Seaford College, Cray Valley Technical High School, Tunbridge Wells Technical High School, Judd School, Skinners School, City of London, St. John's Leatherhead, Sutton Valence, St. Edmund's Canterbury, Tonbridge School, Bethany, and many other schools through the years. But boys still went to Sevenoaks. 1964 was a particularly good year when two scholarships were awarded, Nigel Henson to Sevenoaks and **Nigel Gibson** to Tonbridge.

In 1967, ambitious plans for the reorganisation of secondary education in Sevenoaks were scrapped following consultation with head teachers, governors, and local council officials. The 'comprehensive' scheme involved the setting up of three high schools–Wildernesse and Hatton in Sevenoaks and Churchill in Westerham–to which all children would have gone at 11 without test or selection. There would have been three Upper Schools–Sevenoaks, Walthamstow Hall and Sundridge Convent (Combe Bank)–to which selected pupils would have gone at the age of 13 for a five-year course.

6

Another Cottage, in the Country (1969-77)

The school blossomed in this greatly enlarged environment at Godden Green. Extra classrooms, then a mini theatre that would be the venue of a whole range of successful plays, and then a better equipped science laboratory were all added. The Concert on the Lawn was reinstated in 1973. Football, cricket, athletics, and cross-country began to flourish and outdoor clubs were founded. In 1969, the school was divided into four houses. Vine, Weald, Knole, and Seal and house competitions in work and sport took on greater importance. There was a short-lived experiment to have a few girls at the school. The school was now in the parish of Seal and the carol service and the end-of-year service were held annually in Seal Church. Many boys moved on as they had traditionally done to Sevenoaks School, but many went further afield to an increasing range of senior schools. In 1977, Mr Ely announced that he was going to sell the school and retire the next year, after almost a decade at Godden Green.

Heads and staff
Most of the staff who moved with the school to Godden Green stayed for at least two years, while overall the number of staff remained at about a dozen for the first ten years in the new surroundings. Two long-serving teachers, **Miss Mary Waters** and **Mrs Barbara Clements**, left in 1971. Mrs Waters was a gem; a lovely, gentle, artistic person who loved the boys and gave **Jeremy Crang** the day off because he worked so hard! She could be outspoken, as another member of the staff knew to her cost when told by Mary to sit with her legs crossed so that her knickers weren't on show! Mrs Clements was a disciplinarian with nineteen skirts, as acutely observed by **David Downton**.

Mrs Jo Nunn, who had done so much to expand the boys' horizons by arranging outings and holidays, moved on in 1973. She was described as having 'a big heart, a big voice (she trained as an opera singer), a big dog and a big vision'. In 1975, **Mr Harold Templeman**, who was the first real science teacher the school had employed, retired. Some of the teachers who had been with **Mr Kenneth Ely** at Vine Court Road, notably **Mrs Angela Lucas**, **Mr Peter Larcombe**, and **Mrs Madeleine Dickinson** were still on the staff when he retired. Along with the new teachers Mr Ely had appointed, especially **Mrs Mary Shefford**, **Mrs Chris Thomas**, **Mrs Pat Richardson**, **Mrs Beth Sadler**, and **Mrs Bryony House**, there was a strong group of dedicated teachers to support the new Headmaster when, in 1978, Mr Ely himself retired. Mr Ely had also recruited the well-known local cricketer **Mr Ken Smart** who, although he was already 60 when he started at The Prep in 1969, was fit and experienced enough to coach the boys in cricket and football until 1987. Not all the staff were successful. Mrs Dickinson remembered a lunatic from Billericay who had acne and wore a cloak and who gave her younger son, **Simon**, six of the best for something trivial. He only lasted one term.

For several years running after The Prep moved to Godden Green, Mr Ely had a series of sixth-form boys from the Voluntary Service Unit of Sevenoaks School to help with sports, supervise break times, and fill in when staff were absent.

In February 1977, Mr Ely had sent the following letter to staff and parents:

'At the end of this year I shall have completed 20 years as Head of this school and I have decided to retire at the end of the autumn term and give way to a younger man. My wife and I, however, will not be relinquishing our interest in the school and during 1978 I intend being available for advice if required and shall be involved with the school finances as **Mr Ronald Webb** was in the past.

'My successor will be **Mr Edward Oatley**, who has been Assistant Head at two preparatory schools during the past 10 years and is a member of the Incorporated Association of Preparatory Schools (IAPS). Latterly he has been at Winchester House School and is thus well known in the district. He and his wife will be moving into the school premises in July and he will have one term with me before he takes over.

'I feel sure that Mr Oatley and his wife[6], who is a qualified teacher, will continue to maintain the standard and reputation of the school and arrangements will be made for all parents to meet them before the end of the year.'

It was the end of an era. Approaching his 70th year, Mr Ely retired. A supper dance was organised by the parents at the Wildernesse golf club for Mr and Mrs Ely where they were presented with a silver tray, a decanter, and sherry glasses and a cheque. Mr Ely was living nearby at Hilltop in Stone Street when he died on 1 December 1984 at the age of 75. Mrs Lucas wrote to Mrs Ely on behalf of

---

6 Mr Oatley's first wife, Frances.

her family, Mr Oatley and the school to express condolences. She emphasised 'the firm foundations, the devoted work and the lasting example which Mr Ely bequeathed to us'.

Fabric

At the end of term in December 1968, the younger boys went home while the entire staff and all the older boys helped Quinnells to move the school 'lock, stock and barrel', including the science lab and the new classroom, to the new site at Godden Green. All the furniture was carried outside to the removal van – boys lugging the heavy double desks. In the playground, a group of boys was making a bonfire of old exercise books and registers – source material which the group who wrote the first *Half & Half's* and anyone else interested in the history of The Prep could well have done with! Mr Larcombe took a photo of them at their vandalism.

The most complicated operation was dismantling the library, which was in the topmost room in the front of 4 Vine Court Road. The books were no problem. They were stacked away, with the first Head's novel among them. It was the long shelving that was the problem. To twist the sections through the house, round all the bends in the stairs, was well-nigh impossible, so the shelves were lowered by rope from the window, which added extra excitement to the day. When the van had gone, there remained only one thing still to do. **Mr Smith**, the school's carpenter and odd job man, armed with a large screwdriver, strode out of the gate, and unscrewed the shining brass plaque from the brick gatepost. 4 Vine Court Road was Sevenoaks Preparatory School no longer! According to a report

left Vandalism! Documents that would have been valuable in the writing of *The Half & Half's* were burnt just before the move from Vine Court Road to Godden Green. *right* All the older boys and staff helped Quinnell & Son (a former Prep family).

top left Mr Smith's last job at Vine Court Road.
top right In-house electricians: parent, Mr Peter Hunt and his son Robert.
above Site set out for the first of many building projects at The Prep's new home.
below The cedar and glass classroom under construction.

in the *Chronicle and Courier* in March 1969, the old school house was to be converted into maisoncttes.

The same team worked on many of the days throughout the Christmas holidays to prepare the new school for the spring term. The new wood and glass buildings were already pegged out on the vegetable gardens at Fawke Cottage when the very large dark blue removal van with a ramp attached to the back arrived. **Tim Dickinson** remembers the procession of Form 6 pupils on day one of the move each carrying a box marked with the name of the new classroom and directed by Mr Webb, inevitably smoking a roll-up cigarette. Day two was more varied and enjoyable as the boys helped **Mr Britain**, a gap year teacher, mark out the one and only football pitch. As the boys did such a good job he took **Richard Jenkins**, **Keith Blackmore**, and Tim down to *The Bucks Head* pub for lunch which consisted of a Coke and a sandwich. Tim reflected on the uproar there would be today: child labour, a member of the senior management team smoking throughout the school and an unqualified teacher taking three 12-year olds to a pub for lunch – but for the record, he notes, it was tremendous fun.

During the Christmas holidays, **Mr Alan Hunt** (known as 'Bob') wired up every part of the buildings, including the fire alarm and the buzzer (instead of a bell to start lessons). His son, **Robert**, a boy at the school, was his mate. **Mr Bassett**, the school carpenter, transformed the stable and garage into the science lab under the eye of Mr Templeman and staff came in to sort out books for different classrooms. It was amazing how quickly it all took shape. The staff soon realised how much smaller the new classrooms in Fawke Cottage were than those in Vine Court Road.

First day at Fawke Cottage, Godden Green, January 1969.

So, on a snowy January day in 1969, all was ready when a coach from W. Davis and Sons brought the first group of boys to their new school, with all its welcome expanse of grounds awaiting them. Mrs Lucas travelled in from Sevenoaks on the coach with the boys on that grey dank first morning of the new term. They all wore orange fluorescent armbands, to be seen in the gloom, for road safety. Imagine their mixed feelings as they filed in through the gate to be greeted by the Head and to find their way to the brilliantly lit new classrooms in the mist.

Mr Ely had succeeded in his dream of finding a new home for The Prep. Like the Cottage at Sevenoaks School where it had all begun, the new school building was also a cottage – Fawke Cottage, in Godden Green, a tiny hamlet between Sevenoaks and Fawke Common best known for its pub, *The Bucks Head*. It is perhaps most easily visualised as being exactly the opposite side of Knole Park from The Prep's birthplace, Sevenoaks School. When the school made the move to Godden Green the staff and boys found themselves surrounded by beautifully kept gardens and they soon discovered the reason: the courteous, hard-working gardener, **Mr Arthur Searle**, who was always attending to flower beds and lawns and fruit trees.

Fawke Cottage[7]

Since at least 1635, the land on which The Prep now stands had formed part of a small farm called at first Stakes, and later Stake Farm. By 1729, when it was owned by William Porter, a tanner, and leased to Henry Summers, it consisted of about 30 acres of mixed orchards, arable, pasture, and woodland and, as well as the farmhouse, included two cottages – one to the north of the farmhouse and one to the south. The farm was later owned by the Hayes family before being acquired by the Duke of Dorset of Knole, became part of the Knole Estate, and then was let to tenant farmers. By 1839, when the tithe apportionment maps and schedules were published, it had reduced in size to about 24 acres and was being farmed by Albert George. Later, the cottage to the south of the farm was demolished and replaced by the more substantial Fawke Cottage.

Fawke Cottage was built in 1867, as the date over the front door indicates, by the Knole Estate as a private hospital where people who lived on the estate could be treated if they became ill; the 1870 Ordnance Survey map marks it as such. To emphasise its links with Knole, its chimneys are copies of those on Knole House. In 1873, however, Sevenoaks and Holmesdale Cottage Hospital was opened on the site of the present hospital at the bottom of St John's Hill, and there was no need for the estate to have its own hospital. The house was converted into a private house and let to tenants. For many years **Mr James Martin**, a London stockbroker, and his family lived there but after the First World War it was unoccupied and rather run down, until two sisters, **Miss Dorothy Coleman**

---

7 This short history of Fawke Cottage is based on an interview with Mr Searle, referred to above on page 45. A full transcript of the interview is on the Memories CD.

and **Miss Violet Coleman**, took on the tenancy, consisting of Fawke Cottage, a further cottage in Back Lane and nearly three acres of woodland. There are several references in the school and other records to these sisters being members of the Norfolk mustard family but on available documentation, their surname is spelt with an 'e', while the mustard family name is spelt 'Colman'.

The Coleman sisters brought a gardener with them and Mr Searle was lucky enough, in 1927, to get a job as an under-gardener, eventually becoming the Head Gardener and working there for over 50 years, except during the Second World War when he served in the army, until he retired in 1977 when Fawke Cottage had become The Prep. Born in 1905 on the Isle of Wight, and married to **Miss Ethel Cottenham** in 1933, Mr Searle lived with his family in Seal Croft Cottages in Childsbridge Lane, Seal. Miss Violet died in 1928 at the young age of 33 but her sister continued living at Fawke Cottage until she died in December 1966, aged 76.

The sisters each had their own car, garaged in the old stables, which became the first science lab after The Prep moved in. Mr Searle took on the role of chauffeur in addition to his garden duties. Miss Dorothy's car was remembered as a venerable grey Wolsey registration number DC 60 which she bequeathed to Mr Searle in her will. Before the war, there were usually three live-in servants, a housemaid, a parlour maid and a cook, who occupied the bedrooms in the top right-hand part of the house and had a small sitting room next to the kitchen. After the war, Miss Dorothy had just a housekeeper who became **Mrs Dora Holbrook** living in, with a daily who came in to help with the cleaning. By coincidence, Mrs Holbrook was an aunt of **Mrs Janet Oatley**, the wife of the future Headmaster. All the living rooms had bell pushes which would alert the servants, via a large board in the kitchen, that they were needed by Miss Dorothy. There was an air-raid shelter under the lawn, about 8ft by 12ft with seven or eight steps down to it, with a beech hedge around it. It had a vent with an escape hatch in case the steps became blocked. Mr Searle had helped to dig it out originally. When The Prep came it was felt to be dangerous, especially as it filled with water when it had been raining, and so it was filled in, along with a well.

When The Prep arrived, a series of sheds was converted into changing rooms. The sheds included Mr Searle's dressing room, where he would change into a chauffeur's uniform when necessary, his workshop, a potting shed, a fruit room, a store room used for used furniture, pictures and other redundant household items, and finally a wood store. There was also, after the war, a small pigsty. An unusual aspect of Fawke Cottage was a wooden outdoor tennis court. Miss Dorothy had had Turners of Sevenoaks lay a grass court on the far side of the lawn away from the house but it was always flooding, so she had it converted into a raised wooden court. It looked like the deck of a ship with long narrow boards about 3in wide and tiny gaps in between, although it was painted green. During the Second World War, an incendiary bomb fell on the court and blew

Miss Dorothy Coleman's colourful planting is still enjoyed today but sadly the cedar tree *(right)* planted in 1935 had to be felled in 2009.

a hole in it. Later, despite regular painting by Mr Searle, it began to deteriorate and had to be scrapped. When The Prep arrived, it was laid as a hard tennis court.

Miss Dorothy was a keen arborist and one thing that everyone noticed was the careful landscaping of the trees so that red foliage had a grey colour behind it then yellow in front of the red. According to Mr Searle, Miss Dorothy was fairly well off, could buy any trees she wanted to, and told Mr Searle where to plant them. The horse chestnut near the summer house provided a ready source of conkers for the boys who had been used to harvesting conkers from the trees in St Botolph's Road at the old school and feared there would be no supply at Godden Green, but the tree was already there when Mr Searle arrived. Near the horse chestnut was a Victorian summer house which could swivel 360 degrees on wheels running on a rail so that it could always face the sun. It was painted green and used for many years to store desks and chairs. It was removed in 2006, having become dilapidated and dangerous.

Another tree that was there when Mr Searle arrived was the Ginkgo or Maidenhead Fern Tree, one of the oldest trees known to man. It was thought to be extinct but one was found in Central China in the 19th century and specimens found their way to Kew Gardens. Mr Searle planted the enormous monkey puzzle tree near the road and, in 1935, a cedar on the lawn, to commemorate the silver jubilee of King George V. The plaque attached to the tree had disappeared for some years and was found in 2002 by some boys playing 'camps' in the woods.

In 2009 a limb fell from the cedar onto the new Oakery dining room, causing damage to the roof and guttering. The tree was declared dangerous and was cut back to a three-foot stump later that year.

A school is created

In what had been Fawke Cottage, now the main school building, there were four classrooms upstairs plus Mr Ely's study, Mr and Mrs Ely's bedroom, their daughter **Jane**'s bedroom and a bathroom. Downstairs was the kitchen, dining room/hall, staff room, and a lounge which was used for interviewing prospective parents. The four-classroom wooden block had been transported from Vine Court Road and now sprouted from the house's vegetable patch providing an element of continuity. It was a tribute to the strength and willpower of the removal men that the school's solid, familiar cedar wood furniture sat so well and undamaged in the new classrooms. The textbooks remained suspiciously familiar; even the school plaque from Vine Court Road was now mounted proudly on the front door to welcome visitors.

In the first two years, with parents' help, the partitions between the classrooms were removed so that once a year the block could be turned into a theatre for the school play. This always needed a huge amount of organisation. The garages, the old stables, were converted into a science laboratory and the garden sheds with their corrugated iron roofs became changing rooms. The individual class changing rooms came as a welcome relief from the cramped communal changing area in Vine Court Road. There were extensive kitchen gardens which were used to produce vegetables and fruit for lunches.

The Godden Green site offered an enormously fresh and exciting contrast to 4 Vine Court Road. With their very own games field – the three-acre Cabbage Patch which was bordered by woodland adjoining Knole Park – at their backdoor and the tennis court in the grounds, the tedious routine journeys to Knole Paddock and the Hollybush Recreation Ground were now things of the past. Football and cricket were played on the Cabbage Patch. One problem was that the 4½ acres between The Prep and Stake Farm, the girls' finishing school a few hundred yards to the north, known as the Front Field, had sheep in it. Until the field was acquired in 1979, the sheep were a nuisance coming through the hedge into the school premises. At speech day in July 1969, a cricket stump was placed where a rowan tree was to be planted in the autumn to commemorate the move to Godden Green.

Academic

Mr Ely's last report as Head in 1978 included a homily on the 11 plus which he explained was a grading, not an examination. He said that The Prep was not an 11 plus school and '…if parents think that by sending their boys here they will have a better chance of a free County place, they should really think again.' In the ten years up to Mr Ely's retirement, The Prep sent just over half its leavers to independent schools, 80% of these going to Sevenoaks, a sixth going to Kent grammar schools and a fifth leaving to local non-selective schools or transferring to other preparatory schools (the balance going to schools outside Kent or abroad). Although some of the statistics are not clear, Mr Ely's view had not deterred all parents, as in the ten years since the move to Godden Green an average of three or four boys each year had left The Prep at 11 to take up a free place at Sevenoaks, with a few going to Judd or Tunbridge Wells Grammar.

1971 saw a record number of 14 boys gaining places at Sevenoaks; **Robert House** gained an open scholarship, seven other boys passed Common Entrance, and six took up county places at 11 years old. This number was not reached again until 2014 when, again, 14 pupils (11 girls and 3 boys) gained places at Sevenoaks, although by this time there were no longer county places available.

The school undertook a geological survey of the Sevenoaks area for a 1975 Science Fair held at West Kent College in July 1975. Led by Mr Templeman, boys went to Dunton Green, Stone Street, Ide Hill, Underriver, and other places and found fossils, specimens of minerals, rocks, etc. which were displayed at the fair with suitable explanations.

School life

The old school's small terraced playgrounds – from which, incidentally, many of the alumni still bore the scars of over-enthusiasm – were superseded by a beckoning expanse of manicured lawns, bounded by idyllic woodland walk-ways (which, as luck would have it, incorporated a conker tree) rather than staid Victorian facades, the new site engendered an unaccustomed but welcome sense of space and freedom, and provided substantial mileage for the boys' boundless curiosity.

Of course, the move had cause to be regretted by some. Exposure to the countryside was a hazard hardly known when the school was in the town. During the first summer at Godden Green, Mr Ely promised a local farmer that the boys of the top form would go into a field beyond the sports field to help stack bales of hay. The effect on many of the boys was sudden and alarming. One boy's face began to swell up, and soon he couldn't see because his eyes had all but disappeared. Sportsmen came to fear not only inclement weather, but animal trespassers. It was soon evident that some of the Friesian cattle and horses in the fields surrounding the games field had a tendency to wander. On several occasions, irritating hoof marks were found on the cricket square. The only hoofed visitor to be received with pleasure by the boys was the occasional fallow deer that wandered in from Knole Park.

Adders have always been a particular menace in woodland during summertime and the new school certainly had its fair share. Besides fostering the inevitable posse of would-be break-time snake-charmers, the first adder sighting in the grounds often provoked a minor panic amongst some boys. Keeping rigidly to

above Manicured lawns, flower gardens and the original Victorian greenhouse.
below Younger boys on a wintry woodland walk with Mrs Dickinson.

the pathways, even cowering in classrooms and cloakrooms, these boys prayed for a spell of cold weather to drive the predators back into the woods.

Despite the hazards, however, in general the new school made a favourable impact on the majority of the boys. The staff remember how the boys delighted in the sense of liberation as they faced the possibilities of the new site, and they delighted in the ever-changing beauty of the grounds. Mr Larcombe typically associated his days at Vine Court Road with rain, but those at Godden Green with sunshine.

The official opening ceremony took place a few months after the move, in the summer of 1969. To mark the occasion, **Mr Jack Higgs**, Chairman of the IAPS and Head of Brentwood Prep, planted a rowan tree in the grounds. The

THIS TREE WAS PLANTED
BY
MR. J. R. G. HIGGS M.A.
IN COMMEMORATION OF
THE MOVE OF THE SCHOOL
TO GODDEN GREEN
IN DECEMBER 1968

Brass rubbing of the plaque.

planting of this tree was the continuation of a tradition of tree-planting at Fawke Cottage to celebrate noteworthy events, stretching back to the Jubilee of George V in 1935. This particular specimen was planted because it was the only tree grown in Kent thought not to be growing in the garden. One can only speculate as to why it hadn't been planted before. Perhaps the fact that 14 years later it had plainly refused to grow in the garden provides an answer.

Of course, the price one had to pay for a glorious rural setting was certain inaccessibility. The Vine had been so convenient for the transportation of boys to and from school, but with the new premises three miles outside Sevenoaks certain problems were created. From January 1969, the school hired a Davis coach to pick up boys at the corner of Vine Court Road in the morning and return them there in the evening. Operating five days a week at an inclusive charge of £25 a week payable monthly in arrears, this service originally transported 50 boys under the supervision of Mrs Lucas and Mr Templeman. However, as various lift rotas became organised over time, so the number of boys using the service dropped. As a result, the coach became economically unviable and the remaining 'commuters' were forced to use the Maidstone and District bus route 106 from Sevenoaks. Almost inevitably, despite pleas by Mr Ely, this service was steadily reduced, fares doubled (and increased twice in one week on one occasion) and eventually the buses on the route were withdrawn altogether. By this stage, the number of private vehicles passing through the small front drive, particularly at 4 pm, became almost unmanageable.

The change of environment did not bring any change in the educational philosophy of the school. **Mrs Barbara Laming**, mother of **Paul**, an alumnus, wrote in *Kent Life* in 1972. 'Mr Ely is a tall, impressive figure and as he walks about the grounds with a purposeful air and a watchful eye, I am reminded of the story of a former Headmaster of Eton who, when asked if he knew every boy in the school, replied grimly, "No, but they all know me".'

In the 1970s, Mr Ely still ran the school along traditional 'old school' lines. He rarely moved from his study, except for occasional teaching, assemblies, and to direct the school plays. Many alumni recall being scared of him; he had a gruff, stern look and was very strict, and visits to his study after some misdemeanour were dreaded. Mrs Ely was gentler; she was very kind and looked after the boys if they were poorly. The male teachers were strict and there was frequent use of the slipper and occasionally the cane.

One alumnus who left in 1970 recalled the pupils' dread of Mr Ely and the 'Six of the Best' and his use of a steel ruler as a teaching aid for arithmetic tests;

others mentioned 'slippering'. (But they also had a grudging respect for him, as they found out that he had been a night fighter pilot in the war flying Boulton Paul Defiants.) Mr Webb, with a permanent roll-up dangling from his lower lip, also administered 'The Whacks'. One boy arrived at school one day knowing he had been put in The Black Book enough times to warrant six of the best. He carried a huge walking stick and when Mr Ely asked what it was for he replied, 'to hit you with, Sir, if you hit me'!

The boys could get caned for almost anything. One got the whacks for admitting writing the disgusting word 'willipig' in chalk on the conservatory wall. However, for the boys, worse than the whacks was Digweed. This punishment meant you had to turn up on a Saturday and do the gardening. Even harder to bear was a shaking by **Mrs Kathleen Johns**, the maths teacher. She would grab the boy's shoulders and shake him backwards and forwards until he thought his head was going to drop off. The after-effects left the miscreant in such a daze that it was hard to concentrate. However, the boys still thought that corporal punishment was used as late as the 1980s. **Luke Harrison** recalled that if you turned left outside the back door there was a small loo where Mr Oatley's bike was stored. There was a six-foot long stick with nails sticking out of it and the tale which was passed down from prefects to younger boys was that this was Mr Oatley's cane. No one questioned it until someone realised that it was an architrave waiting to be mended.

Mr Ely had instituted a system of order marks for misdemeanours or bad work and when a boy accumulated five, he would be sent to Mr Ely, who would administer a telling-off for the first set of five, with increasing punishments for further sets of five, culminating in a caning. These, and stars won for good work, were the means by which the work and conduct cup were won. Mr Larcombe remembered that his natural retort in the classroom, 'Do you want an order mark?' became a by-word for generations of boys, many of whom used to try to imitate it!

Another teacher, who will be referred to as Mr W., was amazingly incompetent. Unfortunately, Mr W. had got the wrong end of the stick and would deduct rather than add an order mark for a misdemeanour. One notoriously naughty boy, when he had four order marks from other teachers, would make even more of a nuisance of himself in Mr W.'s class so that he sometimes 'received' four order marks, have them deducted and go to the next lesson with a clean sheet.

Mr W.'s approach to teaching consisted of writing a task up on the blackboard for the boys to do, then opening up his broadsheet newspaper and reading it for the rest of the lesson, with the boys out of his sight. A favourite trick was for the boys to climb out of a window, go round to the classroom door, knock on it, say 'Sir, sorry I'm late', to be received with a grunt from Mr W., and resume his place. **Philip Oldroyd** remembers one golden day when the whole class managed the subterfuge, one by one, with Mr W. none the wiser.

An orienteering briefing in Knole Park with Mr Hodges.

Donald Smith remembers the marble runs from his days as a pupil, when the school still had the old-fashioned desks with inkwells that were no longer used as inkwells. The boys used to punch a hole through the bottom of these and set up their books and rulers within the desk so that the marble, dropped into the inkwell, would roll along the ruler and the books and finally plink-plonk through the hole, when they would catch it. The marble used to make a noise when it reached the edge of the desk, so the boy would cough to cover it up. Did the teachers realise, and just do nothing about it? The boys also went through a Tic Tac phase, when they would nominate a member of staff and try to demolish a packet of Tic Tacs in the lesson. Because they are quite noisy to get out of the box, the challenge was to succeed in finishing them all without the teacher realising. Donald also got involved in a prank as a look-out when some boys decided to raid Mr Ely's vegetable garden, where the science lab was until 2017. Having been caught, the boys had to line up outside the Headmaster's study, knowing full well that Mr Ely used the slipper and sometimes the cane. He left them sweating there for about half an hour before letting them off with a stern, 'Be off with you'.

The scope and variety of school activities increased enormously over the years. Orienteering became a regular exercise for boys in the upper sixth. *The Acorn* of 1973-74 recorded that on Monday 1 July, the upper sixth were engaged in an orienteering exercise organised by **Mr 'Uncle Arthur' Hodges**. Groups of two or three boys set out to reach six points on a course that covered eight and a half to ten miles. Each group was given a piece of paper on which were questions about each point. Marks were deducted if a group arrived back earlier than 3:30 pm or later than 3:45 pm. Everybody enjoyed the expedition and Mr Hodges generously awarded the winner a prize.

An assault course was constructed by **Paul Waite**, of Doodle Master fame, along the woodlands footpath at the top of the lawn. Comprised of a number of tyres, planks of wood, and ropes, it provided an exciting addition to the PE curriculum. Boys were given permission to camp in the grounds during school holidays. In the summer of 1970, during their half term, eight intrepid pupils including **Martin Andrews**, Richard Jenkins, **Roddy Hale**, Robert House, and **David Lucas** braved the elements to spend three nights under canvas in one of the corners of the playing field, and by all accounts had a marvellous time.

A guinea pig club was initiated by Robert House and **John Killick**, Richard Jenkins, and Roddy Hale. According to Robert's mother, Mrs Bryony House, the club began with two guinea pigs, Clemmie and Randy, which were kept in the school's pigsty in the grounds during term-time and in their house during the holidays. The club, with a membership fee of 6d (2½p), was an immediate success and soon mushroomed, with boys performing the duties of midwifery, grave-digging, pall-bearing, and cremation. Then tragedy struck! Paddy, the Ely's dog, got into the pigsty one day and killed one guinea pig and injured others. In the mist of this emergency, the science lesson was interrupted and dramatic efforts were made to revive the animal. Unfortunately, it was to die later at the Houses' home. Yet all was not lost. Mr Ely bought some new guinea pigs and the club was able to continue.

A young ornithological club was founded in 1969 by Mrs Sadler, who organised occasional visits and film-shows for its members. Mrs Ely arranged regular Saturday morning trips to the Royal Festival Hall for the Ernest Reid concerts and one courageous pupil, **Howard Davies**, even made his own film about – in the director's words – 'a cross-country runner (**Guy Bennell**) who after hearing his scripture teacher (Mr Larcombe) talking about a man conversing with Christ, had a vision of Jesus while collapsing after the run. He then goes off into wild fantasies to the music of Webber/Rice's *Jesus Christ Superstar*!'

The Guinea Pig Club and the 'villainous' Paddy.

Packed lunches gave way to meals provided by a caterer and then eventually an in-house team but dining alfresco was always enjoyed as often as the weather allowed.

School lunches have always been a preoccupation of schoolboys. What would they be like at Godden Green? To begin with no one could complain because everybody brought his own and ate it either in the dining room or, if the weather was fine, out of doors. Sometime later, hot meals on aircraft-style trays were brought to the school daily by a catering firm from Tunbridge Wells. The next development saw Mrs Ely cooking meals on the premises with **Mrs Elizabeth Crang** and **Mrs Martin** helping her in the kitchen. Small teams of boys were responsible for setting the tables and cleaning up afterwards. Sweeping the floor might be fun, but the dustpan and brush was a chore every boy avoided if he could.

It would be at lunch time, and during other breaks, that the boys would have noticed that they were not the only pupils at the school. Mr Ely had taken the decision to take a few little girls between the ages of five and seven into the school to assist those parents of boys at The Prep with daughters of school age. This had become an accepted policy of the IAPS. Apparently, however, most parents had already placed their daughters elsewhere as only one little 6-year-old, **Katherine Whitehouse,** joined the school in the bottom form followed by **Beckie George** and **Alison Hands.** Although Mr Ely expected a few more girls to join, the experiment was destined to last only a short time. School Inspectors criticised the lack of female facilities, especially toilet facilities, and on their insistence the scheme, sadly, came to an abrupt end.

Everybody's day began, as it had always done, with assembly, usually with Mr or Mrs Webb at the piano. The boys filed silently into the dining room to sit on wooden benches, whilst the prefects stood along an oak-panelled wall. On the opposite wall stood the school cups grouped above the coloured house names Vine–blue, Weald–red, Knole–yellow, Seal–green. The latter two houses had been inaugurated after the move since Mr Ely expected the number of boys in the school to rise somewhat. In any case, they provided keener competition. School colours were awarded in assembly and comments on the performance of various teams were made by the Head. The hymns the boys enjoyed singing most would be chosen for the end-of-term service in the summer.

Godden Green is in Seal Parish and Mr Ely approached the vicar of Seal, **Canon John Barnard**, to ask if school services could be held in Seal Church. Two services a year, carols at Christmas and thanksgiving at the end of the year, were held in the church of St Peter and St Paul. To begin with Mr Ely trained the choir, then Mrs Shefford took over. A succession of staff, boys and alumni read the lessons and Mr Larcombe assisted the vicar in conducting the worship.

An alarming event occurred in the middle of the carol service at Seal on 14 December 1977, the day after a new one-way system had been introduced in the village. As the congregation was enthusiastically singing the words *Suddenly the Lord descending, in his temple shall appear*, two policemen, caps under arms, marched up the aisle and went into conference with the vicar. The service adjourned for 15 minutes while the parents who had parked in the wrong places were given time to move their cars. A number of people present wrote either to the police or the ecclesiastical authorities claiming that this was an illegal act under the Law of Sanctuary!

The Sevenoaks Chronicle reported the incident as follows:

'Police interrupted the recent carol service for Sevenoaks Preparatory School pupils and parents at St Peter's and St Paul's Church, Seal. No, it wasn't a raid but bad parking by members of the congregation. Canon John Barnard who conducted the service said "It was an unfortunate occurrence but the cars had to be moved. The police were only doing their duty by stopping the service, and they carried out the task with the minimum of fuss".'

As The Prep settled in to its new environment at Godden Green, the opportunity was taken to utilise the spaciousness. In the 1973 summer term, two new events took place: the concert on the lawn and, not least, the fête. The latter involved the parents much more than they had been previously and this new approach was confirmed when the school was used as a parking and rallying point for a new activity for parents, a car point-to-point. This was followed in 1974 by the first mothers' cricket match against a school side and, in 1975, an orienteering day in Knole Park involving 90 parents, friends, and boys.

1973 was a landmark year in the life of The Prep as it was the year that the Oldroyd family first came to the school–the start of a long association with The Prep. **Mr Jim** and **Mrs Janet Oldroyd** moved back to Kent from Yorkshire and bought a house in Seal when Mr Oldroyd's work brought him to London. Mrs Oldroyd was from the Sevenoaks area, having attended St Hilary's School in

Bradbourne Park Road, while Jim was an alumnus of Sevenoaks School. They had two boys, **Philip**, then aged 7, and **Richard**, aged 4, who had been born in Kent but brought up at first in Yorkshire. The Oldroyds looked at the local primary school in Seal but decided to seek out alternatives, including The Prep. After what he recalled was a good lunch, Mr Oldroyd had a meeting with Mr Ely and agreed that the two boys could join The Prep even though Richard was officially a year too young for the Reception class. In 1978, the Oldroyds presented an enormous number of books for the junior school library. The look on the faces of the staff was something to behold – they thought the school had won the pools.

Philip's first impressions of The Prep were of green open spaces and a beautiful kitchen garden, but the sharpest memory of his first day was of being introduced to his first form teacher, Mrs Pat Richardson, upon which he promptly burst into tears and ran and locked himself in the family car. After much persuasion he finally let himself out and went back to the class to sit next to **Tom Pridham**, with whom he went through The Prep and Judd, and they have remained lifelong friends.

Both boys went through the school and on to The Judd School. By this time their parents had separated and Mrs Oldroyd was working at The Prep. She took on a major role in its management when she married the Headmaster, Mr Oatley, in 1985. Later, in 1994, Philip came back to teach at The Prep and became Headmaster in 2005; both his sons were at the school in the first decade of the 21st century.

Drama and music

The school year followed a familiar, seasonal pattern, culminating in the end-of-year summer shows, the junior classes performing their offerings on the lawn whilst the senior boys, with their more challenging productions, usually performing in three classrooms transformed into a hall. Mostly they were musicals, where Mrs Shefford provided the musical input but with Mr Ely firmly in charge. His daughter, Jane, invariably took the leading female role and was joined by two or three sisters of boys who were taking part – often quite a distraction! Jane went on to have a career in the theatre, as a stage manager, and her daughter followed in her footsteps by performing in plays at her school.

The initial spring term at Godden Green was too busy with the settling-in for a play to be arranged, so the first one to be produced at the new site was, in the absence of a suitable indoor location, *Toad of Toad Hall* performed outdoors twice on hot and sunny afternoons at the end of the summer term.

The vast Johnson Hall at Sevenoaks School then became the venue for two major productions, *Hans Christian Anderson* (in 1970) and *Where the Rainbow Ends* (in 1971) yet, as Mrs Ely recalled, the arrangement was not a particularly convenient one and both she and her husband longed for their own drama facilities at the Godden Green site. As Hans in the former play, **Christian Dodd** achieved the remarkable hat trick of playing the lead in three consecutive productions.

Just before Christmas 1971, the school celebrated its 50th anniversary (two years late!) with a wine and cheese party in the dining room at Sevenoaks School, and nearly £100 was raised towards an anniversary fund. Significantly, the main beneficiary was a mini theatre for the new school. The money collected by the fund was used to construct this mini theatre by partitioning the walls of three of the outside classrooms. Mr Bassett made a stage, **Mrs Waite** made the curtains and Mr Hunt erected a very efficient and professional lighting system. Having their own theatre made the task of producing the annual play very much easier and everyone felt at home in their own cosy little theatre.

Although some members of staff recall that the task of dismantling the inside walls from the cedar-wood classrooms and the removal of all the furniture once a year was at times onerous, nevertheless the intimate atmosphere between performers and audiences engendered in the mini theatre proved a great success. From 1972 such ambitious productions as *The King and I, Salad Days, Eliza Doolittle, Me and My Girl, Charlie Girl, and Oklahoma!* were enthusiastically performed in the new arena. There were many memorable performances over the years. David Downton's performance as the King of Siam was particularly memorable, **Tom Denyer** played Eliza Doolittle's father with great gusto, Jane Ely, a veteran Prep performer, played the flirtatious Ado Annie in *Oklahoma!*, and the wonderful **Simon Riley** was Wainwright in *Charlie Girl*: a born comedian and mimic who had the audience in stitches. Offstage, his impersonations of members of staff were famous. A terrific sense of fun and excitement ran throughout the entire cast during the play productions. From the first rehearsal to the last performance, the experience was delightful and for many an enduring memory of the school. In 1978, several sisters of boys had parts in the school production of *Oliver*.

Of course a redoubtable team had been built up behind the scenes: Mr Ely expertly produced and directed the productions; Mr Larcombe and a posse of helpers gallantly designed and painted the scenery; Mr Webb pulled the curtain; Mr Hodges acted as box office manager; Mrs Lucas and Mrs Sadler efficiently produced props at crucial moments; **Mrs E. Lee** organised the colourful costumes; **Mrs Maureen Perks** choreographed; Mr Templeman and two senior boys manned the lighting; and Mrs Dickinson, Mrs Richardson, Mrs Thomas and **Mrs Margaret Hodges** all at some stage supervised the make-up.

Last but not least amongst all these talents was Mrs Shefford who, with her small band of musicians, which included one year the youngest member of staff **Mr Matthew Best**, regularly produced music lively enough to do justice to a much larger audience. Mr Best taught at The Prep for one year before going to King's College, Cambridge as a choral scholar. In 1973, at the age of 16, he had already founded and conducted his own Corydon Singers and he went on to become one of Britain's leading opera singers.

Concerts on the Lawn

left Cast from the 1976 performance of *Hiawatha*.

below A later version with the artistic talents of Messrs Larcombe and Crang on display and the school orchestra comprising boys and staff.

Whilst great deeds were being conceived within the new mini theatre, The Prep tradition, stretching back to the 1920s, of performing on the school lawn, was not forgotten. Initiated by Mr Ely, an annual junior concert on the lawn became a feature of the school calendar. In the charming setting of the gardens, beneath the shade of the horse chestnut tree, the audience of grandparents, parents, and tiny brothers and sisters would sit facing the magnolia and wisteria-covered facade of the school with its windows peeping out through the leaves.

Here Mr Ely conducted the performance of *Noah and His Floating Zoo* supported by the school orchestra as the clouds above grew more ominous. The moment he put down his baton the heavens opened and everyone scurried for shelter in the downpour!

The school choir continued to flourish, although **Brian Whittaker** recalled that boys at 13 years of age going through the biological change that can take the soprano out of their voice were often dismissed from the choir to join the growing ranks of what Mr Ely called 'the groaners'. Boys tried very hard to make their voices break early so that they could achieve the accolade of joining this key group, especially as Mr Ely would allow them to play mini golf on the course he had laid out on the lawn at the side of the house by the towering monkey puzzle tree during choir practice.

In 1977, Mrs Shefford had masterminded an Elizabethan spectacular on the lawn to celebrate the Queen's Silver Jubilee, centered around the first Elizabeth to celebrate 25 years of the second. The producer suggested that perhaps the outside wall of the house might be adapted to make a more suitable backdrop for the concerts so for several years the windows were filled in with paper and Mr Larcombe and Jeremy Crang, who had returned in a gap year to help out at the school, painted mountains, water and trees wherever they could, Jeremy discovering he had a genius for mass producing fir trees with a household paint brush! This certainly added a new dimension to the concerts. By its very nature, the school orchestra was always changing its size and sound, losing players who were leaving but gaining new boys often with experience of new instruments. Whatever changes there were, however, did not stop the regular playing for hymns at assembly and the special services in Seal Church.

Sport and recreation

Because the school moved in January, the first sport played at Godden Green was football. The 1st XI pitch was marked out across the farthest end of the field. Boys of earlier years well remember the idiosyncrasies of various pitches at Knole Paddock, but the early boys at Godden Green were unlikely to forget stumbling across the ridge that bedevilled the new one. The 'third game' played their football near the entrance to the field, on a pitch that most will remember as being a veritable mud-bath. Under the eagle eyes of Mr Ely and Mr Smart, who had replaced the veteran **Mr Ronnie Marchant** as games coach during the academic year 1969-70, football continued to thrive. In the early years at Godden Green **Richard Bennett** is remembered by many as being the outstanding football star at the school. In 1970, he scored eight goals against Halstead Place in the first match of the season and went on to score 18 of The Prep's 19 against other schools. **Paul Ellison** took on his mantle in the mid-1970s.

The first cricket season at Godden Green was a disaster. The square wasn't exactly flat and it wasn't a great side. The 1st XI lost all their games and Mr Ely refused to have a photo taken as the season was so bad. Things could only get better and they did in 1970, recording five wins and six losses. Plenty of attention was lavished on the cricket square, which lay between the two original football pitches, and a dedicated succession of masters strived to get the best out of the boys. The astute coaching of Mr Smart, a Vine cricketer of distinction like Mr Marchant, was a feature of these years, supported by the determination of the

Head. Junior sides were knocked into shape by such staff as the young **Mr Tim Ruck,** older brother of Prep boys **Paul** and **Mark Ruck**, **Mr Derek Ellison** and the popular Mr Hodges. In 1973, the 1st XI beat all their prep school opponents, losing only to Sevenoaks School.

The school produced a number of excellent cricketers during this era. Many will remember the hard-hitting **Richard Keeley** who once scored 41, 78 not out and 79 not out against Streete Court, Solefield and Hilden Grange within the space of a week; the elegant and talented **Willie Stewart**; Paul Ellison, who could terrorize the opposition with his batting and fast bowling; his brother **Mark Ellison**; **Ian Hitchcock**; **Martin Steyn** and **Jimmy Page**, son of **Colin**, the former Kent Cricket Club manager.

In the drought summer of 1976, the cricket square got so hard that Mr Ken Smart asked Philip Oldroyd, who was a useful bowler, to stop aiming at the stumps as it was very difficult to put them back into the hard ground.

One lunchtime in 1968, an embarrassed young **Chris Alcock** was the first recipient of the Alcock Squash Cup, which he had received from the hands of his own father, who had presented it to the school. Squash was now being played regularly on the court belonging to the neighbouring school, Stake Farm College. Supervised at various times by **Mr Waite**, Mr Best, Mr Ely – when his daughter Jane joined in – and later by **Mr Mark Thomas**, who came to the school in 1978, the squash club took place every Wednesday after school throughout the year.

Meanwhile, back at the new school with its velvety lawns, smartly-dressed boys in their twos and threes sedately indulged in a civilised post-lunch round of putting. A nine-hole course had been constructed in the gardens in 1968 and

A post-lunch round of putting on a 'velvety' lawn.

a popular putting tournament for the senior forms took place in the summer term, sometimes attracting nearly 40 entrants. The finals were often riveting. Interestingly enough, in three consecutive years, 1975, 1976 and 1977, **Russell Edwards**, **Jeremy Edwards**, and **Andrew Stephen** all won the close contests at the very last hole. Russell won £1 and Andrew was awarded four golf balls.

To the great delight of the boys, there was a hard tennis court in the new school grounds and tennis quickly became an extremely popular activity, especially during Wimbledon fortnight. During breaks and lunch hours, keen young tennis players were seen hitting balls left, right, and centre all over the court, though there were some boys who had greater control over the ball than others. Mr Ely gave special permission to boys who enjoyed tennis and had their own rackets to play during games times instead of playing cricket. If any balls were lost they had to be replaced, but the faithful ball-finder, Paddy, often came along with the lost ball in his mouth. During Mr Ely's years, Mr Webb and **Richard Rawlings** – an old Tonbridgian who was on the staff before going to university – coached the young tennis players and began a regular tennis tournament.

It was the combination of his advancing years and the difficulty of transporting the young boys some three miles to Sevenoaks baths that persuaded Mr Webb not to continue his swimming instruction. However, boys did continue to train with outside clubs. Most notably, **David Rickward** swam regularly for Kent and competed in the national championships in Leeds.

The school's new grounds provided a lovely setting for sports days. The athletics track, although a little bumpy, was first marked out across the original playing field (always a complicated geometrical task). Boys will remember badgering Mr Larcombe to show them the starting pistol and let them have the empty cartridges, or peering over Mr Webb's shoulder to see how the house points were progressing as he calmly recorded race results under the big oak tree, or racing hard towards Mrs Lucas at the finishing tape.

But for some, sports day was a fearful and dreaded day in the school calendar. **Peter Harbord** remembered that the complete lack of ability of the majority of young boys was revealed, although as he got bigger he discovered that by lifting a lighter lad completely off the ground he could simply run and win the wheelbarrow race every year! His place in glory was assured until the ruse was spotted and the rules updated – hands had to actually touch the ground, he was informed. Most unfair on the boys with no ability!

Outings and holidays

For some, the most spectacular event of the period was the school's holiday to Dartmoor in 1970. Mr Larcombe, Mrs Nunn and Mrs Lucas, along with **Mr Derek Lucas** and their daughter **Helen**, bravely accompanied a number of boys to Manor Farm near Lydford on a pony-trekking holiday. They travelled by rail and countless buses to get to an authentic farm on the edge of the moor,

1970 school holiday to Dartmoor.

which had that wonderful fresh smell associated with farms and horses. According to Mrs Lucas the holiday was full of surprises. Apart from the rare sight of seeing Mr Larcombe in jeans and the exceptional eagerness with which the boys got up early in the morning to help the rather flirtatious stable girl muck out the horses, two boys in particular seemed to court disaster in the saddle. No matter which pony **Nicholas Scoble-Hodgins** sat on, it proceeded to develop inexplicable, violent eccentricities and **Mark Graves-Gidney**, in the best traditions of a Thelwell cartoon, had the dubious pleasure of being astride a pony one day that suddenly developed an itch and without warning rolled on its back in the mud with Mark just scurrying out from underneath in time! Tim Dickinson remembers riding in the fog over Dartmoor, being kicked by a horse whilst grooming, as well as taking a shine to the beautiful stable girl. One evening Mr Larcombe and Mr Lucas gave a recital of Chopsticks, the former maintaining the bass chords and the latter improvising very flashy trebles.

— 7 —

Young Oatley Does Well with His Boys (1978-86)

In December 1977, Mr Ely retired, handing the school on to Mr Edward Oatley, who came from his post as Deputy Head at Winchester House School. Mr Oatley took over 141 pupils and 13 staff. The school facilities were much the same as ten years before, both inside and out. Soon, a new car park was laid followed by a new hall. In 1981, Mrs Rosemary Cooke, who ran a nursery school in her home in Seal, brought her children up to Godden Green and became part of The Prep. She began with 18 boys and girls under the age of 5 in a room in the recently built hall. Meanwhile, in 1983, Sevenoaks School announced that it had set up a committee under the chairmanship of the relatively new Headmaster, Mr Richard Barker, to consider the desirability of extending co-education throughout the school with the objective, if approved, of admitting 11 and 13-year-old girls from September 1984. The repercussions of this proposal were to change the face of private education in the Sevenoaks area fundamentally. In 1985, Winchester House suddenly closed and Mr Oatley generously offered places to a number of boys and some of the staff. In 1985 Mr Oatley and Mrs Janet Oldroyd married, the start of a long and successful partnership which had a major influence on the progress of The Prep. Numbers had been growing gradually since Mr Oatley took over, and the influx from Winchester House put the numbers up to 216 pupils and 22 staff in the academic year 1985-86. That year also saw the retirement of three stalwart teachers, Mr Peter Larcombe, Mrs Angela Lucas, and Mrs Madeleine Dickinson.

Heads and staff

Mr Edward Oatley joined The Prep in September 1977 and worked with **Mr Kenneth Ely** until the latter's retirement in December of that year. Mr Oatley had been brought up in Northwood and went to Aldenham School in Elstree, Hertfordshire. In 1962, he left Aldenham and **Mr Michael Hobbs**, a fellow alumnus, and recently appointed Headmaster of Winchester House School in Sevenoaks, asked him to join the school as a gap year student. After completing a successful first year, he decided that teaching was the way forward and Mr Hobbs offered him the opportunity of training while working through the then IAPS training scheme. During his time at Winchester House he taught maths, geography, history, RE, and all sports; in 1969 he was appointed Assistant Head and joined the IAPS. He came to The Prep with his wife **Frances** and 8-year-old daughter **Claire** and the family moved into Fawke Cottage when the Elys moved into a house in nearby Stone Street.

During Mr Ely's headship, his wife **Betty** had looked after the kitchen and dining room. When she retired she asked **Mrs Elizabeth Crang**, who had been helping her in the kitchen, if she would become cook and organise the lunches. In turn Mrs Crang asked **Mrs Janet Oldroyd** if she would help her; then, when she left to become a matron at one of the Sevenoaks School boarding houses, Mrs Crang asked Mrs Oldroyd if she would take over from her. Later on, **Mrs Pauline Burden** took charge of the kitchen. The kitchen is remembered as being very small and the room next to it, which became a store room and housed the fridge and freezer, had originally been Mr and Mrs Ely's dining room.

When Mr Oatley took over The Prep, there were 141 boys and 13 staff, much the same numbers as ten years previously when the school moved to Godden Green. The core of the staff was half a dozen experienced ladies, all of whom (say it quietly) were older than Mr Oatley. **Mrs Angela Lucas** had started in 1966 when The Prep was still at Vine Court Road, the others were **Mrs Madeleine Dickinson** (who started in 1967), **Mrs Mary Shefford** (1969), **Mrs Chris Thomas** (1969), **Mrs Pat Richardson** (1971), **Mrs Beth Sadler** (1973), and **Mrs Bryony House** (1975). The male staff included **Mr Peter Larcombe**, who had been a pupil at The Prep in the 1940s and had joined the staff soon after qualifying as a teacher in 1959, and **Mr Ken Smart**, the very experienced and notable local sportsman who had been responsible for overseeing sport since 1969. **Mr James Cooke** was another member of staff who had been appointed in 1975 by Mr Ely to teach science when **Mr Harold Templeman** retired. In addition, Mrs Frances Oatley was a member of the staff until, in November 1980, the Oatleys separated and she left the school. Their daughter Claire continued living with Mr Oatley in Fawke Cottage but for most of the next decade attended a boarding school in Tunbridge Wells, returning home at weekends and during the school holidays.

Mrs Sadler started teaching at The Prep in 1973 when Mr Ely was Headmaster. She recalls that Mr Ely (as he was always called[8]) was rather austere and stern and she felt he ran the school on a shoestring. Although classroom resources were basic, the teaching staff seemed to make up for that; Mrs Sadler found them all most welcoming and helpful when she joined and some of those with whom she worked became lifelong friends.

Although Mr Oatley joined as Headmaster in September 1977, Mr Ely stayed on as Joint Headmaster until December. He then continued to work as Bursar, take the top form for music and, with Mrs Shefford, produced the 1979 school play, *Treasure Island*. This, together with the fact that most of the staff he inherited were older than himself, must have been quite tricky and daunting for Mr Oatley. Mrs Sadler remembers an early staff meeting after Mr Ely had gone when they were all rather taken aback, as Mrs Thomas just came out with the fact that it was time that the staff were all paid properly and on the Burnham scale. That would never have happened in Mr Ely's time, but Mr Oatley settled it amicably and the meeting continued. It was the shape of things to come.

Mrs House recalls that when she and her husband **Patrick** moved to Kent in the late 1960s and were looking for a school for their two sons, **Robert** and **Timothy**, they were told 'Sevenoaks Prep has few facilities, but old Ely does well with his boys.' This was an accurate description and after looking at various schools, they plumped for 'old Ely'. The boys did well there, Robert becoming head boy, and both went on to excellent secondary education. More importantly, their years at The Prep were very happy years and they both look back with affection on their time at the school.

In 1975, Mr Ely had asked Mrs House to join the staff for a term to stand in for Mrs Lucas who was away for a short period. She stayed nine years, not to replace Mrs Lucas, but to take over Form 3. Mrs House taught in the junior school where the four lady teachers co-operated closely over the pupils' progress with Mrs Thomas' robust support, as well as occasional criticisms. When the family moved away from Kent in 1984, Mrs House summed up her family's time involved with The Prep by adapting the original advice they had received to 'Sevenoaks Prep has all the facilities and young Oatley does well with <u>his</u> boys'. She added, as her swan song, a series of limericks about the staff and the school, which are included in Appendix 4.

To start with, much necessarily remained the same, but there were noticeable changes too. Around the school, the feeling was more relaxed and supportive with Mr Oatley working hard to 'get it right', even turning his hand to catering with, initially maybe, mixed results. In contrast to Mr Ely, Mr Oatley was much more in evidence in the school and far more active, positively fizzing with ideas.

---

8 This formality was illustrated by a letter written in 1976 by Mr Peter Larcombe, an alumnus and long-standing member of staff, which started 'Dear Mr Ely'.

He was very keen on technology, especially on the use of overhead projectors for explaining his lessons and ideas, but he relied heavily on the boys to show him exactly how the equipment worked.

It was a time of change and development with numbers increasing, a flourishing Kindergarten, and new buildings acquired. The staff felt it was a very happy environment in which to teach and it was Mr Oatley's philosophy not to cram but to always be helping to bring out the best, in every way, in each youngster. Under Mr Oatley, the school went from strength to strength and expanded considerably as he introduced many changes and improvements. His youth and tireless vigour spurred the staff on, and each year a new building appeared. By then, the staff were a particularly united group and much discussion, advice, and considerable laughter took place in the staff room during break times.

There were some staff changes soon after Mr Oatley took over: **Mr Bill Stroude** left in July 1978; **Mrs Pam Burrows** left in April 1978 to have a baby; **Mrs Jane Priestley** covered for Mr Cooke who was ill and she stayed on from September 1978; **Mr Eric Tozer** returned to teach games from September 1978, although Mr Oatley and Mr Smart continued with the 1st and 2nd football and cricket XIs. **Mr Arthur Searle,** the gardener inherited with Fawke Cottage, officially retired in December 1977 at the age of 70, although he kept being called back to help. He died in February 1985, aged 78.

Staff 1982
back row Mr J. Cooke, Mr M. Hall *(gap year student)*, Mr P. Larcombe,
Mr K. Smart, Mr E. Oatley.
middle row Mr L. Baldwin, Mrs A. Culley, Mrs J. Biggs, Mrs J. Oldroyd, Mrs M. Laidlaw,
Mrs T. Burns, Mr I. Culley.
front row Mrs M. Dickinson, Mrs M. Perks, Mrs B. Sadler, Mrs C .Thomas,
Mrs B. House, Mrs A. Lucas, Mrs M. Shefford, Mrs R. Cooke.

In September 1980, The Prep was under pressure, being unavoidably short staffed, especially when Mrs Frances Oatley – who had been the Form 5 teacher – left the school. This crisis resulted in **Mr Ian Culley**'s first contact with The Prep. He was teaching at Skippers Hill school near Mayfield in Sussex and, being a good all-round sportsman, was playing cricket with Mrs Lucas' nephew. He must have said after a particularly bad cricket match that it might be time to change his job and her nephew told Mrs Lucas that there was a prep school teacher he knew looking for a job and contact was made. Although Mr Culley wasn't actively looking for a job, he was interested enough to come for an interview. He did his homework by looking up The Prep in the IAPS handbook and was very impressed that the school had an all-weather athletics track. At his interview, after being given a tour of the school and grounds by Mr Oatley, he asked where the track was and was told: 'Oh yes, you see that creosote line round there, that's the running track and we use it all the year round'. This so appealed to Mr Culley's sense of humour that he thought: 'I've got to come and work here'. He was offered the job but couldn't start until the next school year and this led to another notable acquisition for the school when, in October, **Mrs June Biggs** arrived and the original problem dissolved. Initially she took on Form 5 and taught them English and maths, but it was soon clear that her first love and her most marked ability lay in teaching English and with Mr Culley joining in 1981, Mrs Biggs began to teach senior English. During her time at The Prep she was to have major roles to play over the next few years as editor of *The Acorn*, preparing boys for the Three Arts Festival and as school librarian.

Mr Culley initially came to The Prep to be Head of Sport and to be the class teacher for Form 5, but within a few years he became Head of Geography, teaching the subject to the Common Entrance form and tackling the very demanding job of guiding boys in their compulsory geography projects. This required hard work from the teacher as well as the pupil, but Mr Culley inspired the boys; the results were excellent, with the boys gaining a great deal from his teaching. As Head of Sport he showed his organisational skills with major events, sports days, swimming galas, and cross-country championships being his hallmark. **Mrs Angela Culley** also joined the staff. When Mr Culley started she had been eight months pregnant with **Simon**, and then in January 1982 she answered an urgent call for a biology teacher for two terms. She stayed for over five years, mostly teaching maths and English to Forms 5 and 6 then left to become Head of The Mead School, a prep school in Tunbridge Wells, where she was Head for 30 years, retiring in 2017.

Luke Harrison, later to teach at The Prep and then become Headmaster, was at the school in the 1980s. He remembers his first encounter with Mr Culley in 1981. Mr Culley was wearing a polyester jacket, bell bottoms, and black loafers. He strode up to the blackboard, chalk in hand, and wrote: 'My name is Mr Culley. That's Culley. C-U-L-L-E-Y. My name is Culley. I am NOT Mr Curry.

Mrs Cooke and KG in their first home at The Prep, part of the 'new' 1981 hall building.

Got it? Culley. C-U-L-L-E-Y. Culley'. 'Blimey', the boys all thought, 'Magnum, PI[9] has just arrived at Sevenoaks Prep!' Terrified as they were, over the coming weeks, they soon worked out that Mr Curry, sorry, Culley, was all right. In fact, he was quite cool. The memory of that first impression stayed with the boys as they proudly told the rest of the school that their teacher was Mr Magnum, PI. Another memory was when Mr Culley re-introduced rugby to the school; the first set of rugby posts were obtained when Mr Culley and Mr Oatley frogmarched a number of the boys into the woods between the school and Knole Park to find some suitable fallen trees and then run them back to school quickly so they could be painted and hauled into position on their new pitch before anyone could ask any questions.

In February 1981, Mr Oatley wrote to the parents to tell them that **Mrs Rosemary Cooke** was to bring her Kindergarten and her assistants, **Mrs Tiggy Burns** and **Mrs Shirley Berryman**, to The Prep with 15 little boys and girls. For 16 years, Mrs Cooke had been running Peter Pan Nursery at her house in Seal. As a result, The Prep was now to have some girls, up to five years of age. Initially, the class was mornings only. Mrs Cooke's philosophy was to provide the first steps in education, plus lots of fun; sharing with each other; and, above all, love and understanding. By the time the children left for full-time schooling, they were well prepared and found the transition easy and natural as

---

9 *Magnum, PI* was an American crime drama television series starring Tom Selleck as Thomas Magnum, a private investigator, which ran from 1980-88.

well as having some knowledge of reading and writing. Initially it was a mixed class of 3, 4 and sometimes 5-year-olds situated in Fawke Cottage; later, when the Kindergarten moved to Stake Farm, it was divided into two groups, Teddies and Bunnies.

At the end of the summer term of 1983, two of the stalwarts who had provided their considerable experience to Mr Oatley after he took over as Headmaster retired. Mrs Thomas had been at The Prep since 1969 with responsibility for the junior school. She had always been a keen runner and had made the most of the opportunities offered by the proximity of Knole Park after the move to Godden Green to encourage cross-country running for the boys. Her memory continues with the Thomas Trophy awarded to the champion school in the annual cross-country competition for neighbouring prep schools organised by The Prep. She started her retirement with a six-year Open University course and Mr Oatley threatened to re-employ her when she qualified! Mr James Cooke had taught science since 1975 and felt it was time he reduced his workload, although he continued to teach five maths lessons a week to the scholarship boys. The example of real care and interest by both Mrs Thomas and Mr Cooke in every child they had taught was second to none.

In 1983, **Mr David Clark**, an alumnus who had taught at the school briefly in the 1960s before becoming completely blind, returned. He had qualified as a teacher and taught blind children for a number of years. He had worked a lot with children who had learning difficulties, and with much enlightened help and encouragement from Mr Oatley, he started teaching pupils at The Prep who had difficulties with reading and spelling as well as other difficulties. A few of the children he taught had quite severe emotional, behavioural, or family problems and he spent a considerable amount of time over several years helping these pupils. It was a totally fulfilling and rewarding activity in which to be engaged. **Donald Smith** remembers playing chess with Mr Clark, who had a special chess board, and they often played games over the telephone.

In 1984, there were two new members of staff who were to have a considerable influence, in their own ways, in the future development of The Prep. **Mrs Marjorie Shea**, whose son **Paul** was at the school while her younger daughter **Helen** had also been in the Kindergarten for the previous year, was approached by Mr Oatley. He needed another teacher for the junior school and was told by **Mrs Sue Bullock**, then teaching Form 2 and with her son **Ben** in the school, that Mrs Shea might be available and possibly interested. Mrs Shea initially taught for three years, then returned in 1992 to head the Pre-Prep, which she did until 2011. **Mr Michael Barnard** joined as Bursar, a post he was to fill until 1998. By 1984, Mr Oatley had been at The Prep for seven years and, as the school increased in size, was finding it difficult to look after all the administration and accounting side of the school as well as being Headmaster and teaching, so Mr Barnard joined The Prep family. He had been a respected accountant but needed a change, and whilst on

Staff 1985 *back row* Mrs M. Perks, Mrs J. Biggs, Mrs T. Burns, Mr D. Cochrane,
Mrs J. Oatley, Mrs J. Bailey, Mrs P. Burden.
middle row Mrs A. Culley, Mrs M. Shea, Mr J. Pegg, Mr M. Barnard, Mr E. Oatley,
Mr I. Culley, Mr K. Smart, Mrs M. Meredith, Mrs G. Bosley.
front row Mrs M. Shefford, Mrs S. Bullock, Mr J. Cooke, Mrs M. Dickinson,
Mr P. Larcombe, Mrs R. Cooke, Mrs B. Sadler.
sitting on the grass Mr P. Oldroyd, Sinbad, Mr D. Smith.

a week's holiday he came and invigilated the November 1984 Common Entrance examinations. Then, as a favour, he helped with the monthly PAYE, started taking on the payment of bills and, at the end of the summer holidays, found he had a full-time job at The Prep as Mr Oatley could no longer do without him. Right from the start he took on every imaginable task to make the whole school tick over more smoothly; one minute he was secretary, the next Bursar, then first-aid man and even, occasionally, washer-up. He was invited to the first ever Kent school bursars' meeting and took on the official title of School Bursar; within a year he had taken on board all the financial administration of the school.

Mrs Liz Harrison also joined in 1984 to head up the catering. She was another current parent whom Mr Oatley approached in the car park and offered a job. She was understandably nervous as, in her own words, she had been 'known to burn four sides of a sausage'. She soon settled in, however, with instructions, as the school cook, to be discreet as when staff popped into the kitchen to make coffee she would overhear all manner of conversations. Mr Oatley normally started his day cycling to Sevenoaks swimming pool and Mrs Harrison would arrive in her kitchen most mornings to find a dripping pair of beige swimming shorts hanging out to dry over the boiler. There was compensation, however, if Mr Oatley had also started his day by making the puddings for lunch.

In April 1985, Mr Oatley told parents in a newsletter that he and Mrs Oldroyd were to be married during the Easter holidays. This was to be a long and happy partnership which is still benefitting the school. She brought along her dog, Sinbad, soon known as the school dog. In the same newsletter, Mr Oatley announced that Mr Culley was to become Assistant Head. He paid tribute to the loyalty and energy Mr Culley had shown in the four years he had been at The Prep.

At the end of the summer term 1986, three long-serving teachers left the staff: Mr Larcombe who had joined the staff in 1959 as an assistant master under **Mrs Agnes Lang** and had taught throughout the Ely era; Mrs Lucas who had joined Mr Ely in 1965 as a parent as well as a teacher; and Mrs Dickinson, who also had had boys at the school and joined the staff in 1967.

Mr Larcombe first came to Mrs Lucas' notice in 1964 when she and her husband brought their son to meet Mr Ely and to see the school. They were immediately impressed by the breadth of subjects Mr Larcombe taught. One of these was scripture, but he did not just teach it, he practised what he preached. He thought out all the assemblies and school services with themes appropriate to the boys' lives and a balanced mixture of lively contemporary Christian songs and much respected, well-known hymns. He ran a school branch of the Scripture Union and every year he and his contingent set off with homemade banners waving, along the road to the Cornwall Hall for the annual rally and bun tea. He introduced pastoral care at The Prep long before the term became part of educational jargon. His concern extended to every boy in the school so that when tragedy struck, as when a boy's father was drowned on holiday, the son and indeed the whole family knew that they were not alone.

Soon after the school moved to Godden Green, he was officially appointed Assistant Head and continued, in addition to his full timetable, to take a little games, to run a music society, to fill in for junior French, to let off the unreliable starting pistol on sports day, and to combine some geography with the history. All this proved to be too much for him and he had to take time off in 1969 and 1970, but he rested for as short a period as possible and returned to take up all his responsibilities again. In the early 1980s, he masterminded the project to write a history of The Prep which was published as *The Half & Half's*, contacting alumni from the 1920s, 30s, 40s, and

'The Half & Half's'

The History of Sevenoaks Prep.

RESEARCHED BY

James Bampton	Alistair Cormack
Christopher Geer	Matthew Hammond
Robert Hartley	Ian Ivory
Guy Mitson	Clifford Mitchell
James Ryman	Russell Smart
Lawrence Springall	Jeremy Tidmarsh
Paul Thompson	Stuart Wallinger
Paul Wishart	Richard Wolfgang

Written by

PETER LARCOMBE

&

JEREMY CRANG

Mr Larcombe's original handwritten version of *The Half & Half's* written with Jeremy Crang.

50s for their contributions, involving the boys in research and interviews and, literally, writing the history in his distinctive, beautiful script.

Some alumni remember Mr Larcombe as 'a great teacher that we all wanted to impress', others recall his immaculately coiffured jet-black quiff styled, they thought, on Elvis Presley's, along with an array of Pentel pens in his jacket pocket. He had around 20 of them, all colour co-ordinated, which the boys were never allowed to borrow. Another alumnus, however, recalled that Mr Larcombe could suddenly lose his temper. He taught scripture from a black leather Bible which had been annotated and colour coded with the Pentel pens and with different coloured stickers to mark appropriate passages. In one lesson, a boy wound up Mr Larcombe with dire results. He was at his desk, bent forward with an open Bible balanced on the back of his head. When asked by Mr Larcombe what he was doing, his reply of 'Reading the Bible, Sir, I have eyes in the back of my head' resulted in him being dragged in a direct line to the door, bumping into and over any desks and chairs in the way and thrown out.

Mr Larcombe was an incredible artist and he often taught from his A2 drawings and parable boards from the Bible which he carried around in a black art folder. He was a wonderful disciplinarian with a loud and imposing voice. On sports day, Mr Oatley used to hire a caravan with a tannoy system in which Mr Larcombe spent the whole day recording results. Everyone was in awe of this man announcing the results in his booming voice.

Through all the changes and excitements of the succeeding years he continued his full involvement at the school while assuming another vocation, as Pastor of Dunton Green Free Church. By 1986, he had decided to devote the majority of his time to his Church while agreeing to remain with The Prep on the pastoral side and also to help with practical history. When he left, Mr Oatley remarked that 'he has been admired and respected by generations of boys and parents for his devotion, understanding, and sincerity and for the marvellous example he has set in all walks of life'. Mr Larcombe continued to be involved with the Church as full-time minister of Cranbrook Congregational Church. He died in North Wales in May 2015 at the age of 80; a memorial service held in Cranbrook church was attended by Mr and Mrs Oatley, **Jeremy Crang** and his mother Elizabeth, Mrs Sadler and Mrs Cooke.

Mrs Lucas had been, like Mr Larcombe, connected with the school for more years than she could remember, having initially come as a parent but soon being recruited by Mr Ely to teach. From 1965 she taught English up to Common Entrance level and Latin to 8-year-olds. Gradually as Mr Ely taught fewer lessons she took more. For over 20 years, Mrs Lucas was a tower of strength for the two Headmasters she worked under. Her broad perception of people in general was coupled with a deeply caring nature and a gentle, though firm, manner in dealing with individuals who were, each and every one, important to her. Her command of English and the spoken word was without parallel and the high standard of work which was produced by the boys in her care reflected the high quality of her teaching.

For many years she was property mistress for the school plays. She, and her husband **Derek**, produced a vast range of 'props', including two ships' wheels. One year, Mr Lucas forged several famous masterpieces to be props for one of the plays; then Mrs Lucas was forced to watch from the wings as these skilful works of art were smashed into pieces over the boys' heads. For many years she was the first violinist in the school orchestra. Not only did she show a gritty determination to perfect her playing, but she was always there to encourage struggling players around her.

After over 20 years of teaching at The Prep, Mrs Lucas decided to retire from full-time teaching, but continued to be in close contact, contributing enormously to *The Souvenir Post* produced in 2000 for the school reunion and to the update and revision of *The Half & Half's* in the early 2000s. **Mrs Lillian Hutchinson** took over the Latin teaching on Mrs Lucas' retirement and was followed by **Mrs Gillian Hankey** who continued to teach Latin on a non-compulsory basis until it was phased out later in the 1990s.

Mrs Dickinson was another gem of a person who looked after generations of little ones and gave them the full benefit of her experience in art, handwork and nature. Her first contact with The Prep was as a parent. Her sons, **Tim** and **Simon**, were pupils of the school during the years 1966-71 and she joined them to teach in 1967. She was taken on by Mr Ely to teach poetry and handwork to the younger pupils while to the boys in Form 1 she was the teacher 'who looks after us in the afternoons'. She opened up a wonderful new world for all the little ones whether on duty at break, or on walks, or in the classroom, as she never missed an opportunity to point out something boys might have missed otherwise – the first snowdrop, a fascinating insect, the changing colour of a leaf. Her own love of nature passed on to boys without number. She was always firm but kind with a marvellous sense of humour. She even became senior art teacher for a while but following a heart operation in 1984 she decided to take life a little easier.

Mr Paul Sykes was one of the teachers who came to The Prep after the closure of Winchester House in 1985. He taught science and in his two years at The Prep significantly advanced the use and knowledge of computers. He left to join the newly established Sackville School in 1987. Another was **Mr Peter Rogers** who taught geography and sport and was Assistant Head in 1988-89, after which he left to take up a position at Gravesend Grammar School and was replaced by **Mr Martin Harris**. The third ex-Winchester House teacher who joined The Prep with her son **Christophe** was **Mme Jacqueline Homer**, which was fortunate timing as **Mrs Maggie Meredith**, who had been the senior French teacher and a vibrant member of The Prep family for a number of years, left in the summer of 1985 to have a baby. Mme Homer taught French to the senior pupils for a further 26 years until she retired in 2011.

Mr Oatley was happy to employ alumni on a temporary or part-time basis as gap year students between school and university or in school holidays. Donald Smith was one of the alumni who Mr Oatley had employed on a gap year, in this case 1984-85. There is a staff photograph from that year in which Donald and **Philip Oldroyd**, who helped out at The Prep after he had finished his university term, are sitting on the grass in the front garden. Following reading French and Spanish at university, Donald became a graduate trainee in an office, thinking 'now I'll be earning lots of money', but he hated it. One evening in 1990 he was driving home from this job he hated on auto-pilot and suddenly found he was sitting in The Prep's car park. He said to himself 'you know what, I want to work here'. So he got out of the car and went up to see Mr Oatley, who welcomed him in. Mr Oatley eventually said: 'Do you really want to work here?' Donald replied, 'I do' and he was hired there and then. Later he did his teacher training at Roehampton along with Philip Oldroyd, which was a hard year fitting it in with full-time teaching. He managed it with the support of **Mr Tom Bowen**. Nearly 30 years later, Donald is still teaching at The Prep.

Fabric

When Mr Oatley took over in 1978, the school's facilities were much the same as in 1968 both inside the house and outside and there was a need for bigger and better facilities. Very soon he managed to galvanise the parents into action and was lucky enough to find one, **Mr David Fry**, who worked for Wiltshires, the building firm.

The new green hall, the first of many buildings to appear over the next few years.

The first project was for a car park. On the first day of the autumn term the school heard that planning permission had been granted after a year's wait; unfortunately, in that time the estimated cost had doubled. However, they decided to go ahead. On Friday 29 September, 87 tons of stone was delivered and early next day the hired machinery and an army of parents and staff arrived in the pouring rain and got to work. By the evening, they had built a car park. Mr Fry had drawn up the plans and applied for planning permission; then, under his direction, diggers and lorries were hired. **Mr Jim Oldroyd** ran everywhere with the roller, **Mrs Cornwell** dug everything up, **Mr Pridham** cut up large trees as if they were matchsticks, **Mr Jackson** and **Mr Watkins** dug a very deep hole and **Mr Thomas** and his two sons with **Mr Shaw** on, and in, the drains, the team were well away and all wishing they had never started! On most of the projects that Mr Fry directed he relied heavily on **Alfie** (no one can remember his surname) who would cheerfully lay tarmac, mix concrete, and generally guide the willing fathers as they went about their labouring.

It was amazing how quickly it was all done and the 'army' had made it possible for the school to complete the job at the original estimate. The dreadful winter of continuous snow, ice, and rain did the car park no good and in the middle of the spring term the same army arrived one Saturday and repaired the entrance. It certainly made a tremendous difference to the school and everyone felt much safer now that the boys could get in and out of cars away from the 'racetrack' outside the main gate.

1978-79 was a terrible year for weather. In November the roof blew off one of the changing rooms, but it was quickly repaired by Mr Searle, gardener and Jack of all trades; there was heavy snow in January and virtually no rugby was played in the spring term.

The start of the summer term 1979 saw planning permission granted for a new hall and immediately The Prep team got going again under Mr Fry's direction. Once more the cost had doubled, so they decided to lay the foundations themselves and, with the same machinery arriving early one Saturday morning (again in the pouring rain), they got to work. Fourteen fathers turned up on two mornings and managed to finish the entire project, although the work was physically very hard. On 2 July, two carpenters arrived and in two and a half days the hall was up. Three days later another two men arrived and the roof was felted. Next day the electricity was all wired up and by this time the outside had had a coat of primer and undercoat. The end of term saw everybody in and out of the hall, looking forward to it being used the following term. The new hall was to be used as a gym, an assembly hall, and an art room.

With the new hall in place, **Mr Brooks** completed the Herculean task of laying lino over the floors of all the school buildings. He spent many evenings making the school a more pleasant place to work in and the result was a tribute to his willpower, patience, and the school coffee and cake!

above 1981 hall under construction.

right A place for the whole school to gather. This must be an 'own clothes day' and whatever they are watching is clearly captivating.

below By 1982, the school was a village of wooden huts, ending in the woods.

At much the same time in 1979 the school acquired the lease of the 4½ acre field next door to the school, known as Front Field. **Mr Charles** and **Mrs Mary Montague** from Stake Farm College had been very helpful in the negotiations with the Knole Estate. Over the years there had been mutual co-operation between the two schools. The Prep pupils had been able to use the Stake Farm squash court and the Montagues' swimming pool, and in return about 20 girls had cookery lessons from an outside teacher at The Prep while every Tuesday Mrs Frances Oatley took some girls for keep-fit in the new hall.

Landscape gardeners were hired to cut, roll, and level Front Field and within a week of their starting it was back to how it used to be 50 years previously when it was a cricket pitch. The earth from the foundations of the new hall was transported to the hollows on the field and it was hoped that by the start of the next term, the grass would have grown. A huge long-jump pit was dug and filled with sand and an athletics track marked out. The field was also used for two football pitches with a cricket square re-established between them. The new sports field was inaugurated with a special family sports and games festival on Sunday 1 July, which included welly-boot throwing, putting, darts, tennis, bowls, badminton, and marbles. There was a fathers' cricket match, a mothers' tennis match and rounders with the event ending with tea, cheese and wine.

In December 1979, **Mr Len Baldwin** helped (and hindered) by Mr Oatley erected the new small hut to be used as a changing room for Forms 1 and 2. This had originally been Mr Oatley's family beach hut in Minnis Bay, Birchington. Mr Baldwin had been gardener, cleaner and handyman for over ten years, initially working with Mr Searle. Since the latter's retirement a couple of years earlier Mr Baldwin had been responsible for maintenance at the school. He is remembered as always wearing a beanie hat and driving an old 1960s car, in which he would sit at lunch time to eat his sandwiches. **Mr David Cochrane** (known by everybody as 'David the Gardener') joined him in about 1984 to help tend the ever-growing estate. Mr Baldwin was remarkable in that he had celebrated his 75th birthday earlier in 1979 when the school gave him some special gifts. He had lived in the area all his life and for the majority of it had been a coalman. He died in September 1984 in his 80th year.

Before long, the hall was being used for classrooms on a semi-permanent basis and it was clear that a further building was needed. Fortunately, in 1980, a parent had seen that a school in East Grinstead was closing down and had a hall with partitions for sale at the knock-down price of £100, providing the purchaser paid for taking it down and transporting it away.

The chosen site for this new hall was where the air raid shelter had been in the garden. The foundations were dug out, the building moved to its new site, and the landscaping completed over two weekends in February by a workforce of 45 fathers, four mothers, three alumni and 12 pupils. With the help of volunteers from the Territorial Army, a team of staff, parents, and pupils filled in the shelter and erected the hall during the 1981 summer term. The weekend of 20-21 June was one to remember as Mr Oatley organised a 36 hour 'paint-in'. The Head started the non-stop painting at 5am on the Saturday and during the weekend no less than 70 people popped in and out to help paint the entire new building. By 5pm on the Sunday it was completely finished. Form 8 looked after the young ones and some kind mothers supplied food and drink. The Head was kept at it all night by various helpers, including **Mrs Mills** and **Mr Sheffield**. Not to be outdone, some of the boys formed themselves into a workforce in subsequent options and painted the changing rooms to prove themselves to be just as good as the parents!

The new hall was opened at the end-of-term service in July 1981 and represented the most important step in a five-year programme of changes undertaken by Mr Oatley, the staff, and the parents. Two of the older rooms in the main house had already been made into subject classrooms, one for maths and the other temporarily for art, and three more outside classrooms were made available for individual subjects. A further building was erected in summer 1981 which provided permanent art and history rooms. With the science lab being used as a dedicated science classroom, each subject for senior boys now had its own classroom. All this meant that from the autumn term 1981, the senior boys were now taught on a subject-classroom basis with the boys moving backwards and forwards according to which subject they were going to. In the autumn 1981 copy of *The Acorn* a poem by **Jeremy Hill** summed up Mr Oatley's efforts from a boy's perspective. It is included in Appendix 4.

1981-82 saw the last phase of the initial building programme. In the winter holiday, the old changing rooms were gutted and rebuilt for classrooms, the science room renovated, and the car park was doubled in size. Although the weather that winter was dreadful (the alumni football match had to be cancelled) it made no difference to the workmen who seemed to get used to working in rain and snow storms. By the end of the fifth week of the spring 1982 term, the renovations to the science room were completed and the extra classrooms, (along with a dedicated school shop for second-hand uniform) were erected and painted. **Mrs Christa Dando**, mother of **Nicholas**, who had been running a second-hand uniform shop since Mr Ely's day, officially opened the shop after half-term and by the beginning of the summer term it was in regular use. It was much appreciated by many parents.

Throughout the spring term of 1982 mothers were seen popping in and out of the hall with tape-measures, needles and cotton; and by the end of term the boys all saw why – marvellous curtaining all around the hall. The school was greatly indebted to **Mrs Lewis** and **Mrs Ivory** who masterminded the whole project. It was about this time that the hall was taking shape as a theatre. The stage blocks had been completed earlier in the term and Mrs Lewis and her army of helpers put the finishing touches to the stage curtains – a mammoth task.

By the summer term of 1982, this massive rebuilding programme initiated by Mr Oatley was completed. Building had gone on and on and now what was once part of the garden of Fawke Cottage had become a village of wooden buildings ending in the woods. The green sheds where Mr Searle, Miss Dorothy Coleman's gardener, had done much of his work became one long changing room inside and, by 1986, the Victorian greenhouse had disappeared, together with its Heath Robinson machinery.

A school prospectus from around 1982 summed up the progress that had been made since Mr Oatley had taken over. 'The main house (Fawke Cottage) has been converted into a school with four classrooms inside, and seven purpose-built classrooms outside. There is also a 50ft x 25ft assembly hall and gym, and a dining room, an art room, fully equipped science block, individual class cloakrooms with washing facilities and the school has its own playing fields of seven acres. There is a tarmac playing area, which is used for all sports, surrounded by lawns and gardens for the children to play in and enjoy. We have use of a squash court adjoining the school. Swimming is taught at the local baths during the summer term. Each form has its own extensive library and there is also a reference library. The school possesses a colour television and full radio and recording facilities for all schools' broadcasts and is fully centrally heated by gas. There is a school mini-caravette for matches and outings.' What the prospectus didn't say was that Mr Oatley was living in Fawke Cottage with his daughter Claire. When he married Janet, her two boys moved in as well, so the top of the main house was fairly crowded.

Forms 4, 5, and 6 were situated in wooden classrooms outside, with all the others being upstairs in Fawke Cottage in amongst the Oatleys' living area. Luke

A Form 1 class on the first floor of Fawke Cottage with Mrs Bryony House.

Harrison's office in 2018 used to be Form 1's classroom and he still gets occasional flashbacks as to where his seat was. Many of his contemporaries now have their own children at The Prep and whenever they come up to see the Headmaster in his office, they are often keen to look around the top floors of the house to remind themselves of where their desks were. When **Mrs Penny Spencer-Allen**'s son, **Lynden**, was in **Mrs Maureen Perks**' Form 1, on arrival at school in the early mornings she would often find poor **Mrs Janet Oatley** bringing her washing down the stairs as they went up to the classroom, which was more or less opposite the Oatleys' kitchen. They also passed a very typical teenage bedroom of Janet's sons, Philip and **Richard**, which was at the top of the stairs. Later, when they came back from university, the boys would often be seen appearing, bleary-eyed, out of their bedroom! Philip was later to become Headmaster of The Prep when Mr Oatley retired.

Mr Oatley never locked up anything and the back and front doors were always open. The staff knew if they forgot something or couldn't sleep, they could drive over, the back door would be open and they would enter with 'Hi Edward, can I just talk something through with you'? Similarly, if the boys forgot their homework or left their sports kit or whatever behind, their parents could just pop up and get it, even in the middle of the night if necessary. The school was always open for business, whether deep in snow, bombarded with wind and rain or floods as, of course, the Oatleys were stuck on site. Mr Oatley and his willing team would ensure this was possible and were prepared to rise extremely early to clear accesses, the car park, and the paths. If anyone needed to go to the school at the weekend they would find Mrs Oatley there weeding the garden and Mr Oatley (usually in his school vest and shorts) cutting the grass. They were always very welcoming and ready for a chat despite the invasion of their privacy. The irony is that, although the Oatleys lived in the house, they never had burglaries, compared with the present day when every other week something seems to happen. One day, **Mr Peter Ratcliffe** announced that the only thing locked in the school was the toilet roll holder.

The green sheds that had been the first ever hall were converted into what were euphemistically known as classrooms. They were lacking in several niceties, not the least being insulation. One winter, the goldfish bowl in Mrs Shea's classroom froze over during the night and stayed like that for a week. Conversely, in summer 1979 the boys grew grass seed around their model Ancient British Village and the heat and humidity caused such a luxuriant growth that **Daniel Collings** invented a motorised Lego hover mower to keep it under control.

In February 1984, Mr Oatley announced that a new music room was to be built with a large room for orchestra, choir, and singing lessons and with three smaller rooms leading from it, two for individual music lessons and one to be a computer room. At sports day in July 1984, Mr Oatley followed this up by saying that a brand-new science block was to be built in the summer holidays and at the beginning of the autumn term 1984, the original science room was refurbished to become the Form 8 changing room with a new floor and another shed attached, which became Mr Rogers' geography room. On the arrival of a new science portakabin in 1989, much to the delight of **Mr Mike Wadsworth**, the Crafty Cabin had to go and the wooden science room was moved to become the workshop which it still is!

Academic

The first science lab had been in the old stables and had a corrugated tin roof, so when it rained it was extremely noisy. Mr Cooke taught science, a very debonair gentleman who would doff his cap to every mother. One thing he allowed the boys to do was to heat and bend shards of glass; they used to walk around with trays of these and many a time burnt glass was tipped onto the desks. It was extremely cold in the lab and Bunsen burners were on most of the time.

In February 1979, a new-style booklet for reports was issued to all parents. The old report sheets, so familiar to parents from their own schooldays, were replaced by individual subject sheets – 6in by 4in – and these were clipped together inside a folder which had a key to the new grading method printed inside for reference. Thus parents could work out what their sons had achieved. With capital letters for effort, and figures to indicate attainment, you just hoped your son would never get 'F', which meant 'downright lazy'!

The numbering of the forms was changed for the 1980-81 academic year, with the top form (normally for boys aged 12 at the beginning of the autumn term) becoming Form 8 and the bottom one (for boys aged 5) Form 1. The numbers in each form varied; from 8 to 1 numbers were 21, 16, 22, 25, 22, 20, 13, 12 making a total of 151.

In 1982, a School Inspector paid a visit and was extremely complimentary on all aspects of the school and its teaching. By the early 1980s, Latin was no longer compulsory for Common Entrance examinations, but Mrs Lucas continued teaching it to small groups of the more academic boys. The Prep had always recognised endeavour as being as important as achievement and in 1982 the C.D.L. Heath endeavour cup was presented by the parents of **Christopher Heath** 'in recognition of the excellent guidance and encouragement Christopher received', to be awarded annually to a boy who, like Christopher, tried hard but without formal recognition.

When Sevenoaks School, from which The Prep sprang, announced that it was going fully co-educational from 1984, the enthusiasm which many parents had had for their sons to go there evaporated and there was an immediate emphasis on alternative schools. Mr Oatley himself led the opposition to the policy instigated by the Head of Sevenoaks. There was a fear that this would make a difference to the tradition that had passed on so many Prep boys to 'the big school' but this was overtaken a few years later when, in 1991, The Prep itself started taking girls again.

Drama and music

After Mr Ely, the mantle of producer of the annual school play fell upon Mrs Shefford. At the end of the 1979 spring term the school play was *Treasure Island* with an attractively enigmatic Long John Silver (**Simon Herbert**), an appealing, gallant Jim Hawkins (**Francis Griffiths**), two highly dignified gentlemen Squire Trelawney (**Andrew Bond**) and Dr Livesey (**Jonathan Gottelier**), a commanding Captain Smollett (**Julian Claydon**), a successfully deceptive Blind Pew (**Tom Pridham**), a wild yet likeable Ben Gunn (Tom Pridham again), an aggressive Black Dog (**William Bliss**), a gentle Tom Redruth (**John Coote**) and a secretive, condemned Billy Bones (**John Cornwell**). The finishing touch was the young goats, resplendent in spectacular masks and fleeces. Mr Lucas constructed a convincing, free-standing ship's wheel which was commandeered by Captain Smollett throughout rehearsals and performances, fending off all the boys who wanted a turn at steering.

As she would do for all forthcoming performances, **Jonathan Bowen**'s mother **Mrs Gwen Bowen** provided the sympathetic piano accompaniment and on this occasion was assisted on the double bass by **Christopher Lang** and on drums and percussion by the producer's son and alumnus **Justin Shefford**.

The 1980 production of *Old Father Time* was perhaps the most difficult play put on by the school to date. This mammoth project had been started in the previous autumn term, when scripts were read through and it was decided who should play each part. The nine major parts were allotted – Jonathan Gottelier became the old and wobbly Old Father Time with Richard Oldroyd as Watchdog (Old Father Time's constant, mechanical and lovable companion). **Luke Gottelier** turned himself into Mrs Sparkle, a cockney charlady, and **Jake George** (with the help of some make-up) was turned into what at first looked like a large, fearsome dinosaur, but who proved to be a young and endearing one. **Mark Williams** was given the part of Sergeant Watchit, a guardsman, **Richard Weaver** the part of the pompous Prime Minister. Dodger and Bodger the two likeable buskers, were played by **Andrew Howard** and **Tim Herbert** respectively and **Darren Fry** was set the task of becoming the green-faced, gruesome and despicable Flying Sauceress.

Then with the spring term came Saturday morning rehearsals where the choreography was taken over by **Mrs Maureen Perks** and, thanks to her, the dances were kept to their usual high standard. Mrs Shefford had everybody singing as she wanted them to, the words as they should be said and the actions as they should be done. Towards the end of the term props, sound effects and the lighting people began to come in to get everything synchronised, while, at the same time, the costumes started to take shape. Then, just two days before the

top
Higgins the
Highwayman,
half of the
1983 double
bill.

above
1985 reprise
of *Treasure
Island*.

left Worzel
Gummidge,
1986.

dress rehearsal, disaster struck. Darren Fry (Flying Sauceress) was ill and could not take part, so Mark Williams (one-time Sergeant Watchit) took Darren's place and **Stuart Burden**, who had been helping with the props, took his place as Sergeant Watchit.

At the dress rehearsal all went well (except one of the major actors forgot his lines) until the end when Big Ben was meant to strike the New Year. This was the signal for the Prime Minister to go forward and ask the audience to sing Auld Lang Syne, but nothing happened! Luke Gottelier saved the performance by coming forward and announcing that it was nearly the New Year and asking everybody to sing. Then came the part in every performance where everybody had a good laugh, as in came the lovable bundle of fun, Puppy Watchdog. After that disastrous New Year Mr Oatley was relieved of his post in charge of sound effects, and **Andrew McLaren** took his place.

The following year saw an equally modern play called *Hijack Over Hygenia* starring **Richard Charlwood** and **Guy Watkins**. *The Acorn's* report listed the behind-the-scenes team of staff who regularly functioned together during a school play: Mrs Perks (dances); Mrs Dickinson, **Mrs Monique Barton** and Mrs House (make-up – Mrs Sadler was to take over later from Mrs Barton); Mrs Lucas (properties); Mr Larcombe (scenery and scene changing); Mrs Oldroyd (curtains and stage management). One of the best pranks in years was in this play. **Douglas Maynard** was the queen and was saying goodnight to the princess (who was acted by **Jeremy Robson**). While the queen was distracted drawing the curtains, the beast in the story was to sneak in and put a pill in the princess's drink. Normally a Smartie, this time it was a big marshmallow. The audience burst out laughing and Douglas had to stand there watching as Jeremy tried to swallow a marshmallow without success. He soon joined in the laughter and had to hide his face behind the curls of his wig.

1983 saw a double bill: *Higgins the Highwayman* starring **Alistair Cormack** and *According to the Rules*, Mrs Shefford's own adaptation of *The Reluctant Dragon*, starring **Christopher Watts**, **Matthias Gruninger** (as the dragon) and **Lawrence Springall** (as St George).

The inspiration of Mrs Shefford could not be confined to drama. Every summer the dramatic and musical gifts of the junior school were displayed in the Concert on the Lawn. The school was trying to broaden its music teaching, adding violin and brass to the piano and guitar lessons already on offer. The 1980 junior concert went exceedingly well with an extraordinary number of parents turning up to see their children perform. The orchestra consisted of members of staff, a parent (the leader of the London Philharmonic Orchestra, **Mr Barry Griffiths**), and about a dozen boys of different ages, all of whom played marvellously. There was also a number of soloists on the piano and on the violin. Form 4 danced as Wombles and Form 3 had a picnic dressed as bears in the wood to the music of *The Teddy Bears' Picnic*.

Painting of a *Concert on the Lawn* by Mr Derek Lucas presented to the school by Mrs Angela Lucas on her retirement. The last full junior concert here was in 1990 but Form 3 continued the tradition for a number of years.

Pupils who had been learning other instruments also had their turn. The guitarists and recorder players played Annie's song and the guitarists played *Any Dream Will Do* from *Joseph and the Amazing Technicolor Dreamcoat*, trained by **Mrs Geraldine Bosley**. Forms 1 and 2 sang songs and performed dances to them; Form 5 acted a short play entitled *Come to the Zoo* (produced by Mrs Shefford) with singing by Form 4 and music from the orchestra. Many wonderful masks had been made for Forms 1 and 2 and for *Come to the Zoo* by members of staff; each form teacher had put in a great deal of hard work rehearsing their own forms. Mrs Shefford trained the junior choir for their sensitive and musical singing of 'Rats'. One of the memorable solos this time was the tall **James Mayo** brandishing a glittering trombone.

Sevenoaks was, and still is, lucky enough to have an annual competitive festival in which schools are encouraged to take part. The Three Arts Festival (for spoken word, instruments and singing) was first held in 1951 and is still going strong. It had the advantage of allowing a less extroverted child to make a stage debut in decent obscurity rather than in front of his peers at school. Whatever the motive – self-expression or self-sacrifice – an astonishing number of boys expressed a fervent wish to appear at the festival. The school supported the Three Arts Festival in many ways, helping with refreshments, photo copying, and setting it up, especially by organising the choir morning. Mr Oatley has been on the organising committee for many years and still is.

A report in *The Acorn* in 1980 illustrated the breadth and depth of the boys' participation in that year's festival. Mrs Richardson organised a mini-festival so that the numbers could be whittled down to a reasonable number. Mrs Lucas and Mrs Priestley sat in solemn judgment on an enthusiastic horde reading prose or poetry at will. Tongue-twisters were mastered, difficult diphthongs practised excruciatingly, the subtleties of different phrases probed expertly, and boys actually learnt poems; even the prose passages were memorised with accidental repetition! At the festival itself, the choir gave an excellent performance – sweet in tone, clear in diction – and was second, just one mark behind the winning choir. (On one memorable occasion, choirboy **Douglas Ruffhead** made things very difficult for the rest of the choir by being sick while they were singing!) Later **Mrs Elizabeth Dwinell** had great success with her violinists and string ensembles.

In the Bible reading, Guy Watkins and **Christopher Crang** received honours certificates. Luke Gottelier and Richard Oldroyd were just behind them. In prose reading, the boys excelled themselves. Richard Weaver and Richard Oldroyd were both first in their groups. **Lawrence Springall** and **Timothy Bampton** received honours certificates and Andrew Howard gave a good performance.

The poetry section was always the loneliest and most difficult and performance depended on experience and natural voice quality. There was the usual crop of colds and coughs. Christopher Crang, a potential star, developed hay fever and anti-histamine robbed his performance of its sparkle. **Andrew Johnson** came first, followed by **Clive Seabrook**, Jonathan Gottelier, Jonathan Bowen, and **Robert Lewis**. In the other class, **Gareth Seabrook** was second and Alistair Cormack third. Richard Charlwood and Luke Gottelier were close behind.

The year 1982 saw the best day yet for The Prep in the festival. There were two firsts (**Ross Anderson** and **Ian Ivory**), four seconds (Jonathan Bowen, **St John Anderson, Richard Wolfgang**, and Richard Charlwood), four thirds (Alistair Cormack, Gareth Seabrook, Matthias Gruninger, and **Alexander Johnson**) plus seven distinctions and 19 merits. In all, 33 boys were trained by Mrs Biggs and Mrs Sadler. Mrs Biggs recalled that one of her favourite times of the year was early summer when they began to research and rehearse prose and poetry to perform at the festival. Works by Roald Dahl, Kenneth Grahame, Robert Frost and others were chosen to be practised at every spare moment of the day. The boys did very well and were proud to show off their certificates of merit and distinction after the competition was over.

The Prep's participation in the Sevenoaks Three Arts Festival continued to prosper. For a prose reading the reader had to time his passage to end within four minutes; if over, he was disqualified. At Mrs Lucas' last festival in 1986, **Dominic Low** received the highest mark of all for his reading from *The BFG* by Roald Dahl. When he ended with 'But that was before we found the dead rat!' he lifted his head from the text and delivered the punch line straight to the judge. It was a striking moment.

The new music room was opened in 1984. In the autumn 1984 edition of *The Acorn*, Mrs Shefford recalled that it scarcely seemed possible that when she started, the school had one or two recorder players and a couple of violinists. In the new space, there was room for 32 members of an orchestra, as well as two practice rooms. The project had so captured everyone's imagination that a staggering sum of £2,000 was raised in most varied and enterprising ways by parents, boys, and staff to properly equip the room.

1979

1985

above Snowy scenes from two
of the significant winters in
Mr Oatley's early years at The Prep.

left Fun was always guaranteed for
those who made it into school as
shown in this more recent photo.
Outings to the slopes in Knole Park
were on the timetable!

School life

The spring term of 1979 started with snow everywhere and ended 12 weeks later with snow still falling. There was still snow on the ground when the summer term started on 24 April. Tuesday 23 January was possibly the worst day, when 74 boys made it to school (including three who skied across Knole Park) but 73 didn't.

Mr Oatley and his staff made many changes, some successfully and some not so successfully. School photos changed from black-and-white to colour. What had been gained in prettiness had, on certain occasions, been lost in definition; it was not always possible to make out who some people were, compared with the crisp, bold definition of the unadorned black-and-white. Apart from photos of sports teams in colour, parents could now have portrait photographs of their sons, together with brothers if they wished. It was even possible to have a pastel or charcoal portrait drawn by an artist, at rather higher cost, naturally, rather than a photo.

One day, the school's brass nameplate, which had once glittered in Vine Court Road and was screwed to the oak front door of Fawke Cottage, disappeared without trace. It was at the weekend and it became obvious to the Head, after a thorough search, that it must have been stolen. He called the police, but before their inquiries revealed anything, Monday morning came and there, at break time, was the plaque, shining brightly on the front door as if nothing had happened. What had happened was that Mr Baldwin, the conscientious gardener and odd job man, had taken it home to give it a proper clean!

In 1981, it was noted that the prefects, especially Andrew McLaren and Christopher Crang, were becoming experts at showing new parents round the school and were doing the job extremely well. It always used to be the Headmaster who did this public relations job but once put in the hands of prefects it proved a beguiling introduction to The Prep for many prospective parents and many terrified young prospective pupils.

Dogs were an important part of The Prep family. The Ely's dog, Paddy, had featured on many of the photographs from the Ely years. Later, Mrs Janet Oatley would walk around the school and through the woods each morning with her Cairn terrier Sinbad, armed with a spiked litter picker-up made by **Mr Michael Heal** to save her bending down to collect wayward crisp packets etc. When Donald Smith's mother came to help Mrs Oatley in the kitchen,

The not-so-saintly Sinbad who in 1985 was even considered to be a member of staff—he certainly appeared in the official staff photo!

she often brought along their dog, Susie, another Cairn terrier that looked like an old-fashioned mop. Sinbad was quite a character and wandered happily around the school, his home, either with Mrs Oatley or on his own. Cricket matches were quite often interrupted by Sinbad. He thought nothing of joining young cricketers in the middle of a match and preventing play until he was forcibly removed from the pitch with much amusement from all concerned.

Sinbad was usually well behaved but Mrs Spencer-Allen recalls one sunny afternoon after giving Mrs Oatley and the 'saintly Sinbad' a lift in her car, Mrs Oatley was witnessed intently cleaning the inside of the now very smelly car: Sinbad had disgraced himself. Everyone was curious but Mrs Oatley was so ashamed that both ladies vowed not to reveal the real reason – sorry, Sinbad, but the shameful tale is now told! Sadly, the much-loved Sinbad died in 1992 and in 1995 Mrs Oatley was given a cross poodle/collie called Skipper by **James Boorman** and the Form 8 leavers. Unfortunately, the collie in Skipper meant he couldn't resist trying to round up the children so, despite many efforts at training him otherwise, he had to return to the Boormans, who found him a new home.

Mrs Shefford had her black Labrador, Jasper, and Mr Clark his retriever guide dog, Dan. Mr Clark and Dan were obviously inseparable and together they walked to and from school along Back Lane, the track behind the stables in Godden Green and across the playing fields from David's home in Blackhall Lane. If there was a match taking place he and Dan would wait for someone to come and lead them round the pitch. In more recent years, **Alice Bramall** remembered that **Mr John Baynes**, the science teacher, had a beautiful collie named Roxie that would wander around the lab benches during lessons until Mr Baynes called her back to her bed.

Ever since the move to Godden Green, trees had been a feature of life at The Prep. When the school moved, they inherited the wonderful well-tended garden of Fawke Cottage which included a number of specimen trees of fond memory; Mrs Shea recalled sitting under the walnut tree at The Prep with Mr Oatley when he appointed her to teach Form 3. She was fascinated by the incredible selection of trees. She found the Gingko Biloba very useful when teaching the Jurassic Period. On rainy days, the magnificent Cedar tree was a wonderful shelter and the Monkey Puzzle tree offered a great stimulus for creative work. One of Philip Oldroyd's earliest memories of the school was to eat the fresh walnuts that fell from the tree that was located around the entrance to what became the language block and it was appropriate that when he left the school in

The gingko tree, photographed here in 2003, pre-dates The Prep at Fawke Cottage.

2012, having been Headmaster, he and his wife **Niki** were given two walnut trees by the leavers to plant at the school.

When Mr Oatley took over the school, the problem of the inadequate size of the car park and how boys were to get to and from the school were two of the first things to be addressed. Maidstone and District buses had recently withdrawn their 106 service which linked Sevenoaks and Fawke Common and which passed the school, and more and more boys were being delivered and taken home by car. The first project initiated by Mr Oatley was to establish a proper car park, which was achieved with considerable help from some parents, in 1978. This car park was doubled in size in 1982, and again, after Stake Farm was acquired, in 1987. With the school having increased in size by nearly 90%, this was sorely needed. In addition, and also reflecting that the school was now attracting boys from further afield, two school minibuses, driven by two members of staff, picked up boys from various locations starting from Tunbridge Wells and New Ash Green.

The car park, of course, became more than just somewhere to drop off and pick up pupils. It was a recruitment ground for Mr Oatley, who initiated many interviews there; it was a place for potential members of staff to reflect having undergone one of Mr Oatley's unusual interviews; for some boys it was where they learnt to drive; and it was where parents would spend many hours hearing of scandals, infidelities, and both good and bad gossip. The rumours and revelations were exciting and numerous. Mrs Spencer-Allen claims that she was to know so much more about the school and its goings on than she was ever to know when she became a member of staff. She also learnt not to believe everything that she heard!

Mrs Angela Pickering, who later joined the staff, recalled the unconventional introduction she had to The Prep. Her family had moved to Sevenoaks from abroad and were looking for schools. They met Mrs Bullock, one of the teachers, who advised them to make an appointment to meet the Headmaster and see the school. She also advised them not to take any notice of the furniture. The Pickerings duly arrived at the school, Mr dressed in his suit, and Mrs in her Sunday best, to meet the Headmaster and view the school. They were ushered into the staff room, which was furnished with an odd collection of well-worn sofas and chairs, and were soon met by the Headmaster, dressed in short red running shorts, and the head boy. Mr Oatley explained that the head boy would usher them round the school, and that they would meet him again after their tour.

They were immediately impressed by the trust given to this young lad, who was polite, personable, and seemed well able to answer most of their questions. They were less impressed by the collection of old sheds which served as classrooms but as they were ushered into each one they became successively aware that all the boys were friendly, actively employed, and very happy. There was a real family atmosphere, and the boys were busy. The old school desks were recognisable from the 1950s, and the Pickerings then understood the warning about the furniture and fittings. At the end of the tour, Mrs Pickering had decided that they should look no further—this would be the school for their boys, but Mr Pickering deemed the science lab to be a potting shed, and a fire risk. After some discussion, however, they decided that they liked what they had seen enough to put up with the fire risk, and their eldest son **Matthew**, soon to be followed by his brother **Jamie**, started in the Kindergarten, which was then housed in the old school hall. He loved it.

Not all tours of the school went as planned. On one occasion, prospective parents were being taken on the mandatory tour of the school and, as the door of the science lab was opened, the science master (who shall be nameless) was holding a boy's head under a tap. The master in question was loved by all—staff and boys alike, and when he came into the staff room afterwards, embarrassed and depressed in equal parts, he said that he expected the prospective parents would not enrol their son because of what they had seen. Shortly after that, the Bursar came in and announced that these parents had been very keen to enrol their son, as the discipline was so good!

'General' periods were introduced into the timetable in 1981 to broaden the boys' awareness of the world in which they lived. Computer studies were added but Friday afternoon 'options' had to be dropped for lack of time. A scholarship set was re-introduced in the top form.

A new uniform was introduced in 1984. Smart prep tracksuits and sports gear could be bought from **Mrs Pauline Burden**, who had taken over the running of the school shop from Mrs Dando, as could the new grey prefects' ties with a monogram of SPS in maroon filigree. The games ties were of the same design but with a navy-blue background and the drama and music ties were maroon with a navy blue monogram. **Bruce Tanner** had the distinction of being the first head boy to wear the new head boy's tie which was, and still is, grey with a maroon acorn. Soon after she married Mr Oatley in 1985, Mrs Oatley took over the running of the school shop with the help of **Mrs Rosemary Kember**, mother of **Simon** and **Michael**.

Most of the boys started wearing the new school tie, which bore no resemblance to the superseded maroon and black tie, nor to its predecessor with maroon and grey stripes. The new tie had stripes of grey, maroon, and navy blue. Alumni could still recognise a Prep boy by his blazer and cap, or even more easily by the name of the school splendidly emblazoned on the back of the maroon tracksuit or across the chest of the grey sweater—white on the tracksuit with the acorn badge, and the same in maroon on the sweaters.

In the April 1985 newsletter to parents, Mr Oatley raised the subject of caps and asked parents whether they were in favour of keeping them as part of the school uniform. This prompted some lively correspondence, mostly in favour of keeping them. As a result, it was decided to keep caps for Forms 1 to 4 only.

One of the first changes Mr Oatley brought about when he took over as Headmaster had been to abandon the old-style *Acorn* magazine which was then printed externally and contained a limited selection of brief articles, essays, and poems by a few of the boys, in favour of an expanded edition with a printed cover and limitless pages of duplicated contributions which included a detailed diary of what everyone had done of note – serious or otherwise – more or less for every day of the year! The whole was held together by a plastic grip spine and the operation of assembling the magazines was done by senior boys, some of whose mothers had typed the text. Mrs Lucas, and later Mrs Biggs, was the overworked editor. The size was either A4 or the slightly smaller 'letter' and one or two editions had in excess of 100 pages.

Mrs Biggs, who taught English to the senior boys, had been editor of *The Acorn* for a couple of years when she introduced some changes in its format beginning with the autumn 1985 issue (covering the academic year 1984-85). She organised a competition for the cover, which had to include the name of the school and the name of the magazine. The competition was won by **Mark Whiting** and featured the school badge with seven acorns and a line of seven oak trees. The new style magazine was still A4 size but was properly bound, had more images than before, and included advertisements for the first time, which were a very random collection: a pub in Edenbridge; a garage in Crawley; a chartered architect (with the same name as one of the prefects!); a fashion house in Riverhead; builders; crop sprayers; and an insurance broker.

Mr Oatley's 40th birthday (10 October 1984) was celebrated in an unusual fashion with the arrival during lunch time of a gorilla clutching a bunch of bananas and a birthday card. He clambered onto tables and tried to join in the boys' lunch before running the length of the tables kneeling in front of anyone he came across, asking in a deep voice 'Are you Mr Oatley?'. When he finally found the Headmaster, he gave him a banana and the card, which had a gorilla on the front, from 'all the gorillas in the jungle'. It was pandemonium and by then Mr Oatley was in hysterics, but he sat down and ate his banana, even though he hates bananas! **Mr John Pegg** steadfastly carried on with his meal, trying to ignore the hairy beast. In came the cake, which had been made to form the word 'Sir'. Mr Oatley managed to cut the cake into about 200 pieces, enough to feed every boy in the school. The boys all thought it hilarious; Mr Pegg was left to restore sanity.

The gorilla then toured the classrooms where the unsuspecting younger children were back at work. They either squealed with delight or shook with fear, watching the creature swaying from desk to desk, and when he departed Mrs Bullock and Mrs Shea were left trying to restore order from the chaos. With seemingly the whole school following him, the gorilla vanished upstairs. No one knew where he had come from or where he went, but the grin from ear to ear on Mr Culley's face as the gorilla created havoc may have had something to do with it!

A special visitor at lunch time for Mr Oatley's 40th birthday, 1984. Today this dining room is divided into two rooms: the staff room and the Admissions Office.

Mr Oatley was, and remains, quite extraordinary in that he genuinely did do everything from meeting parents to cleaning and cooking. If any of the staff or parents arrived at the school at what they considered to be an early hour, they would be greeted by Mr Oatley, who would tell them that so far since he had been up he'd had his cycle ride, been for a swim, collected the post, mown the 1st XI cricket pitch, prepared the pudding for lunch that day and done the staff salaries, all by just after 8.00 am. If anyone came back after school for any reason and walked through the house, they would see Mr Oatley either downstairs in the old kitchen (now where the Development Office is) whipping up 70 sponges for lunch the next day, or in the side room where the medical room is now running off a school newsletter on a huge old-fashioned printing machine with his hands covered in purple ink. His routine for the day was always written on the backs of old envelopes to save paper.

On 15 December 1984, a prominent Seal resident wrote on Kent Special Constabulary notepaper complaining about the parking around Seal Church when the carol service took place, noting the 'deliberate flaunting of the law by both parents and ... staff'. He cited the following offences: ignoring double yellow lines; parking within 15 yards of a junction; parking facing the wrong way after dark; parking between 'no waiting' cones; deliberate obstruction of the entrance to commercial premises; and parking in a dangerous position. On 10 December 1991 he was at it again: 'Prep mothers are not renowned for their good driving nor, indeed, their good manners – it seems strange to me just how rude 'new money' can be...'.

In April 1986, a phone call one morning from a gentleman with a heavy Scottish accent caused great consternation. First Mr Culley and then Mr Barnard took the call from the British Society for the Preservation of Hedgerows who wanted an explanation of the school's intention to remove a hedge from between two fields. Concern was expressed that not enough consideration had been given to the two chaffinches and a thrush nesting in the hedge, and what was the Headmaster going to do about it? A representative would call at 12:00 pm to hear Mr Oatley's explanation. This caused much alarm because the hedge had already been removed! Mr Barnard was panicking – where was Mr Oatley and what answers would he have ready? As midday approached Mr Oatley was hovering in the office as ready as he could be when in walked a police officer[10] followed by **Mr Chris Bailey** (father of **Roddy**). In his wonderfully charming way, Chris began to pass the time of day and then broke into a strong Scottish accent. Mr Barnard nearly exploded as he realised that he and the Oatleys had all been hoodwinked. There was uncontrollable laughter – it was, of course, April Fool's Day! Mr Bailey was awarded his games' tie.

The boys were capable of pranks as well. In the mid-1980s there was a very high-brow teacher who taught English and who used to do a lot of marking in class. She used to get the boys to line up at her desk with their books and they got a bit bored waiting, so they realised that they could move the clock on the wall behind her forward five minutes and then would say 'Mrs X it seems to be the end of the lesson.' To start with this worked fine, but when the boys changed it to 10 minutes some staff became puzzled that pupils were out of lessons early, and when it got to 15 minutes they were rumbled and the game was up.

The employment of Donald Smith and Philip Oldroyd as gap year students gave them the opportunity to revive the competition to see who could eat the most fish fingers in one sitting that had occupied their lunch hours a few years earlier – Donald thinks this got up to some ridiculous number like 30. The competition continued on both junior and senior sides of the school until one member of staff, Mr Wadsworth, worked out that you could have one lunch in the junior school and be back on the senior side for a second lunch as the timings were different. Donald cottoned on to this and occasionally managed it himself, but Mr Wadsworth was a professional. He used to ask whoever was doing the timetabling to try to make sure he wasn't teaching last period before lunch.

Sport and recreation

Mr Oatley's period as Headmaster started off auspiciously on the football field when the 1st and 2nd XI football teams beat their counterparts from The New Beacon 2-1 and 4-2 respectively. In the former game, Philip Oldroyd scored one and claimed another, but it was deemed to have been an own goal. If he had been credited with that goal, he would have been joint top scorer (with 10 goals) for the season with Donald Smith.

---

10   The police officer was Mr Tony Donnelly, father of Luke and Tom.

First XI football
team 1978
standing:
J. Claydon
C. Williams
W. Bliss
F. Griffiths
Mr Smart
sitting:
D. Fry
D. Smith
P. Oldroyd *(capt)*
J. Coote
M. Williams
kneeling:
R. Weaver

To make the inter-house seven-a-side football tournaments which took place at the beginning of the autumn terms more interesting (and competitive) Mr Oatley invited Winchester House to take part from 1977 to 1984 with four Prep houses and three from the visitors. The Prep also took part in an annual tournament organised by The New Beacon.

In 1978-79, the school had its best overall football season since records had been consistently kept from 1958 – and probably long before that as well. Of all the matches played that season by five age groups (a new development in itself) only two were lost. This creditable record included being the first visitors to win at The New Beacon for six years. One person who must have appreciated the season was Mr Tozer, who returned to the school to teach for a short while after an absence of 30 years.

In 1980, **James Coote**, the 1st XI goalkeeper, had a trial for Gillingham FC and during the 1982-83 season **Jeffrey Bickley** scored a staggering 51 goals in 11 matches, an undoubted school record. After several years of competing, The Prep finally won The New Beacon seven-a-side competition in October 1982. Mr Culley, who had joined the school to teach both in the classroom and on the games field, pointed out that having been losing finalists for the two previous years, it was a great relief! It was hoped that the newly constructed hard court, as well as being used for regular Saturday morning practices, would contribute towards further football successes.

Of course, there were hazards with which to contend on the football pitch, as some boys like **James London** will never forget. Mr Larcombe remembered

A rugby sevens tournament squad, 1984.

being summoned to the main pitch to console James, who had broken his leg in a tackle. The goalkeeper was insistent that he had heard the leg snap 50 yards away. Meanwhile, Mr Oatley phoned for an ambulance which later reversed onto the field. The Head, still in football shorts and boots, travelled with the patient to Farnborough Hospital (now the Princess Royal University Hospital). His appearance somewhat surprised the pin-striped commuters with whom he had to return home later on the train!

About this time there was a further modification of The Prep's rugby and football strips. The traditional maroon shirts could still be worn but maroon shorts were replaced with navy blue, and the white shirts, having been relegated to practice games in earlier days, disappeared. In their place the boys now had smart maroon and grey hoops for the new rugby shirts while the new football shirts were maroon and grey stripes.

In January 1983, The Prep had a visit from a Maltese U14 football group. Four games were organised for them including ones against Winchester House and the Old Boys.

With the arrival of Mr Culley at The Prep, rugby, started by **Mr Ronald Webb** some 25 years before was reintroduced. Although it had lapsed in recent times it had been played as an after-school club activity run by two alumni, the **Alcock** brothers. Mr Culley decided that The Prep should have a proper rugby team and play against other schools. The first serious fixtures took place in the spring term of 1982. They won their first match against Skippers Hill 8-4 (only four points for a try in those days) and then faced Solefield who were the most formidable team in the area at the time. They had a very tall boy called

First XI cricket team with Mr Smart and Mr Culley, 1982.

Adam who was the star – really, it was a one-man team. It was Richard Oldroyd, the captain, who took him out with a massive tackle and The Prep held out for a draw. Solefield were really miffed as they had beaten The New Beacon and Yardley Court that season. There was an awful lot of muttering from the Solefield dads about Mr Culley's refereeing, the only time in his whole career that his refereeing had been brought into question. The next year, The Prep played seven 1st XV games and Mr Culley managed to get a colts team out as well. Overall, the results were disappointing, but the boys played well and the foundations had been firmly set for rugby to be a regular feature on The Prep's sporting calendar.

In the spring term, a number of seven-a-side fixtures were played and The Prep hosted Castle Court boys from Dorset. Perhaps inspired by Mr Larcombe's film on the history of the Sevenoaks area in the morning, the Castle Court boys proceeded to abuse their hospitality somewhat in the afternoon by beating their hosts 0-30! Yet in tribute to Mr Culley, it was the school's only defeat in its first full term of rugby. At the end of the year Mr Culley wrote in *The Acorn*. 'Who knows, with a little help from the Head, I may yet turn Sevenoaks Prep into a rugger school!'. The improvement in 1984 was such that several games were won and the school was confident enough to send a team to play in the Rosslyn Park National Schools Sevens tournament. Rugby tours began to be a regular feature of the school's calendar. The first was organised by **Mr Bill Shea**, father of Paul and husband of the teacher Mrs Shea, during half term in February 1986 to Newcastle. They lost well-contested games to two local schools before defeating a junior side from Percy Park RFC.

above The earliest Thomas Trophy photo we could find, 1991.

below An early athletics team at an away meeting.

bottom A smarter athletics team from 1985 with Mr Culley!

On the cricket field, the 1st XI had an undefeated season in 1980, coached by Mr Ken Smart, winning seven and drawing one match. By that time there were enough boys in the senior school for The Prep to field a 3rd XI, winning both their matches. A couple of years later, under Mr Oatley and with the coaching of Mr Cooke and Mr Culley, individuals continued to shine, perhaps most notably **Julian Fry**. To add to his 30 wickets in the 1983 season, he emerged with a batting average of 46.4, a tremendous achievement for a prep school boy and, as far as documents show, a then school record.

The tradition of annual football and cricket matches against the fathers continued enthusiastically, but not to be outdone in recent years a mothers' match became a regular and often daunting fixture for the 2nd XI. It should not be thought that **Paul Downton** has been the only wicket keeper of note that the school has produced. In the mothers' (and occasionally the fathers') matches Mrs Lucas, a proud grandmother, gave textbook performances behind the stumps!

The first cross-country inter-school tournament for the Thomas Trophy was hosted by The Prep in March 1983 and has continued to be held each year since, apart from the odd occasion when bad weather or water-logged fields led to a cancellation. Initially there were two races, senior (U14) and junior (U12) for boys only and only three schools took part. The combined points winner received the trophy, donated by Mrs Thomas, who had been in charge of cross-country for many years and retired from teaching later that same year. The event proved extremely popular. Within a few years, a dozen schools and 120 boys were taking part. By 2016 there were six events, including three for girls and races for U10s with more than 600 runners from 14 regional schools taking part.

Another feature of these years was the hilarity of the slow bicycle race, and, following the fashion of the times, the space hopper races. Mr Culley organised the sports days brilliantly. Heats were completed in record time and the running track, which now stretched across the two new playing fields, was meticulously prepared. There was now even a public address system to announce results.

Athletics matches against Halstead Place continued for several years at Godden Green and cross-country was given a tremendous boost by the fact that the school was now so close to Knole Park. However, with the arrival of Mr Oatley, athletics really flourished. Regular athletics competitions at Sutton Valence, Sevenoaks, Rose Hill, and Claremont School were held. Mrs Frances Oatley and **Mr Fowler** made valuable contributions to the coaching of the boys, and later the enthusiasm and dedication of the indefatigable Mrs Thomas brought further success.

Competing for the Manley Swimming Shield.

Compared with the restrictive confines of Vine Court Road, Godden Green proved an ideal setting for physical education – which had superseded physical training. Pupils no longer performed regimented exercises but were encouraged to join in more creative physical activities.

Basketball, rounders, circuit training, British Bulldog, '52 Bunker', even some gymnastics, were all experienced by the boys during these years.

One of the first things Mr Oatley did was to reintroduce swimming lessons in the summer term, using the invaluable new school minibuses, and some mothers, to ferry the boys. The school took over the old Sevenoaks baths in Eardley Road on Monday mornings and practically the whole school took part. Mr Oatley assisted at the baths, with the aid of two mothers, **Mrs Tanner** and **Mrs Nixon**. The Prep participated keenly in swimming competitions and a noisy and exciting school swimming gala was enthusiastically contended. **Russell Manley** was the proud winner of the inaugural event; his family then donated a swimming shield to the school.

Tennis continued to be played on the court in the back garden. Mrs Frances Oatley and Mrs Janet Oldroyd led the coaching and produced a number of talented players, perhaps notably Richard Weaver, Mark Williams, and Jeffrey Bickley. Tennis matches began against local schools and there was a keenly contested school tournament annually when Mr Oatley usually challenged the champion in his early years as Headmaster! Mr Oatley was also a keen table-tennis player. The school hall housed a number of table tennis tables and in 1983 The Prep had its first tournament, won by **Philip Smith**. In the evenings the Phoenix Club, including some parents, played at the school.

To those up at the crack of dawn, the sight of Mr Oatley cycling in and around Sevenoaks must have been familiar. Mr Oatley was a cycling enthusiast and his enthusiasm spread to the boys. School cycle rides through the Kent countryside were regular events, with the Head usually bringing up the rear, mending chains or brakes and picking up cans of Coke or hats. Mrs Shea, before she joined the staff, remembers one summer activity week in the early 1980s dropping her son Paul at school with his bike and a picnic. When she returned that evening to collect Paul, she asked the usual questions, 'Everything OK? Did you have a good time? Where did you go?'. 'Yes', 'Yes', 'Hyde Park Corner!' When she was helped up from the ground, it was confirmed that they had indeed cycled to Hyde Park Corner, around it, and returned. Mr Oatley said it was flat all the way! That was even before helmets were worn. Mrs Shea's comments—'Marvellous, Unbelievable'. For those less adventurous boys, the grounds provided ideal terrain for their BMX bicycles.

Luke Harrison loved cycling and remembered the craze in the 1980s for BMX bikes. Boys would bring their bikes to school and ride round all the paths. They asked Mr Oatley if they could build a track in the woods, behind what is now the Oakery and where there happened to be a public footpath. The older boys spent three or four months staying on after Saturday school to build a proper BMX track, the design copied from Bucknell Park in Medway. The track went from the road to around where Forest School is now, so it was quite long. They had to navigate the trees and build mounds and ramps. The lovely thing is that there are still traces of

Fabulous framed photo entitled 'The BMX Boys 1984' on display in Fawke Cottage.

it there today. As time went on, this craze turned into a love of motorbikes and a few boys decided to dig out the old motorcycles their parents had from the back of garages and sheds. Luke had a birthday party one Sunday and brought a motorbike and scrambler bike to school. Mr Oatley said they could use the school field, but unfortunately some of the boys decided to use the cricket square as a skid pan. Luke

Trampolining fun for all – boys, staff and a candid cameraman upstairs in Fawke Cottage!

doesn't remember Mr Oatley complaining!

Mr Oatley was always keen that the children should use the school and its grounds outside normal school hours. When Luke Harrison was in his last year, he became very interested in golf. Mr Pegg was a keen golfer and was eager to help, recommending that Luke join Knole Park Golf Club. Mr Pegg would bring his clubs into school and let Luke go onto the field at break time to practise. After Saturday school a group of four or five boys would stay on until late afternoon using the grounds as a driving range and, if they were lucky, Mr or Mrs Oatley would bring out sandwiches.

There were two more new activities for the boys. **Mrs Smith,** mother of **Gareth Smith**, was able to obtain a trampoline for the school. The boys were trained to use it by Mrs Frances Oatley and then by Mrs Smith herself – a qualified trampoline coach. Success came quickly to the trampolining team; the first competition the school entered was won easily because The Prep was the only

Judo squad with Mr Burkett, 1986.

team that entered! The school went on to walk away with the under-18, under-15 and under-13 team trophies from the next competition for the same reason and Gareth Smith became the Kent under-12 champion. Through the hall windows after lunch it was possible to watch small boys in white struggle with each other under the expert eye of **Mr Malcolm Burkett**, the school's judo instructor who began with a class of up to 35 boys in September 1980. One wondered what may happen to little brothers and sisters at home at the end of the school day! Mr Burkett arranged a five-hour judo marathon in December 1985 which raised £500 towards the purchase of new mats.

The Prep's approach to sport was clearly having a good effect on the boys and laying a foundation for a lifetime's enjoyment of sport. As one of the school's most famous sporting alumni Paul Downton wrote after his cricket career was over, 'The real importance of prep school sport is surely that you are introduced to the team element of games probably for the first time. So it is at this level you first begin to learn the values of comradeship and spirit – the essence of playing for your team. Individuals sometimes win games but well-disciplined units do most often. And, after all, the thrill of winning is the same whatever game you play. You are taught how to accept defeat in the right way but nobody needs to explain the feeling of winning. So prep school sports shoulder a lot of responsibility. Not only are the basics of technique taught but, maybe more importantly, the values of the game are instilled. I enjoyed sport then and I enjoy it now. Sevenoaks Prep School was my first contact with organised sport; I have a lot to thank the school for.'

By 1982, The Prep was offering its facilities to local sports organisations including Sevenoaks Athletics Club, the Phoenix Table Tennis Club, Sennocke Cricket Club for their junior cricket, and later by opening up its sports field for Sevenoaks RFC's veterans on a Saturday and its junior section on a Sunday, when one of their pitches at Knole Paddock was out of action.

The first family fun run was held on Saturday 30 November 1985, open to parents, alumni, and children around the senior cross-country course. About 40 people took part with the winner being **Luke Baldock** (who had left in 1982 and gone on to Sevenoaks School).

Outings and holidays

From 1979, the end of the summer term did not now bring an end to the excitements and activities of The Prep. Before July was out, one of Mr Oatley's new initiatives, Holiday Adventure Week, was on. It was decided to have different activities every day for a week for boys in Forms 6, 7, and 8, and the itinerary was as follows – Monday: walk to Ightham Mote and back; Tuesday: trip to London; Wednesday: cycle ride (35 miles around Kent) for the middle school; Thursday: senior cycle ride (50 miles); and Friday: sports day at school. The next year, the week included a day trip to France and a day at Lords to

Holiday Adventure Week included a session in the pool next door (the Montagues').
One year Mr Oatley was pushed in – the name of the culprit is unrecorded!

watch the John Player one-day cricket final with Mr Oatley's team, Middlesex, playing Kent, obviously the choice of most of the boys (Kent won). These weeks became a regular feature in the calendar and the boys (as well as some of the staff) got to know the beautiful Kent countryside and local attractions. Later, these weeks were confined to the school premises as health and safety deemed such adventures ill-advised.

In 1982, Mr and Mrs Culley organised a boating holiday on the River Thames. An extract from the ship's log on Sunday 29 August said 'Weather still holding but by the time we reached Clifton Hampden the wind was very strong. Very pretty stop for lunch at the Barley Mow. Three fell in – Nicky, Alistair and Peter. Although beautifully sunny all inside while wind so strong. Passed through Clifton Lock which had a mad Irishwoman in charge. Pip and Mrs Culley got out at Culham Lock and walked to Abingdon. We all met at Abingdon boatyard, moored in great wind below the bridge and saw a modern 12-berth cruiser called the Osprey with which the boys fell in love'.

With the school minibuses it was comparatively easy for staff to take their classes on interesting outings. *The Acorn* listed a few of them: Ernest Read concerts at the Royal Festival Hall (monthly visits on Saturday mornings in autumn and spring terms 1972-73); a seniors' visit to a pig farm at Stanstead; the London Experience and St Paul's Cathedral; a visit to the Ford Works at Dagenham (October 1979); a day at the London Theatre (Westminster); a visit to Dover Castle; visit after visit to Lullingstone Villa; a trip to see stone carving at Canterbury Cathedral; a trip to the Friars, Aylesford; a visit to the Science and Geological Museums; a trip to *The Daily Telegraph* (June 1981); a day at Charlton Manor Farm, owned by the father of **Hugh Goldsworthy** (when **Mrs Zutshi** tried sheep-shearing!); a visit to the Horton Kirby

Farm Centre; a day in Rochester; a trip to Michelham Priory; a tour of Bodiam Castle; and several day trips to London with Mr Larcombe and other staff.

Mr Culley started geography field trips for the boys. The first one was on rivers. The school hired two long boats from Guildford, went on the River Wey and then onto the Thames, under Putney Bridge and almost as far as Oxford. Unfortunately, one of the boats kept breaking down, but despite this it was good fun. By chance, on the Saturday night, they met up with a party from Homewood House Prep who were on the river as well. There were some mothers on the trip who offered to look after the boys while the teachers went to the pub, which was something you wouldn't get away with nowadays.

In 1986, Mr Oatley decided that all the children who had done the cycling proficiency test would take part in the London to Brighton bike ride. In June some 27 boys, alumni, staff and parents took part. Five energetic (or foolish) adults started by cycling up to London; **Mr Dennison** drove the cattle truck with the other bikes loaded on while **Mrs Cantellow** and **Mr Hammond** ferried the more sensible entrants in the school buses. The weather was glorious with the notable achievement of **Alex Wright**, the youngest entrant, beating his father by two hours.

Other schools

From the mid-1970s, fundamental changes in educational arrangements in the country, the county, and the town had far-reaching effects on the junior and senior independent schools of Sevenoaks. One was the withdrawal of free places at Sevenoaks School (for boys) and Walthamstow School (for girls) provided by Kent County Council for the brightest local children at the end of the 1970s.

For several years, Sevenoaks School had co-operated with Walthamstow Hall, an independent girls school in Sevenoaks, allowing girls to study subjects at Sevenoaks that were not offered at their own school. In 1976, Sevenoaks admitted the first seven full-time girls into the sixth form; by 1982, there were over 100 in the sixth form. In 1983, Sevenoaks School announced that it had set up a committee under the chairmanship of the relatively new Headmaster, Mr Barker, to consider the desirability of extending co-education throughout the school with the objective, if approved, of admitting 11 and 13-year-old girls from September 1984. The announcement created a storm of protest in the local press including a letter signed by seven principals of local preparatory and secondary fee-paying schools (including Mr Oatley) condemning the proposal and listing a number of concerns. The controversy raged all summer in the press, in the town, and within the school itself. However, towards the end of 1983 the school Governors, convinced by Mr Barker's arguments and the support of 85% of the staff, decided to admit girls at all levels from the following academic year.

In late 1984, Mr Oatley proposed a merger between The Prep and Winchester House. He was very familiar with the latter school after his spell as Assistant Head there before becoming Headmaster of The Prep, and was aware that it was suffering from falling numbers. The proposal was for the combined school to occupy an expanded Godden Green site, to be called Sevenoaks Preparatory School, with Mr Oatley as Headmaster and Mr Michael Hobbs, the Headmaster of Winchester House, as his deputy.

School sign gleaned by Mr Oatley.

Nothing came of the subsequent discussions, however, as the Governors of Winchester House rejected the proposals. In April 1985, **Mr R.W. Vickers**, Chairman of the Governors, wrote to the parents announcing that it was going to close on 19 July that year, at the end of the summer term. Winchester House had been started by **Mr Percy Wilson** in 1936 in a house in Granville Road with just four boys. After the Second World War, it relocated to a large house with two acres of land in Hitchen Hatch Lane and prospered for the next 35 years. But in the early 1980s, the school was in trouble. In his letter, Mr Vickers explained that numbers in the school had declined from around 125 a few years earlier, while the forecast for the next academic year was 77, and this meant that it was not economic to continue. The Governors had considered staff reductions or an increase in fees but neither was practicable. They had looked at the possibilities of moving to an out-of-town location (as The Prep had done some years before) or of merging with another school but had made no progress on either count.

Attached to the letter was a note from Mr Hobbs, the Headmaster, offering to be available to discuss the alternatives with parents with a list of local schools and their possible vacancies. The Prep was prominent with the offer to take more than any other school, especially the older boys. In a letter to The Prep parents, Mr Oatley explained that this influx would allow The Prep to have two Forms 7 and 8 and recruit some ex-Winchester House staff. There was sufficient accommodation already to absorb the newcomers. In the event, The Prep took 20 boys and three members of staff.

The trauma that this sudden closure generated for parents of boys at Winchester House was recalled by Mrs Spencer-Allen. Although as a young girl she had lived next door to The Prep in Vine Court Road, her brothers had enjoyed Winchester House school so much that Mrs Spencer-Allen had decided her own sons should also go there. **Corin**, her eldest son, was happily settled in Form 1 at Winchester House and second son, **Lynden**, had just started and was enjoying the Kindergarten. One Saturday morning, and totally out of the blue, the Spencer-Allens received the letter saying the school was closing down and they needed to find a new one as soon as possible. Suddenly phones were ringing and many anxious parents didn't know what to do – it was a difficult and most concerning time. Mrs Spencer-Allen rang a couple of schools that she knew of but received some rather snooty and unhelpful replies. Speaking about it to her parents, who had lived in Vine Court Road, they suggested ringing The Prep, which was now at Godden Green and where they thought Mr Oatley was now the Headmaster. She remembered that name from the past; he had been her brothers' favourite teacher at Winchester House. She rang immediately and amazingly Mr Oatley answered the phone.

He was delightful, remembered her brothers, and offered both her boys a place immediately with the proviso that the whole family could cope with the mud! He wanted no complaints about it. The Spencer-Allens were invited to a meeting at The Prep, along with others in the same dire situation, to find out more about the school. They did not know then but Mr Oatley had postponed his wedding to Janet to hold this meeting, and to sort out the families who would be joining his small school that potentially could double in numbers overnight!

So, on a cold wet evening, they walked up the muddy path to the old school hall to be warmly welcomed by Mr Oatley. He explained what The Prep was all about. He told the prospective parents that most of the classrooms were really no more than shacks and mentioned the mud again and also the lack of facilities. He told them exactly how it was and they knew despite these odd problems that their sons and they would absolutely love it. While all the staff, parents, and pupils at The Prep must have felt overwhelmed by the arrival en masse of all these new boys and their parents, the newcomers were welcomed and looked after like one big, happy family. The superb ethos of The Prep shone through magically then and hopefully always will.

Although no-one complained about the mud or the shacks, it was clear that Mr Oatley had not undersold his school. The mud was actually more white than brown but the boys really didn't mind. The washing was quite plentiful at weekends but strangely one mother rarely washed her own boys' kit as they usually came home with another boy's grubby gear instead and she often wondered which poor mother washed her boys' stuff! The 'shack' classrooms were also not an understatement and were just as Mr Oatley had described, except that they had no central heating either. Boys in those days where hardy and so, it seems, were the staff.

Parental involvement

Mr Oatley had taken over as Headmaster of The Prep in January 1978 on Mr Ely's retirement. By the summer of that year, he was beginning to put into place some of his ideas to improve the school for pupils, parents, and staff and to create his vision for the future of the school. He was, as ever, optimistic about the future, despite the economic and political situation in the country with a continuing recession, high unemployment, inflation, and conflicts with the trade unions. The problems of the Labour government led to the 1978-79 'Winter of Discontent' and the decisive Conservative victory in the 1979 general election.

Mr Oatley organised three open days for parents in May 1978 and followed these up with a questionnaire to all parents. He stated the school's aim was first and foremost to give the boys a high standard of all round education, and that new buildings and equipment would give them more space for learning, recreation, and reading and would allow project and art work to be a long-term activity. All this, he believed, would give the boys more incentive and opportunity for learning and would give the staff more scope to explore their many talents. The questionnaire asked for the parents' reaction to ideas on possible building and educational projects. It also suggested ways in which some of the necessary money might be raised and how parents could provide expertise in various areas. There were also questions on the day-to-day organisation of the school against the background of contemporary trends in education, with the purpose of eliciting the parents' reaction to these. These trends included such diverse subjects as the establishment of a parent teacher association (PTA), social functions involving the whole family, open days, holiday activities, reports, sex education and the dropping of Latin as a compulsory subject.

The response to the questionnaire was excellent, with 92 of the 108 sent out being returned. In a letter to the parents in June with the results and the decisions the school had subsequently made, Mr Oatley thanked the parents for their interest and care in answering the questions 'a great source of help and information to [the school] in so many different and useful ways'. There was overwhelming support for a PTA (87%); various suggestions for fundraising but with only 27% in favour of gifts; general support for functions, with a garden fête the favourite (81%); library books (74%) and an art room (70%) topped the wish list for money raising; open days were wanted by all respondents; there was support for continuing school reports, for basic sex education, and for dropping Latin; holiday activities were supported by 75% (but not abroad); and finally only 40% were in favour of a week's holiday at half term.

Given this support, Mr Oatley was not backward in coming forward to ask for help from the parents and the laying of the car park and the hall building in 1978 would not have been possible without considerable parental brawn and brain. Mr Oatley later recalled that nearly all the groundwork, upkeep of buildings etc. during much of his first 15 years as Head was done by parents, staff, and pupils in the holidays, half terms, and weekends.

As a result of the questionnaire and the many detailed comments, the school took a number of decisions immediately; the formation of a PTA would be looked at, perhaps called 'The Friends of Sevenoaks Prep', as a fund-raising committee with no influence on how the school was to be run; many parents had already given gifts and plans for a hall/gymnasium and car park were finalised; two open days a year would be held; reports in booklet form would be twice a year; there would be some sex and drug education for the top two forms; Latin would no longer be compulsory; there was to be a joint camp with Winchester House in South Wales in the forthcoming summer holidays; and half terms would be three days only. In fact, by 1980, Latin was no longer compulsory for Common Entrance (the only compulsory subjects were science, maths, English and French).

Not all parents were supportive of Mr Oatley's initiatives, however. One wrote 'the main reason for sending my two sons to [The Prep] was to enable them to enjoy the benefits of what may be termed an old-fashioned style of education that concentrated upon academic and sporting achievements' and continued 'I am not in favour of allowing boys an increasing amount of freedom of thought and action as to how and what they do'.

The years from 1978 saw a range of events, which had the dual purpose of enjoyment for boys, parents, and staff and at the same time fundraising either for the school or for outside causes. Many of these became regular features of the school calendar.

Parental involvement was emphasised in 1978 when the first school social was held, a summer dance organised by Mrs Dando and **Mrs Elsa Broadhurst** in St John's Church Hall. The first garden fête was held in June 1980, the inspiration of Mrs Dando and organised by a team of parents. Over £900 was raised for the building fund while the star attraction was the T.A. bomb squad from Chatham led by a parent **Mr Klewn**. In the same year, the first school dance held at The Prep itself took place in July when 180 parents, staff and friends enjoyed a very successful and friendly evening. The food was outstanding thanks to **Mrs Sue Carmichael**, Mrs Oldroyd and their many helpers. The decorations made by Mrs Bullock, **Mrs Holland**, Mrs Ivory and **Mrs Grindley** were greatly admired. The first joint Prep/Russell House fashion show was held in 1985 and continued

Mrs Joan Harrison *(far left)*, the current Headmaster's mother was the mastermind behind a parent cabaret at one of the early dances held in The Prep's own hall.

The parents' fashion shows continued intermittently for some years, sponsored by local shops. Bat and Balls Sports was one contributor that is still trading.

intermittently for some years, sponsored by local shops (often owned by parents of pupils at the two schools) with the clothes on show available at discounted prices.

The school grounds saw a succession of garden fêtes, jumble sales, and Christmas bazaars arranged by the parents to raise money for one or other project for the school, with children and parents often working hard together as a team. A most successful garden fête was a May Fair organised by **Mr Peter Christian-Lim** in 1986 when a record £2,000 was raised.

Mrs Spencer-Allen remembered that the fêtes began as very small affairs with a few stalls, bat 'n' trap, wet sponges to throw at the teachers, a homemade cake stall and a sweet stall. It was the latter, the sweet stall, where she was to offer her services for her first time at a school fête. Rather nervous about this, she thought perhaps doing the early stint would be easiest – but how very wrong she was! From the moment she put the first sweets out on the clothed table she was bombarded by eager children and their pennies. The later stints would have definitely been better as the sweets, by then, were long gone. In later years, the fête changed and Mrs Spencer-Allen remembered one year it was more like a horse show with an arena in the big field and riders showing off their horse-riding skills, or lack thereof. Another year there was a fairground.

Parental involvement could also take other forms as parental talents were tapped regularly by Mr Oatley. Anyone keen on drama or music or someone good at dressmaking was roped in to assist Mrs Shefford with the school plays and concerts; others helped with the sports' coaching and ferrying boys to and from sports' fixtures, the Three Arts Festival and various outings. Any parents involved in the early days of computers were brought in to teach the basics to the boys, initially **Mrs Tina Hubbard**, mother of **Philip** and **Andrew**. By 1983, **Mr John Cantellow**, was helping by holding regular Saturday morning computing classes for Forms 7 and 8. 1984 saw the culinary knowledge of parents

left The ever-popular plant stall was a must at any fête or bazaar.
right Early computing at The Prep was taught by volunteer parents.

and staff transcribed into a cookbook and published by **Mrs Janet Appleton**, which sold for £1.50. Two more cookbooks were to follow, the first in 1991 produced by **Mrs Suzanne Brunton** and the next in 2009 by **Frances Ramji**, **Eva Veldhuizen**, **Fenella McLuskie** and **Emma Storkey** as their Form 8 Social Entrepreneurs Project.

One of the enduring traditions of The Prep has been the early November bonfire and firework display. The first was organised in 1983 by the **Creed** and **Richardson** families. It was originally a low-key affair aimed at the younger

(l-r) Mr Rupert Creed, Philip Creed and Mr Barry Richardson, the original bonfire team, joined here in 1991 by Mr Brian Smith and Mr Mark Parrett.

members of the school with a charge of 50p for children and 75p for adults. The 1983 display, including a competition for the best guy, was a great success and the next year featured twice as many fireworks and a caravan to burn on the bonfire. Bonfire night was also an opportunity for Mr Pegg, the brilliant, mischievous science master to bring his subject into real life. Each year, around the 5 November, Mrs Shea and her class would watch, in great excitement, the flashes, sparks and explosions that banged and crackled as Mr Pegg and his class experimented with explosive materials.

The parents were allowed to make use of the school facilities for gentle exercise, popmobility, which took place one day a week in an early afternoon for mums who could exercise, then have a cup of tea and a chat before collecting their children. This was run by **Mrs Judy Bailey** and **Mrs Terry Bateman** who both had sons at the school, **Roddy** and **Maxim** respectively. There was a small charge which went towards the general fund-raising for the school and in 1984 it went towards science equipment. **Mrs Carole Picket**, mother of **Andrew** and **Martin** ran a tap dance class for staff and parents which Mrs Shefford continued in later years. The parents also organised another fund-raising initiative in 1983 in the form of a 100 club, run by **Mr Tim Baldock**.

In 1983, the sons of two parents who had been of immense help to the school over several years left. Mr David Fry had been responsible for buildings; he had organised the work forces and brought in outside and parental help when necessary although becoming a former parent made little difference and he continued to help the school for some years. Mrs Christa Dando had been running out of school activities including the organisation of Christmas bazaars (1983) and the school shop for eight years. Mr Oatley described her as 'a one-woman industrial complex'.

At the end of the 1985-86 academic year, a disgruntled parent wrote to Mr Oatley 'Yet again [my son] has been passed over as a form prize winner when all the evidence available to me suggests that no one is more deserving of a prize than [my son]. I would be grateful if you would explain to me this consistent inconsistency.' Mr Oatley replied with vigour, 'The explanation was in my speech. There are many young boys who deserve prizes throughout the school and there could have been another 30 letters like yours this morning but I am glad to say only yours turned up'.

8

Disruption and Consolidation (1986-95)

Having spent almost ten years improving the facilities and setting the groundwork for changing the ethos of the school from a largely traditional one to a family-based inclusive school, the next ten years saw Mr Oatley dealing with the repercussions of Sevenoaks School going co-ed and schools in the Sevenoaks district closing. One thing he identified was the need for a private school option for boys' secondary education, and he worked with others to establish a new school, Sackville, initially for 13 to16-year-old boys, and later proposed a three-way merger between The Prep, Sackville and St Hilary's, a private school for girls from Kindergarten to seniors. A lease on neighbouring Stake Farm was secured but Sackville in fact started in Hildenborough and The Prep took on the Stake Farm lease as a base for its junior school. For a year Mr Oatley acted as temporary Headmaster of Sackville. In 1991, The Prep took the decision to go co-educational and the first girls moved from the Kindergarten to Form 1. St Hilary's eventually merged with Walthamstow Hall. Overall numbers at The Prep increased steadily, reaching 268 (including 32 girls) and 32 staff in the academic year 1993-94. Many staff were recruited by Mr Oatley from the parents, often persuading mothers who had given up teaching for various reasons to return. The Stake Farm lease came with over six acres of fields and, once these were cleared of stones and drained properly, allowed the school to have a better athletics track, a floodlit five-a-side football pitch and all-weather cricket nets. By the beginning of the academic year 1995-96, The Prep was in a strong position with an ambitious and dynamic Headmaster, experienced staff, and a vastly improved environment.

Head and staff

Mr Edward Oatley often had an unconventional way of recruiting staff. In 1986, the **Pickering** family had returned to the UK and the two boys returned to The Prep. It was at this time that numbers in the school had increased to the extent that a second year group was needed for most forms. **Mrs Sue Bullock**, who had been teaching at The Prep for a couple of years, suggested to **Mrs Angela Pickering** that she should apply to be a class teacher, but Mrs Pickering had not taught for a few years, so was a little reticent and said that she would need a stiff gin first. A couple of days later, her elder son, **Matthew**, came home with a bulky envelope saying that Mr Oatley had asked him to pass this to his mother. Inside was a mini bottle of gin, together with a brief letter saying, 'Please drink this and come and see me'. She did both, and was soon installed as a Form 4 teacher, alongside **Mrs Beth Sadler**.

Staff 1990
back row Mrs M. Agnew, Mrs M. Heal, Mrs B. Sadler, Mrs J. Oatley,
Mrs R. Cooke. Mrs C. Ruprecht, Mrs A. Pickering, Mrs W. Woolf, *Unidentified.*
middle row Mr E. Oatley, Mrs C. Jeffers, Mme J. Homer, Mrs S. Bullock, Mr P. Rogers,
Mr M. Wadsworth, Mr R. Gledhill *(gap year student)*, Mr P. Ratcliffe, Mrs J. Wilkes,
Mrs L. Hutchinson, Mrs S. Berryman, Miss P. Kemp.
front row Mr A. Searle, Mrs G. Virgo, Mrs S. Lewis, Mr M. Barnard, Mrs M. Perks,
Mr J. Pegg, Mrs M. Shefford, Mr D. Clark, Mrs J. Low, Mrs B. Lloyd, Mr P. Valentine.

In 1988, Mr Oatley persuaded **Mrs Jackie Low**, whom he knew well as her son **Dominic** was just starting his last year at The Prep, to come back into teaching after an extended period of maternity leave. She fondly remembers Mr Oatley requesting she started 'next Monday morning' before she had actually agreed to take the role and he said he would not take no for answer. He believed she would be a great teacher for The Prep and he was right; she taught English and maths for 16 years. At about this time, **Mr Peter Valentine**, who had recently retired as head of PE at Wildernesse School, joined the school to strengthen the PE department until he finally retired from teaching in 1994.

In 1990, **Mrs Lyn Witton**'s interview for a kindergarten teacher position took place in a truck whilst being driven around the school grounds by Mr Oatley and finished up in the kitchen of the Oatley's flat in Fawke Cottage where the upstairs offices are now. Her first assistant was **Miss Sally Perks**, **Mrs Maureen Perks**' daughter, who two years previously had started her 30 plus years as a member of staff, and her second was **Mrs Alison Bellwood**, who retired in 2018 after 26 years in the Pre-Prep.

Mrs Penny Spencer-Allen had an unusual recruitment story to tell. In 1991, she had just finished watching one of her sons playing cricket at The Prep; it was one of her first outings after having a rather ghastly riding accident followed by two operations and months of physiotherapy. The accident had actually happened outside The Prep and it was **Mrs Janet Oatley** who had come to her rescue and extremely kindly driven her straight to hospital. Meanwhile, **Mr Michael Barnard**, the Bursar at that time, had bravely led the spooked horse to the Godden Green stables down the lane to be looked after. Back to the cricket and to Mr Oatley, who had also been watching the exciting match. He did not know it then, but he was about to ask Mrs Spencer-Allen a life-changing question! 'Would [she] be interested in helping out in the Kindergarten as they desperately needed a spare pair of hands'? She pointed to her useless arm in its sling and said she didn't actually have a 'pair' of hands. However, Mr Oatley was totally undaunted by this, saying she would be fine. (She had been a nursery teacher before having her own children.) A couple of days later she found herself in the Kindergarten with **Mrs Barbara Lloyd** and **Mrs Cheryl Ruprecht**. Both of these teachers had boys at the school, Mrs Lloyd with **Alex** and **Christopher** and Mrs Ruprecht with **Jonathan**. Mrs Spencer-Allen couldn't be a huge help to them in the early days because of her injury, but as it improved she was able to do more and eventually started running a pre-kindergarten group for younger siblings.

Mr Oatley continued to employ alumni on a temporary or part-time basis. While he was at Tonbridge and university, Dominic Low, Mrs Jackie Low's son, was given the opportunity to earn some money during his holidays by Mr Oatley. A phone call used to arrive on Sunday evening – no email, Facebook or WhatsApp then – and Dominic would turn up at the school at 8am on the Monday morning to be greeted by a list written in virtually illegible doctor's-type scrawl on a torn envelope. He then set to work completing the tasks that he thought Mr Oatley had written! It was impossible to know whether he was doing the right job but he did them anyway, painting Kindergarten windows, mowing the 1st XI cricket square, assisting the French class, assisting the science class, clipping the laurel hedge, cleaning the pond, marking the white lines for the athletics track, invigilating exams, manning the office, teaching all sports…

Having applied for a teaching post at The Prep, **Mr Peter Ratcliffe** received an invitation from Mr Oatley to go over to the school for a 'chat '. He'd been through formal interviews before at other establishments, so prepared himself mentally as he donned jacket and tie and drove through the wooded country lanes to the school. All was quiet as it must have been a Saturday afternoon or summer half term. A little keyed up, he pressed the doorbell and heard what sounded like a 'raspberry', reminiscent of a disapproving 'Miss' response to a new record release in the 1960's BBC television programme *Juke Box Jury* – no reply; he tried twice more without success, being greeted with two more raspberries then knocked on the door – no reply. He went to the rear and knocked on the back door. A track-suited gentleman opened the door. 'I'm looking for Edward Oatley', he said. 'I am he', was the reply. 'Come on in!'

Having mentioned who he was and realising that some time had passed in his attempts to get into the building, he commented that he'd been knocking on the front door. Mr Oatley replied with a little smile, 'No one knocks here, they just walk in!' In the office he was surprised to see a Manchester United scarf draped across a wall. As a United fan, Mr Ratcliffe saw they had something in common and chatted happily about football. He began to relax, but not for long. 'I'll show you around. Get in', instructed Mr Oatley. Outside, he'd barely shut the door of the estate car before the vehicle was accelerating across a playing field at high velocity, through a gap in a hedge, then came to a stop. Mr Oatley got out of the car walking away, enthusiastically explaining about the new athletics track. 'Where are you? Come on!' he exclaimed, but Mr Ratcliffe was still in the car looking for his seat belt.

Mr Ratcliffe could see that The Prep was a school with a difference and this was confirmed when he was shown the green huts, particularly the science lab, which resembled a classroom from the 19th century, if not earlier. The smell of chemicals pervaded the atmosphere. In the corridor, coat pegs seemed to be about two feet from the floor. He'd previously taught for years in a comprehensive school and was often used to looking up when facing pupils. He would need to get used to looking down at The Prep. After a second visit and chat, it was agreed that he would start in September. 'This is a great day!', exclaimed Mr Oatley as they walked out of the staff room. Never before had Mr Ratcliffe experienced such a feeling of support, rapport, and encouragement from an employer. He taught at The Prep for 23 years.

When **Luke Harrison** finished his schooling at Tonbridge in the early 1990s, he came back to The Prep for five months as a gap year student, earning £10 a day. He would arrive at midday, have lunch and then set up the fields for matches, help with training, and then leave at 4.00pm to collect his sister from the bus station in Sevenoaks. During one Easter holidays, he painted the entire interior of Stake Farm.

Mrs June Biggs retired in 1988, having taught English in the senior school, edited *The Acorn* and been the school librarian. She had been particularly

The current Headmaster, Mr Harrison, spent five months at The Prep during his gap year – this was taken on his last day.

successful with scholarship and remedial boys, Common Entrance and the steady work leading towards it. One alumnus, already at his senior school, was heard commenting to his younger brother 'Don't worry, you can't fail with Mrs Biggs, she's a super teacher!' and another boy remarked 'Nobody minds if Mrs Biggs seems cross, it is only because she wants us to do things really well'. Boys' successes over the years in the Three Arts Festival where competitors earned honours, distinctions and merits in spoken poetry and prose readings, reflected her taste and endless patience in helping and encouraging them – the Groves Poetry Cup for composition seemed to be won by The Prep every year. The literature section of *The Acorn* reflected the enthusiasm for writing inspired by Mrs Biggs in her class work. She also played in the orchestra, helped with the music and readings at assembly and the readings for the church services, made up actors for the play, arranged and conducted outings, judged on sports days and above all was always there, with her high standards of conduct, her dedication to effort and her ceaseless care for her pupils.

Mr Ian Culley, who had been Head of Sport and Geography at The Prep, also left in 1988 to take up a post at Claremont School in Sussex. No member of staff had given more time to the school in the previous few years than Mr Culley. He had always been prepared to be around to do the boring tasks of organising the changing rooms, the school lists, the timetable, marking the pitches, sorting out the games shed, and doing the 101 other jobs that have to be done but which no-one else sees. He organised camps, sailing holidays, adventure weeks, and rugby tours while his coaching of team sports produced very competent and hardworking sides. He brought serious rugby to the school with the patience and expertise to be able to do it through all age groups. He was not away for long and, two years later, returned briefly to The Prep.

Mr David Clark had been a pupil and had had two spells of teaching at The Prep. Latterly, he had been helping children who were having reading difficulties or any general problems. He retired in 1990 after an association with the school which spanned more than 60 years. He said that it had been a great privilege and pleasure. In July 1992, Mrs Sadler, who had taught at The Prep for nearly 20 years and spanned the Ely and Oatley eras, retired, as did Mrs Perks, who had had two spells teaching at The Prep, one under **Mr Kenneth Ely** and one under Mr Oatley. Now the only teaching staff link with Mr Ely's time was **Mrs Mary Shefford**, the Head of Drama and Music. Mr Oatley paid tribute to the two retirees, both Scots, who had brought to their teaching the kindness but firmness of Scottish schools. He said that they were the two teachers he could trust to put the pupils and the school first in their working lives. Both had helped Mrs Shefford enormously with the staging of plays and concerts. Mrs Perks' natural talent for dance and her ability to put together such a variety of dance routines gave many children their first opportunity to show their ability on the stage. She expected a high standard and the children responded to her encouragement – on the day! Mrs Sadler was always there backstage giving her artistic expertise to the makeup and costumes.

Mrs Sadler's strongest memories were of the many boys she had taught, which had made it all so worthwhile. She remembered **Mr David Cochrane** being delighted to let her know that a boy in her class 'much preferred man teachers'! **Donald Smith**, an alumnus who came back to The Prep to teach (and is still there), recalled Mrs Sadler as his first teacher in Form 4 as being very kind but strict. 'You knew when to draw the line. With a stern look and a stern voice, which was never raised, the boys knew when to stop and think "now I must get on with my work".' As one alumnus remarked to Mrs Sadler at a reunion, 'I liked it in your class Mrs Sadler because you never shouted BUT you could LOOK'. Having come from a state school with 30 pupils in the class where he had been totally lost, Donald Smith found that suddenly this teacher was paying good attention to him and was really interested in what he was doing.

Two other teachers left in July 1992: Mrs Pickering and her husband moved to California with their sons boarding at King's Rochester, and Mr Culley left for the second time having taken a teaching post at Ashdown House School, moving later to a Headship at his previous school, Claremont. Both, however, were destined to return, Mrs Pickering after just one year and Mr Culley in 2006 after another 14 years. After Mr Culley left, **Mr Bob Anderson** joined as Assistant Head and to teach maths and sport. Although he was at the school for only two years, leaving in 1994 to take up a position in Guernsey, he had a strong influence on the development of the school, in particular encouraging and developing after-school clubs. **Mr Tom Bowen** was another teacher who came to The Prep in 1992, having been an extremely successful Head of Seal Primary School for nine years, and who was to prove an excellent Form 4 teacher and a coach for many sports. Many will remember Form 4's entertaining puppet shows at the end of the summer term, when the children made their own puppets and produced their own play.

In August 1992, *The Sevenoaks Chronicle* recorded the death at the age of 96 of **Mr Ronnie Marchant**, who had taught games at The Prep for over 40 years, from 1927 to 1969. He was a former member of the Royal Medical Corps who won the Military Medal for his deeds during the Battle of Passchendaele in 1917. A former pupil of Weald primary school and a gardener at Hever Castle from the age of 14, Mr Marchant became a sports reporter with *The Sevenoaks Chronicle* and also a groundsman at Sevenoaks Vine Cricket Club. With Major Donald Campbell (later Lord Colgrain), he was the founder of Weald British Legion and was also a past Chairman of Sevenoaks Rural District Council.

Mr John Pegg retired from his second career as a teacher in 1993. He had just taken early retirement from I.C.I. in 1983 when the school put an advertisement in *The Sevenoaks Chronicle* for a science master to take over from **Mr James Cooke** and it was spotted by Mrs Pegg. With a degree in maths and a scientific background, as well as being an old friend of Mr Oatley, Mr Pegg was a shoo-in. He taught all the sciences until 1991 and took Form 8 for maths from 1988. His infectious enthusiasm and personality helped the boys with their science and maths but, just as importantly, also with their social problems. He was a delightful man and caused great hilarity with some of his legendary escapades. His contributions to the pyrotechnics of bonfire night have already been noted. He was also known to have shown the Form 8 pupils how to distil alcohol and, so the rumour goes, test it on the staff. He certainly arrived at least once in the staff room at break time with a big grin on his face and a beaker full of neat alcohol, almost 100% proof. At other times there were clouds of smoke billowing out of the lab and, again, he would emerge grinning broadly.

Fabric

Since its move to Godden Green in 1969, The Prep had had a friendly, neighbourly relationship with the college which was located in the buildings immediately north of The Prep around Stake Farm and also leased from the Knole Estate. Originally the farm house for a small farm, the building had been substantially rebuilt in about 1890 to a design by Frederick Moore Simpson ARIBA (1855-1928). The alterations included the removal of the front door from the centre and turning the entrance-passage into the dining room, the dining room into the hall. The cow shed became the drawing room with a new bedroom and dressing room over, the stables were turned into accommodation and new drainage, plumbing and heating installed. It was then leased as a private house with substantial land to a civil engineer Anthony Henley.

In the 1960s, Stake Farm College had been established by **Mr Charles** and **Mrs Mary Montague** for foreign girl students wishing to 'be finished' over here and the Montagues lived in the converted farmhouse with their two children.

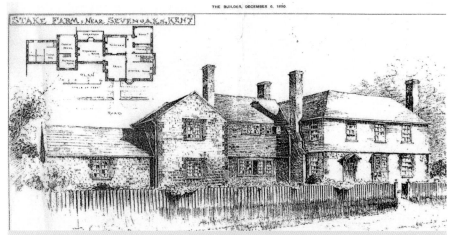

Artist's impression and floor plan of Stake Farm published in an architectural journal 'The Builder' dated 6 December 1890.

In 1972, **Mr Michael Heal** had come to Stake Farm to take a job as a gardener and handyman for the college with his wife **Mary** and children Janet and Brian and moved into 1 Cherry Tree Cottages opposite The Prep. Mrs Heal helped the Montagues with their own children as well as the college girls and eventually became the college's cook. The Montagues moved out of Stake Farm to Little Steading, behind Cherry Tree Cottages, and the number of dormitories in Stake Farm increased. As the whole idea of debutantes and finishing schools became less appealing and fewer girls were coming from abroad, the school changed its focus, becoming a school for boarders and local girls taking their A levels (Mrs Heal remembers there being between 20 and 25 pupils in dormitories named after

Mr and Mrs Heal with Mr Cochrane on a Prep staff outing in the early 1990s.

London streets and six or seven members of staff) and having a summer school for foreign girls to be taught 'to be ladies' by Mrs Montague. Most of the girls were housed in Stake Farm but local families also had them to stay (Mrs Oatley's sister **Mrs Sue Birch**, whose son **Patrick** was a pupil at The Prep had two of the girls staying with her and husband **Chris** for a while). By 1984, the Montagues had sold the college to the two Jeffery sisters and moved away from Little Steading. Soon after this, as there were fewer and fewer pupils at the college, the two already elderly ladies decided to retire to Sussex and the school closed.

One of the consequences of Sevenoaks School going fully co-educational from 1984 had been to reduce the number of secondary school places available for boys in the Sevenoaks area. Mr Oatley was obviously aware of this and identified a need for a non-selective private boys' school in the area. When he became aware that Stake Farm College was closing, he saw the opportunity to establish a secondary school for boys on its premises and, after consulting with the Knole Estate, the lease was taken up initially by The Prep and an idea began to take shape. Mr Oatley began a process which would culminate in the foundation of Sackville School and the formation of a company, PES. (Kent) Limited, which would own both The Prep and Sackville School.

In September 1986, Mr Oatley had written to the parents of The Prep boys to say that Sackville School was to open in September 1987 on the Stake Farm site, taking boys from 13 to 16 and following the new GCSE syllabus. **Mr Harold Edwards**, who was a housemaster and registrar at Tonbridge School, had been appointed as Headmaster. The Stake Farm site had seven acres of playing fields and 1½ acres available for building classrooms with a further 6 acres, while a house suitable for the Headmaster would be available within three years. Mr Oatley emphasised that this new enterprise would be entirely separate from The Prep and was backed by a consortium led by **Mr Tony Donnelly**. It had the full support and co-operation of local schools and would provide the middle school that had been needed for so long in the area. The Donnellys had bought Little Steading from the Montagues and their two sons, **Luke** and **Tom**, joined The Prep in 1985. As neighbours, the Donnellys became close friends with the Oatleys and Mr Donnelly approached Mr Oatley to discuss how he could help when it became known that Mr Oatley wished to start Sackville in Stake Farm. The members of the consortium also included **Mr Tony Wallinger**, a local architect and father of pupil **Stuart**, and he was extremely helpful in designing the changes necessary to Stake Farm.

However, early in 1987, Foxbush School in Hildenborough, a private Catholic boys school, suddenly announced its closure. The opportunity to occupy the large 26-acre site being vacated by Foxbush was too good an opportunity to pass up. In May 1987, Mr Oatley wrote to parents saying that, following the sudden demise of Foxbush, a consortium had purchased its premises and grounds for Sackville School. There were advantages with this site, particularly the fact that the new school would benefit from a fully equipped and up-and-running school on land which it would own, while Stake Farm had a 15-year lease. There would also be less disruption to the running of The Prep. Meanwhile, eight acres of playing fields and a car park had already been established on the Stake Farm site and it was decided that The Prep would take over the lease and convert the Stake Farm buildings into classrooms for the junior school comprising **Mrs Rosemary Cooke**'s Kindergarten, Forms 1, 2 and 3 and a senior art room. There would also be kitchen and dining facilities for the junior school. Mr and Mrs Heal were employed by The Prep, with Mick continuing as handyman and gardener and Mary as cook. She also helped Mrs Oatley with cricket teas.

The Prep took over the lease of Stake Farm in 1987 and the junior school moved in. Two fields came with the lease, but they couldn't be played on for two years because they had to be drained and flattened. When this was done hundreds of stones appeared on the surface and the school had stone patrols filling up endless buckets. Even when the boys started playing rugby on these fields in the early 1990s they still had to be inspected closely for any stones. When the work was finished there was a significant extension to the playing fields, with an athletics track with long and high jump pits, a full-sized rugby pitch and more. This gave space on the field between the school and Stake Farm for a floodlit tennis court that doubled as a five-a-side football pitch and later, nearer Stake Farm, all-weather cricket nets. Sometimes boys would go into Knole Park, where a plateau on the top of a hill became an extra football pitch and this was known as the Golan Heights because it was high, bleak and cold in the winter months. The field behind Stake Farm was known as the athletics field in the summer but rugby and football were played in the winter.

On 10 February 1987, another building programme was announced. By the end of the summer term it was hoped to build a new English room with a library; to extend the hall to include a storage area; to double the size of the car park; and to erect a covered way by the back door. This was all achieved under **Mr David Fry**'s supervision (who was still helping the school, even though his boys had left) and by the parents assisted by Mr Cochrane. In addition, the outsides of nearly all the classrooms and changing rooms were painted and major repairs were made to the history room. Another shed was erected next to the greenhouse where Form 8 were able to run their own shop selling tuck and other items. This was a plan by Mr Oatley to teach the boys how to run a business: they had to do all the planning and accounting themselves as well as providing the goods to sell.

When Mrs Witton joined the Pre-Prep staff in 1990 the KG classrooms were temporary buildings, which still remain as a Pre-Prep art block, and were craned into place. The term started with bare walls, a sink, six tables, and paper and pencils. Mrs Witton's husband installed the shelving. One of the more memorable events at Stake Farm took place just before the 1991 spring half-term when Form 3's ceiling collapsed. The Christmas and summer shows were performed by the Pre-Prep in the senior school hall, which was a large wooden building with a stage. It was always chilly and pretty dirty but it made a very lovely little theatre with plush dark red curtains.

By the early 1990s, as the larger numbers in the Pre-Prep started moving to the senior school, it was obvious that more facilities were needed, especially with girls moving into Form 3. So – on with the building programme! The old toilets opposite the back door were demolished and the urinals became the cleaner's cupboard. A new girls' changing room and toilets and new boys' toilets took their place. Form 3 moved again and became two classes in the old Form 4 rooms with Mrs Pickering, who had re-joined the staff in 1993 to be a class teacher with **Mrs Sue Lewis**. Form 3's old classroom became the boys' changing room. Forms 5 and 6's rooms became **Mr Brian Morrow**'s geography/history room and an enormous new portakabin block appeared after a team of staff and parents had demolished the old changing room sheds – very sad for those who felt the last bastions of the original buildings were fast disappearing, but it was time for 'out with the old and in with the new'.

Academic

Mrs Judy Bailey had been teaching art at the school when she decided in 1985 to retrain as a specialist in children who had been diagnosed with dyslexia, a specific learning difficulty. After qualifying, she was wondering where to teach, when Mr Oatley came to her aid. He offered Mrs Bailey the use of a room in the Pre-Prep that at the time was not needed as a classroom. In this way, she was able to begin teaching those children at The Prep who had been diagnosed with dyslexia.

Over the next few years, she taught, with the aid of three more trained specialist teachers, including **Mrs Jenny Dunlop** and **Mrs Sue Barton** (who took over when Mrs Bailey retired), not only children from The Prep but children with dyslexia from many of the other prep and state schools in the area as, at that time, these schools did not cater for children with dyslexia themselves. At first pupils travelled to The Prep, but naturally over time teachers asked The Prep teachers to go into their schools. This avoided the youngsters wasting valuable lesson time travelling to and fro. Finally, many of the schools decided to employ their own dyslexia trained teachers.

The Prep had led the way in catering for these children. Today the unit is an important department of the school. With the appropriate help at the earliest time, specific teaching for children with dyslexia has proved a most valuable and successful outcome for these pupils. They learn to manage their dyslexia and go on to develop their potential. A stirring example of this is a young man now in his thirties who is a well-qualified scientist in Norway!

In October 1987, there was a visit from 16 Japanese educationalists on a fact-finding mission to the UK and Germany, the first of many visits from overseas teachers to the school over the next few years. This first visit was disrupted because it happened in the aftermath of the great hurricane which had devastated Sevenoaks and much of the south-east. Much of the visit was in darkness and Mrs Bullock remembers Mrs Oatley being one step ahead of the visitors, carrying the one vase of flowers she had been able to arrange. These visits enabled teachers from overseas to learn from the British educational system and were serious occasions for Mr Oatley, as the school's reputation for its approach to inclusive teaching and a family atmosphere was increasing, but there were lighter moments. During one Japanese visit, just before they were due to arrive, **Mrs Liz Harrison**, with Mrs Spencer-Allen's help, dressed up as a Japanese lady in a kimono with her hair up (fixed with long curly drinking straws) and with a Japanese style long-handed cleaning brush walked out of the kitchen into the hall muttering to Mr Oatley 'very filthy English school'. Mr Oatley's face really was a picture of horror…briefly!

Mme Jacqueline Homer began an exchange programme with a school in the south of France, starting with a visit from 48 children and four staff from the French school in May 1988.

In June 1988, there was a visit from **Mr Abdulla Al-Mohanna**, a teacher from Kuwait organised by the British Council. He was visiting a variety of private schools in England on a fact-finding mission.

The new English classroom and library transformed Mrs Biggs' working life. On Mrs Lucas' retirement in 1986 she had become the senior English teacher and the official librarian. At that time, books were occasionally and ceremoniously carried by wheelbarrow to the so-called library, a broom cupboard fitted with shelves next to the then art room. It was like a trek to the Arctic and only the most avid readers ever ventured there, usually accompanied by an adult wrapped in furs and thermals. Mrs Biggs arranged the books in order during the holidays while in the English room she guarded her personal collection, only venturing on occasional sorties northward. Later, when the English room moved to a new portakabin, books were housed there too and were accessible when required by Mrs Biggs and her pupils, but not alas to the whole school.

The new library actually looked like one with vast numbers of shelves, and it felt friendly as a library should: warm, light and comfortable, stacked high with books of all sorts and all sizes on a wide range of topics to cater for varying interests. It benefitted from parents and visitors who generously donated gifts. Mrs Biggs was greatly helped when setting it up from the pupil librarians **Gary Anscombe**, **Richard House** and **Greg Pay** who, as she noted 'helped to organise me; quietly, efficiently and without fuss'.

The paper-back bookshop originally stood in a dark corner of the hall outside the dining room. Mrs Biggs remembered small groups of boys peering through the gloom to find the latest editions. The new bookshop now stood flanked by windows with ample room for all to see. Apart from some interesting sound effects in heavy storms, conditions for teaching and learning English were vastly improved.

Co-education and the Pre-Prep

On 29 January 1991, Mr Oatley sent a letter to parents informing them that The Prep was going to become co-educational and that girls would now be able to pass into Form 1 from the Kindergarten. He confirmed that in principle no girls would be added to the existing all-boys forms with the girls joining year by year over the following seven years so that the school would be fully co-educational by September 1998.

Five little girls, four with elder brothers already in the school, started in Form 1 in September 1991. When asked about uniforms, the young mothers of these girls, to the surprise of Mrs Perks the Form 1 teacher, opted for traditional white shirts and ties and 'a proper school hat'. **Gabby Brunton** remembers being measured up for the girls' uniform, choosing the different pinafores and cardies and wondering what was going on. She wasn't bothered as long as she could wear her blue duck wellies, and she was such a tomboy she would have been happy in the boys' kit. A second eye-opener to Mrs Perks came at the end of the first craft lesson of the year. She turned from the sink, where she was dumping paint pots and brushes, to detail some children to help with clearing up the classroom. She did not have to say a word, as some of the girls had already begun! One was on her hands and knees with dustpan and brush; another two were wiping the table-

The first Form I girls in their new uniforms and in class with Mrs Perks in 1991, the year The Prep began its journey towards full co-education. Until then the girls went on to other schools after Kindergarten.

tops with very wet cloths, and the others were carrying the waste-basket to collect the scraps of paper. As Mrs Perks noted, 'Who said there's no difference between boys and girls? A myth, if there ever was one!'

Mrs Rosemary Cooke and **Mrs Shirley Berryman** retired in 1991 and the Kindergarten classes were now the responsibility of Mrs Lloyd, Mrs Ruprecht and Mrs Witton. Mrs Spencer-Allen was recruited in 1991 to help in the Kindergarten and soon began to run an informal group for younger siblings. The groups were designated KG1 for the relatively younger and KG2 for the relatively younger older in the recently installed portakabin in Stake Farm's garden. In April 1992, Mr Oatley wrote to parents saying that KG1 would now be five mornings a week and KG2 five days (up to 3:15pm) from the following academic year with children attending every day. This provoked some letters of complaint from parents who wanted the flexibility of the old arrangements maintained.

From half term (October 1992) there was extended day provision, called the Little Oaks Club, offered for children from the Pre-Prep up to 6:00pm, including tea, under the supervision of **Mrs Barbara Adams**. This valuable child-care

facility after school was charged to the parents, while 'late stay' was offered free of charge, where children with older brothers or sisters in The Prep were looked after until the older siblings were collected.

Mrs Marjorie Shea returned to The Prep in 1992 to head the junior school and to teach Form 1 following the retirement of Mrs Perks. In addition to managing the young children and their parents, her objective was to help the school to become fully co-educational, develop two classes in each year group, and formally establish a nursery for rising threes. At that time, there were about 95 junior school children, including a smattering of girls, housed in Stake Farm along with the senior art room.

The first thing Mrs Shea needed to do was to stop everyone saying 'Stake Farm' when they answered the phone, so that callers would begin to think of them as an educational establishment instead of a farm! By the end of the year, they were calling themselves 'The Pre-Prep'. This was an important move to recognise that their children

Mrs Marjorie Shea, head of the Pre-Prep, taking a harvest assembly circa 1996.

aged from 3 to 7 were mostly infants and not juniors. It coincided with the recognition of pre-preps by the IAPS and the beginning of an association to support, train and meet fellow teachers.

Mrs Sue Binnie started in the Pre-Prep in September 1993 when the Nursery class was established for the rising 3s in two rooms on the ground floor of Stake Farm. The first group of children comprised seven boys and two girls, all with birthdays in the autumn term. In the spring term, **Mrs Vanessa Dussek**, who had been running her own nursery in Shipbourne, joined her and they welcomed another group of children, this time with their third birthdays falling in the spring and summer terms.

Two Kindergarten classes of rising 4s were then housed in the so-called temporary building (this had arrived in 1991, supposedly for two years, but was still the Kindergarten in 2015!) Mrs Spencer-Allen and **Mrs Jane Murphy** (mother of **Robert**, **James** and **William**) had one room for the younger children while Mrs Lloyd and Mrs Ruprecht had another. KG2, the older Kindergarten class for rising 5s, was renamed Reception, which was in line with most other schools and a lot less confusing, and two classes were housed in the main Stake Farm building. The rising 6s, rising 7s and rising 8s in Forms 1, 2 and 3 respectively were also in the main building, along with the senior art room. As the year groups expanded into two classes, it was not long before Mrs Lewis and Form 3, and eventually the senior art room, moved across to the senior school

The KG classes had a hotchpotch of low tables and a mixture of tiny chairs, some puzzles, toys, and – at that stage – not much else. What they did have, though, was a superb shelving unit made by Mrs Witton's husband the previous year. In the early days, their resources were really quite sparse and they relied heavily on old cereal packets, toilet rolls and egg boxes (totally frowned upon nowadays) and other handouts. Mrs Perks regularly used to arrive at the school bringing loads of saved up cardboard boxes etc. Sally, her daughter, was always, and still is, a great help to both the Kindergarten and Nursery classes when extra

The Pre-Prep's first ballerinas, circa 1993.

support was needed and has always helped with Little Oaks Club. In the early days of KG, there were of course no computers, nor did they have the amazing climbing frames and outdoor equipment of nowadays. They did, however, have the beautiful Prep grounds with lots of trees to climb and places to explore, of which they made full use. The building, near Stake Farm's entrance, now changing rooms, was once a squash court and the teachers were allowed to take the children in there to play and throw balls etc. It was a godsend on rainy days. The children also liked the echoing sounds they could make!

The Pre-Prep's first summer concert performed outside at Stake Farm, 1991.

It took about five years to establish even-numbered classes in the Pre-Prep and eight years to become fully co-educational, with two classes of 18 right through and 36 part-time children in the Nursery and Kindergarten. To help encourage girls, different activities such as ballet, with **Mrs Alison Knapp** whose son **Tom** was a pupil, and needlework were offered and **Mrs Linda Underwood** did an amazing job organising girls' games. There was a dedicated team of teachers and assistants with complete understanding and commitment to the children, making the best of their accommodation. They changed classrooms most years, depending on numbers and, in typical Prep fashion, painted them as they went. It was hard work but it was fun and they turned their hands to everything. Previously unknown do-it-yourself talents emerged. One summer holiday, the teachers and assistants all turned up with white paint to freshen up what had been the senior art room (the last outpost for the senior school in Stake Farm). The first day was spent removing staples, the second painting, and the third admiring the different shades of white paint they had all used. **Mrs Lucy Wigley** fitted the sink unit, having taken inspiration from Mrs Witton, who had previously fitted out the Kindergarten rooms. It was a very happy and successful time. As the reputation of the Pre-Prep grew, so did the numbers.

Drama and music

The 1987 play was *1066 and All That*, in which 39 boys acted out 107 parts. With all the changes in costumes and the short scenes, things quickly became manic behind the scenes, except for Mrs Shefford sitting serenely on her stool checking the script. Towards the end of the 1980s, Mrs Shefford started to write her own plays under the pseudonym **Mary Honor**. The first to be performed at The Prep was *Bertie's Genius* in 1990, followed by *Rock A-Round Robin* (1991), *Yeeha* (1993), and *Summer Fun* (1995), while in 1996 *Bertie's Genius* was repeated, the last play she produced for the school. Mrs Shefford's plays continued to be performed at The Prep and in other schools as well.

The 1989 reprise of *Old Father Time* with Tom Butlin as a very memorable Margaret Thatcher.

above A school choir in concert conducted by Mrs Shefford in the early 1990s.
below Two scenes from *Island*, the middle school play in 1992, directed by Mr Culley.

When Mr Luke Harrison, the current Headmaster, shows prospective parents around the school, he always shows them the IT classroom, as it reminds him of all the classrooms in which he was taught. It is one of the two remaining wooden sheds and was originally Mrs Shefford's music room (the other shed is the school shop). Mary was nicknamed Mary Poppins because she acted like her and had the boys singing songs from the musical. Mr Harrison remembers being in the choir when his voice was breaking, but he was so desperate to sing in the Three Arts Festival that Mrs Shefford said he could mime. Unfortunately, during rehearsals, he mistook miming for humming and this was the one and only time he was reprimanded by Mrs Shefford. However, Mrs Biggs entered him in the poetry section and he won the Grove Poetry Award for the best original poem. His winning poem *Sounds* is included in Appendix 4.

In 1993, **Dan Clews**, who went on to have a career in music, and his father **Mr Martin Clews** wrote the lyrics for a song about The Prep, to be sung to the tune of *Wild Rover*, which is also included in Appendix 4.

Mr Oatley in a letter to parents said that the senior concert in December 1991 was the most successful ever, highlighting the devotion of Mrs Shefford and the other peripatetic teachers who helped. Following a play in March 1992, Mrs Shefford wrote a poem of thanks to her principal helpers, Mr Michael and **Mrs Ronnie Barnard** and Mrs Oatley, which is included in Appendix 4.

Mr Culley became involved in drama in the early 1990s, producing the middle school plays *All Clear* and *Island*. His mother was in charge of the props for *All Clear* and the space round the back of the stage was tiny. On the first night she set up camp, regally sitting in a large armchair with all the props around her taking over the whole backstage with no room for the cast. Two teachers from Claremont School, where Mr Culley had been teaching previously, who came along to provide the music were crammed into the showers at the side.

Two unidentified staff pantos *left* Mr Bowen in tights.
right Mrs Biggs and Mr Culley with unknown Father Christmas and dead dragon.

Mr Culley remembers **Robin Collings**, who returned to the school to teach English and drama, and Dan Clews starring in *Island*. Both plays were so popular that Mr Culley produced them again in 2007 and 2008 after he had returned to the school.

The performance that some of the staff dreaded was when Mrs Shefford persuaded them to put on a pantomime for the children on the last day of the autumn term. Some staff, such as Mr Barnard, were in their element, but others wished they had had another glass of wine with their Christmas lunch. In one panto, Mr Morrow was persuaded to wear a tutu, but fortunately no photographic evidence exists. Few of the staff knew their lines, as at the end of term they were all too busy with reports and other paperwork, so they used to put the lines on the lintel at the top of the stage. The performances were, of course, hugely popular with the children.

School life

The sixteenth of October 1987 was the night of the infamous hurricane. In the morning, large oak trees lay on their sides across the playing fields and access to the school was completely cut off from all directions. The last telephone call before the lines went dead was from The New Beacon asking whether the football match was still on that afternoon! There was no electricity and when it did come back it was spasmodic – and a group of Japanese teachers was visiting the school in the cold and dark!

Complete devastation surrounded the school, and it was a week before things started to get back to normal. Luckily, the school buildings remained intact and the only damage to buildings was a tree through the games shed and across the roof of the hall. All the panes of glass in the greenhouse in Stake Farm were smashed and the caravan beside Mr Heal's shed was upside down. The greenhouse had had a most beautiful mature vine and Mr Heal and Mr Cochrane were very sad when it eventually had to be pulled down following the damage sustained. Mrs Witton was very fond of the building, and she tried to take a cutting from the vine but failed, which was a great shame. She still, however, has many of the lovely crockery flower pots which Mr Heal was throwing away.

Dominic Low recalled the aftermath of the hurricane and The Prep's reaction. He woke up on the Friday morning to utter devastation. His father's first reaction was, 'how on earth are we going to get you to school?' They got into his car and started to drive, frequently stopping to remove trees and branches from the road. They managed to get the car as far as Seal, but Park Lane up past the golf course was impassable. They walked up the lane, climbing over trees and helping other people along the route to remove trees from blocking their drives. After what seemed like ages, they arrived at the school, which was unrecognisable, with the sports fields resembling the aftermath of a battle. The school buildings miraculously survived but access was difficult. It was still early in the morning

The games shed was one casualty of the October 1987 hurricane.

but one or two other parents and their sons arrived on foot. They were greeted by Mr Oatley with his fluorescent yellow jacket on – no hard hat, of course, as health and safety rules had not been invented then – and a chainsaw in each hand. **Mr Brian Low** ventured to ask if the school would be closed. 'Closed Brian, of course we're not closed' yelled Mr Oatley followed by 'Brian, will you take this chainsaw, and get started on that fallen oak tree that's blocking the history room. I reckon we'll get lessons going after lunch!' And so the staff, the parents, and the boys, led by Mr Oatley, cleared the school and got it up and running in no time.

The Christmas bazaar, due to take place on 14 November, was cancelled due to the enormous amount of work everyone had to do to get back to normality

Tree planting on The Vine to replace the six of the 'seven oaks' that were lost.

Form 8 in 1989 with the enduring evidence of the storm two years earlier.

after the hurricane in October. Mr Oatley offered work parties to parents who needed help with fallen trees at their homes.

This was quite a year with regard to the weather, as in January the school was cut off for two weeks following the worst snowfall for years. A few people struggled into school in snow boots and two boys even managed to ski across Knole Park! Once again, no electricity; but in true Prep spirit, the staff and pupils who made it in put on extra sweaters and soldiered on. There was a potential problem with the contents of the freezers de-frosting, so it was arranged to distribute the contents around accessible homes which still had power. Mr Oatley answered one knock on the door to be asked, 'I understand you have food to distribute from your freezers. I hardly dare to ask as my son goes to Solefield'! Of course he went home with a selection of fish fingers, chips, and peas.

In 1989, **Mrs Christine Jeffers** took over as editor of *The Acorn* from Mrs Biggs, who had retired. Initially, she did not change the format but, making use of the advances in technology, introduced more and better-quality photographs and other images. The autumn 1992 copy of *The Acorn*, which covered the 1991-92 academic year, was number 29 and the last one, having been published annually since 1962-63. It was replaced by a more regular newsletter *The Prep Post*, with the first issue being produced at the end of the spring term 1993. For the rest of the time that the Oatleys ran the school, usually two a year were produced and in total there were 29 published over the subsequent 13 years. Since 2005, *The Prep Post* has been published annually.

There was a visit from a group of Danish teachers and children in September 1992, and a visit from eight Japanese teachers in May 1993. A Japanese delegation of 26 teachers visited in November 1994 and there were repeated visits

The Japanese delegations always took a formal photo as a memento.

during most of the next few years. Mrs Spencer-Allen recalled some Japanese teachers who came to look at the Pre-Prep. They were all very charming and she was hoping they would be impressed by the Kindergarten children's artwork when visiting their classroom. Alas no, they were much more interested in the fact that a little boy went off to the loo by himself. 'Ah, he do pee by himself', they exclaimed, taking their cameras to the cloakroom. They said that in Japan, all the children would sit on potties in a row at the same time!

The school minibuses featured in many escapades. One of the first was a Sherpa bus, which was used to take sports teams to away fixtures. Mr Oatley would drive with all the bags in the middle aisle, three boys on each bench, with **Piers Baldock** sitting in the sink and another boy on the loo! This was usually parked next to a trampoline with no safety nets outside the main school house and boys used to try and jump over the Sherpa bus from this onto a crash mat. The Sherpa was replaced by an old green Ford Transit with benches on either side and no seat belts, so when the bus braked the boys slid one way then the other; sometimes the door would swing open, but no one ever seemed to fall out. Mr Culley remembered driving down the A21 with the **Creed** twins (**Quentin and Benjamin**) shouting from the back 'Mr Culley, Mr Culley, the back door's open'.

On a Sunday afternoon in September 1988, the day before Mr Ratcliffe was due to start teaching at The Prep, he had been asked to pick up one of the school minibuses so that he could pick up pupils en route from his home to the school in the morning. 'Take the white van', he was instructed. 'The keys are on the hooks outside the study.' He duly arrived at The Prep and walked into the school house. There were several keys on the hooks with one labelled 'White Van' so he took it off the hook and walked out towards the white van at the rear of the house. There was also a red van nearby. The door of the white van was unlocked. He climbed in and pushed the key partially into the ignition. The key wouldn't go in so he moved the steering wheel at the same time to unlock a possible security system on the column. The ignition did not provide a good fit for the key and wouldn't engage. He turned the key over and tried again and it snapped! An hour later a car appeared. Mr Ratcliffe jumped down from the van and explained that there was a problem with the ignition, and that the key had broken inside. 'I did use the white van key,' he uttered defensively as they walked towards the van. 'That's not the white van. That's the white van over there'. 'But that's a red van', he replied as calmly as possible. 'It is now. It used to be white. It's recently been resprayed.'

The next morning, Mr Ratcliffe arrived at The Prep in the red van with a contingent of pupils. He placed the spare set of red van keys on a hook. The office door was wide open and Mr Barnard was sitting behind his desk. 'Ah, you must be the fellow who's been breaking our school van's ignition systems!' he said loudly and confidently with a wry grin. Mr Ratcliffe was starting to explain when he saw a youngish, smart-looking woman standing in the office. He turned to face her. 'Good morning. Do you work here?' he inquired. 'I'm the Headmaster's wife,' she replied. 'Pleased to meet you,' he said and slunk to his classroom.

School staff outings were always fun, with Mr Oatley driving one of the newer school buses, which replaced the Ford Transit. One year, he crunched his way through the gears to Dover, from where the staff proceeded to spend the day in Boulogne.

There was no such thing as personal health and safety, and none of the rules and regulations of today. The staff did not have vast amounts of paperwork, reports, planning etc., etc., to do. There were no boundaries or fences around the school. Amazingly, despite this, there were few – if any – accidents; no one got poisoned by egg boxes, and they never had a burglary, until one day Mrs Spencer-Allen arrived early one morning to find the Kindergarten not as she had left it the night before. There were a few toys scattered haphazardly on the floor, and a chair had been moved near the units where the beautiful clay baskets and little rabbits the children had made for Mother's Day and Easter were placed. She went to check to see if they were hard and ready to paint. There were two missing, one rabbit and one basket. After checking each name, it appeared that the missing objects were both made by the same child, whose mother later in the day told Mrs Spencer-Allen that her son had given her a lump of unidentifiable clay when he came home from school. He, who shall be nameless, had apparently taken himself to the classroom alone while his mother was chatting in the car park awaiting another of her sons. He had managed to climb up onto the chair and somehow pick out his own creations to give to his mother early! Although Mrs Spencer-Allen and the mother weren't very pleased, the little boy got top marks for choosing the right ones.

The school had long been used to inspections from the equivalent of present-day OFSTED but increasingly other inspections were made. Health and Safety inspections by the local council became more frequent and Mrs Liz Harrison remembers one incident when H&S made an impromptu visit and she had to quickly extract an open tin of dog food belonging to Sinbad, the Oatley's dog, out of the fridge pretty sharpish. On another visit, she was asked if she used the small basin (which was covered with a wooden top) to wash her hands before working, which was fine until the Inspector lifted the board to find a dead spider and its web! She promised to do better and made sure the sink was spotless thereafter.

Sport and recreation

Football in the autumn term 1986 was very successful with nine wins and only one loss, and the 2nd XI and the rugby XV (in the spring term) had records which were almost as good. The 1990 football XI won nine of their ten matches in the autumn term, losing the last game 3-4 in the last minutes. They were described by Mr Oatley 'as the best first XI I have seen in my 25 years of teaching'. Top scorers were **Alex Harrington** with ten goals and **Ben Davies** with eight. The 2nd XI was unbeaten and the overall school record was played 36, won 25, drew 5, and lost only 6.

A football team from St George's School, Vancouver, toured in October 1991, playing Hazlewood, The New Beacon and The Prep. Parents were asked to put boys up for three nights. The tour was organised by the brother-in-law of the Head of Combe Bank school, and Combe Bank hosted a cheese and wine party for all the parents who had hosted the visitors, and a disco for the boys with the first and second year Combe Bank girls.

Under Mr Culley's coaching the standard of rugby gradually improved. In March 1987, The Prep got to the quarter-finals of the Rosslyn Park sevens. Mr Culley thinks this was probably the strongest sevens team the school has had, with **Paul Shea**, **Robbie Agnew**, **Stuart Janzse**, and **Ben Bullock** amongst others. They were very sporty, and because weight was less of a factor in sevens play, they did not have the problem of coming up against massive opposition. They just lost out in the quarter-final to Warlborough Hill from Devon by a couple of points. They almost snatched it as Robbie Agnew did have the opportunity to score late on when he broke away, but he had too far to run and was caught just before the line.

There were further rugby tours following the successful one organised by **Mr Bill Shea** to Newcastle in 1986. They were very much a family affair, like the ski holidays, with the parents enjoying themselves as much as the boys and with mostly good memories. One tour was to North Wales and unfortunately produced a less good memory. The Prep played an older Welsh club side who treated it like an England/Wales international. Mr Shea really took the Welsh coach to task

right Dennison 5-a-side Football Cup winners with Mrs Dennison, 1987.

below 1987 Rosslyn Park Sevens quarter finalists with Mr Culley.

bottom Rugby tour to Wales, memorable scenery but unsporting opponents.

The Prep won the Bethany 7s cricket shield in 1990. Pictured here is the winning team with their coach, Mr Harris, and their 1st XI caps.

over their attitude. Better memories came from a tour to Bournemouth, with sporting and really close matches.

In a cricket match at Yardley Court in May 1989, **Jamie Ford** with 115 not out and **Matthew Bensted** with 103 not out put together an unbroken stand for the third wicket of over 200 runs. The Prep's total was 255 for two and at the close, Yardley had struggled to 74 for five. Needless to say, the wickets were shared between Jamie and Matthew. Both were selected to represent Kent U13s later that summer.

In spring 1987, The Prep won the junior (U13) Knole run organised by Sevenoaks School with the second team coming fifth (out of 14). This was The Prep's third win in five years.

The variety of sports available at the school grew, not least because of the increase in the proportion of girls from 1991. The school started playing table tennis, basketball, netball, softball and rounders. In 1992, sailing lessons were offered to Form 8 boys post Common Entrance and later some senior boys tried hockey under **Mr Philip Oldroyd** at the Holly Bush Lane all-weather pitch.

A sports story from around 1995 about cross-country running in Knole Park from Gabby Brunton illustrates the school's inclusive approach to encouragement and getting the best out of the children. Starting from the big oak tree in the middle of the sports fields, Gabby and **Georgia Kemp** were running together and began to slow a bit, probably because they were chatting too much. They decided to walk but Mr Donald Smith spotted them and came up to begin running alongside. They said the things most short-legged 9-year-olds say about not wanting to run but he ran with them and encouraged them with, 'Try, see how you get on; do it together'. They (probably thinking about

A successful cross country team from 1993.

the old adage that teachers had eyes everywhere) tried their best to run all the way back. Neither of them thought much of it, but a few days later in assembly when giving out certificates, Gabby and Georgia were awarded them for cross-country, to their surprise. Gabby went to say thank you to Mr Smith and asked, 'why, I'm not a very good runner?' and he replied, 'because you tried, and you did it together'.

Mrs Spencer-Allen remembered the effect the school had on her apparently non-sporty sons who had been at Winchester House. **Corin**'s final report on leaving Winchester House at only age 5 said he would much prefer reading a good book than play any sport. This was to dramatically change once he went to The Prep and sport was to become one of the most important things in his life. He, and later **Lynden**, were to captain quite a few teams during their time at The Prep and were extremely fortunate to have many inspiring sports masters who helped them on their way to eventually play junior county cricket, and later for their universities. Sportsmanship was always very important at The Prep and losing was never frowned upon; just happily saying, 'we will do better next time' was the encouraging Prep attitude. Winning was, of course, brilliant and celebrated but without boasting. The Spencer-Allens travelled around many schools while playing various sports and she had to admit that The Prep's tea was definitely one of the best, thanks to Mrs Oatley's culinary skill!

Outings and holidays

Mr Oatley encouraged pupils to take up his beloved activity of cycling. The school arranged, for those boys who wished, to take part in charity rides – notably several London to Brighton rides and, in June 1996, London to Oxford. Other family members were also encouraged to take part. In the 1987 Brighton ride, a Form 8 boy, Roddy Bailey, was involved in an incident: his bike was hit in the rear by a fellow cyclist after about 22 miles and his back wheel was so buckled he couldn't continue. Although he found an official repair station, he did not have enough money to pay for it. In the days before mobile phones, it was difficult to contact anybody and, after an adventurous 12 hours, including rides in an official van, a Red Cross car, and an ambulance and meeting a pretty girl with a similar broken bike, he arrived at Ditchling Beacon where he was picked up by his father. Mr Oatley wrote to the organisers about Roddy's difficulties and received an apology.

Charlton Athletic FC returned to their old ground at the Valley after several years sharing Crystal Palace's ground and invited local schools to attend a match against Notts County in January 1993. Over 100 boys, parents, and staff went. Later that year, a number of Charlton players came to the school to provide the children, including several from other schools, with some coaching. The connection with Charlton lasted several years with **Mr Brian Kinsey**, who had been a professional footballer with Charlton, helping the school with coaching in the 2000s.

Mr Culley began organising camping trips for the boys in the summer holidays, usually in South Wales but one year they went to Guernsey. Accompanied by Mr and Mrs Culley, some alumni, and a few intrepid parents, the groups travelled in the ever-deteriorating school minibuses. The memories of those taking part recall breakdowns, getting lost, and accidents but most of all fun, adventure, and food.

At Clapham Common for the start of the 1987 London to Brighton cycle ride.

Summer camp in Wales — a miracle they ever made it in the minibus!

The things they used to do on those school camps, you wouldn't dream of doing now. One favourite was the midnight 'wide' game. From the field outside the village, two adults who were nominated as spies would be dropped some five miles away. The boys were then the defence team and had to try to stop the spies getting back to the field. They were 11 and 12-year-olds who just disappeared into the dark to try and find the spies. Mr Culley recalls that the present Headmaster and his brother just took the boys off and hid. By about half midnight there were some boys missing, and Mr Culley can remember driving round the field in the minibus searching for them and suddenly this head popped up – either Luke or **Guy** – saying, 'Oh, is the game over then?'.

Alumni

In the summer of 1987, alumnus **Richard Wergan**, who had gone to Sevenoaks School in 1980, took part in a British Schools Exploring Society's ornithological expedition to Svalbard, a Norwegian archipelago in the Arctic Ocean. A film of the exhibition was shown on Channel 4 in November.

Jon Clarke, who left in 1980, was trying to raise money to enable him to compete in the London marathon in 1990. He had been born with spina bifida and walked on crutches but wanted to do the marathon in a wheelchair. While at the school his determination had been a great inspiration to everyone, especially on one occasion when he did a sponsored swim of 66 lengths of St John's Pool in Tunbridge Wells and raised over £100 towards the school hall. He went on to Cannock House, where he achieved 8 O-levels, and then to Hadlow College. The Prep planned to sponsor him and Mr Oatley asked parents for some ideas on how to raise further funds towards the £1,000 cost of a racing wheelchair.

A grand sum of £2,200 was raised for the Spina Bifida Society when Jon took part in the London marathon in April 1990, finishing in a creditable four hours, despite having a puncture after 16 miles. He completed his second London marathon in 1993, nine minutes faster than his previous one, and soon afterwards visited the school to thank them for helping him raise £15,000. He reported that he had recently taken up two new sports, golf in a specially adapted buggy with a swivelling chair and water skiing, and was planning a sponsored parachute jump.

Although **Paul Downton** left The Prep after Form 6 to go to Sevenoaks School, he was one of the best schoolboy cricketers the school had seen. While at Sevenoaks he played both cricket and rugby at international schoolboy level. He then went to Exeter University, where he read law, before becoming a professional cricketer as a wicket-keeper batsman. He played for Kent from 1977 to 1979, then Middlesex from 1980 to 1991, with 30 test matches and 28 one-day international appearances for England. In 1990, he was awarded a benefit by Middlesex and, as part of this, a dinner and dance was held at Sevenoaks School in April 1991. The Prep gave a colour TV for the main raffle prize. Paul's cricket career ended in 1991 when he failed to recover from a freak eye injury when a bail lodged in his eye when he was standing up to the stumps during a Sunday League match. He went on to a career as a stockbroker in the City and is now a cricket administrator.

Simon Zutshi, who is partially sighted and had left in 1985, became a member of the Magic Circle and went on to become an entrepreneur and to write a very successful book called *Property Magic*. He and **John Martin** entertained many boys and staff with their magic tricks.

Roddy Bailey left in 1987 to go to Sevenoaks School and then Oxford

Simon Zutchi and John Martin performing at a parents' event.

University, where he is a professor of history as well as being a broadcaster and bestselling author. His first book, published in 2008, *The Wildest Province: SOE in the Land of the Eagle* was about the Special Operations Executive in the Second World War. He has gone on to publish several books specialising in the study of the Second World War and the history of modern war and medicine, as well as appearing in TV programmes about the two world wars. He also served with the British Army in Afghanistan where he won a Queen's Commendation.

Other schools and organisations

Sackville School had been established in Hildenborough in 1987 and immediately became a popular choice for boys to go on to after The Prep. Of the 30 Form 8 leavers in July 1987, 12 went to Sackville (Sevenoaks School was next with four). However, Sackville did not get off to a good start. Mr Edwards, who had been appointed Headmaster, was unable to take up the post due to ill-health and as the founder Mr Oatley felt it was his responsibility to act as Headmaster for an interim period while the Governors sought a replacement. In a letter to parents of The Prep in September 1987, Mr Oatley assured them that he would continue to fulfil his teaching commitments at The Prep and that his strong management team of Mr Culley as Assistant Head and **Mr Peter Rogers** as Director of Studies, together with Mr Barnard and Mrs Oatley, would ensure that The Prep continued with minimum disruption. However, the rumour mill in the car park went into full swing and two days later Mr Oatley had to write to the parents again and repeat more forcibly that he remained as Head of The Prep and fully committed to the school. The search for a new Headmaster proved successful and **Mr Richard Simmons** from Dover College was appointed in February 1988 to take up his post full time at Sackville from September that year. However he did not last long and by the end of 1988 had decided to leave which meant that Mr Oatley had to go back to oversee the running of the school. Finally a very successful appointment was made in September 1989 when **Mr Jonathan Langdale**, who had been head of Hilden Grange Preparatory School for many years, became Headmaster in September 1989.

In autumn 1988, there was a meeting of the Heads of some of the junior and senior independent schools in Sevenoaks with the aim of improving their image and to present a united front to the public. In October, **Rev. Paul Cox**, Headmaster of St Michael's School in Otford, proposed sending a questionnaire to the Heads of some dozen local schools asking if they would support the proposal that collectively the schools give a donation to a charity, and asking for further suggestions. Most schools responded with donations, several (including The Prep) raised money from collections at carol services that Christmas and in February 1989, £500 was given to both the Care Village at Ide Hill and the Crossroads Care Scheme – but the idea fizzled out and the initiative was not repeated.

By the end of the 1980s, another independent school in Sevenoaks was suffering from falling numbers. St Hilary's was a girls-only junior and senior school, founded in 1942 as a kindergarten by **Mrs Dorothy Packman** in a private house in Seal and moving to Bradbourne Vale Road two years later. Discussions took place in late 1989 with the senior staff and Governors of St Hilary's, with the aim of PES. acquiring St Hilary's and merging its junior school with The Prep at Godden Green and its senior school with Sackville in Hildenborough to create two co-educational schools with a common board of Governors to run them. Although draft heads of agreement were drawn up and various plans made for the structure of the new schools, in January 1990 the Governors of St Hilary's decided that it was not in their best interests to proceed with the plans. In December 1991, **Mrs J.S. Lang**, Head of Walthamstow Hall, wrote to Mr Oatley to formally announce the merger of her school and St Hilary's with effect from September 1992, to continue single-sex girls' education in Sevenoaks with the newly enlarged junior school occupying the site in Bradbourne Vale Road.

In 1995, Cannock House in Chelsfield, where a few Prep alumni had gone over the years, closed.

Mr Oatley's policy of opening up the school and grounds to outside organisations continued. The Prep hosted the annual Association of Kent Cricket Clubs 6-a-side competition for local clubs from October 1988. Sevenoaks RFC continued to use The Prep facilities for veterans and junior rugby on winter weekends. A scout activity weekend was hosted in September 1992 for 130 boys from the Sevenoaks area, and this continued for several years. A festival of rugby for boys and girls aged 8 to 13 was hosted in April 1995, and a football day was run by Charlton Athletic FC in May 1995. The Duke of Edinburgh Award scheme used the Stake Farm grounds and house for activity weekends.

Parental involvement

Bonfire nights continued to be organised by a group of parents, helped by the bonfire-building skills of Mr Cochrane. In 1986, over 650 people attended, tempted perhaps by the fact that for the first time there was a bar; over £400 was raised. In 1992, children and parents from Solefield School were invited to participate, an arrangement which continued for about seven years until the combined numbers became too large. Bonfire night on 4 November 1994 was

1994 guy competition for bonfire night.

The early fêtes grew into a day of family activities with an early evening barbecue and barn dance.

the last one organised by the initiators from 1983, parents **Mr Rupert Creed** and **Mr Barry Richardson**.

A family day was held on 1 July 1989 and included music from the school steel band run by **Mr Duncan Dwinell** who taught brass at the school (his wife **Mrs Elizabeth Dwinell** still teaches the violin with great success), stalls run by each class, a fathers' cricket match, mothers' rounders, an early evening barbeque, and a barn dance. That July was particularly exhausting for pupils, staff, and parents. After the family day, a junior concert, a swimming gala, a triathlon, a senior concert, the end-of-term service and sports day all followed within a fortnight. These continued to be successful events. In 1994, over £4,000 was raised for school funds, which went towards an adventure playground for the middle school and the purchase of video recorders.

The school was now operating a resources fund with parents' involvement. The Christmas bazaar paid for the refurbishment of the junior library with new shelving and curtains; the money raised by the school dance in the spring term went towards improving the tennis surrounds and purchasing music stands, while the money raised in the summer term was for the senior library and updating computer equipment. In the two years from 1989, £10,000 was raised through parental initiatives. The junior school with three computers, the senior school with networked BBC computers, the library, the science room, and the junior school reference room all benefitted. Mr Oatley decided to set up a Friends of Sevenoaks Prep Committee and send out a questionnaire (the previous one was 12 years before). A ball to celebrate 25 years at Godden Green was held at Somerhill in summer 1993.

The Old Boy Network, a 1960s rock and roll band, was formed of current and former parents of The Prep, **Mr Rob Wickenden** (bass guitar and vocals), **Mr Allen Mills** (drums), **Mr Chris Bailey** (lead guitar, backing vocals), **Mr Colin**

The Old Boy Network, a band of Prep parents performed at various local events.

Brunton (guitar and vocals), and **Mr Rob Pickering** (guitar and vocals). They played at several local venues in the early 1990s and were also a supporting act for groups such as *The Searchers* and *Gerry and the Pacemakers* at The Stag Theatre in Sevenoaks. The band supported several charities and raised a considerable amount of money over the years, also producing CDs of their music for sale. They played at some of The Prep's events and the school also benefitted financially from some of their charitable gigs.

The structure of the Friends of Sevenoaks Prep and its function was defined in the October and December 1994 newsletters to parents, noting that it had been set up to bridge the gap between Mr Oatley and the form co-ordinators (FCs). There were three functions set out: to ensure that each term's events were included in the school diary; to be a forum for Mr Oatley to be advised of any items arising from the social events committee (SEC) meetings for his attention; and to be a forum for Mr Oatley to advise of his plans for the school which were relevant to be passed to the FCs and therefore the parents. The role of the SEC was to remain that of organising social events for the school, raising funds for the extras that parents would like to provide for the children, and as a forum for the FCs to be able to advise the Headmaster if they had any problems reported to them from the parents in their class.

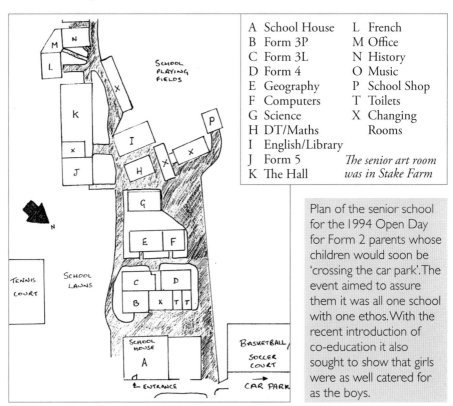

A School House	L French
B Form 3P	M Office
C Form 3L	N History
D Form 4	O Music
E Geography	P School Shop
F Computers	T Toilets
G Science	X Changing
H DT/Maths	Rooms
I English/Library	
J Form 5	*The senior art room*
K The Hall	*was in Stake Farm*

Plan of the senior school for the 1994 Open Day for Form 2 parents whose children would soon be 'crossing the car park'. The event aimed to assure them it was all one school with one ethos. With the recent introduction of co-education it also sought to show that girls were as well catered for as the boys.

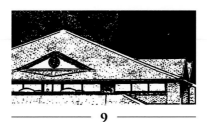

9

Continuity, Co-education and Community (1995-2005)

When Richard Brown, who had left The Prep in 1984 to go to Sevenoaks School, came back for a year in 1995-96 to teach Latin and games, he found that the only familiar faces in the senior school were Mr and Mrs Oatley, Mrs Mary Shefford, and the part-time Mr John Pegg. Mr Oatley, however, had been recruiting carefully and, by 1995, had brought in about a dozen staff who would stay at the school for at least ten years[11], plus three who stayed for at least 24 years[12] and four who were still at the school in 2018.[13] Mr Oatley also recruited wisely four long-serving support staff.[14] As the school entered the new century, Mr Oatley's vision for the school he had taken over more than 20 years before was being realised: to create a family ethos of co-operation and mutual assistance between boys, parents and staff; to lead by example; to develop the potential that is in every child; and to maintain links with local organisations while creating new ones. The first girl, Hannah Bramall, to go right through the school left in 2000. Music and drama continued to excel. In 1998, the school took over The Stag Theatre in Sevenoaks for a spectacular, 'Curtain Up', featuring a senior and a junior play, in which all the pupils and staff took part. In

11 Mrs Sue Bullock, Mrs Janet Wilkes, Mme Jacqueline Homer, Mrs Angela Pickering, Mrs Sue Lewis, Mrs Christine Jeffers, Mrs Cheryl Ruprecht, Mrs Jackie Low, Mrs Penny Spencer-Allen, Mr Tom Bowen, Mrs Sue Ives, Mr Philip Oldroyd, Mrs Gail Leathers and Mrs Linda Underwood.
12 Mrs Marjorie Shea, Mr Peter Ratcliffe and Mrs Lyn Witton.
13 Miss Sally Perks, Mr Donald Smith, Mrs Alison Bellwood and Mrs Alyson Thomas.
14 Mr Michael Barnard, Mr David Cochrane and Mr Graham Taylor.

2000, there was a reunion for alumni, former parents and staff, and friends. Some 1,400 people were contacted and over 600 came on the day. In 1999, planning permission had been granted for a permanent building – a new hall for sport, drama, music, and assemblies – and fund raising by the school with parental support began in earnest. Mr Oatley set out in 2000 on his first overseas fund-raising cycle ride and this – plus a series of events organised by the parents, culminating in a Millennium ball – raised some £30,000 in 1999-2000 alone. The new school hall was opened in October 2001 by Graham Taylor, who had managed the England and Watford FC football teams. The number of pupils had increased by more than 100 over the ten years to 2005, and the aim of having two classes in each year group through the school was almost achieved. This increase was mostly accounted for by the number of girls increasing from 36 in 1995 to 127 in 2005. In 2004, Mr Oatley announced that he would be retiring in July 2005 and that the new Headmaster would be Mrs Oatley's son, Mr Philip Oldroyd, who had been a pupil at the school in the 1980s and had been teaching at The Prep since 1994. It was the end of an era.

Head and staff

In July 1996, **Mrs Mary Shefford** retired. She started teaching at The Prep in 1969, soon after the school moved to Godden Green, but even before that she was helping with the school plays. Her two sons are alumni, so her association goes back even further. She was in charge of teaching music throughout the school until **Mrs Sue Ives**, another parent whose son **William** was at the school, came in 1993 to take the junior classes as Stake Farm expanded. On Mrs Shefford's retirement, Mrs Ives taught senior music as well. Mrs Shefford led the choir, organised the orchestra, ran a dance club, gave individual piano lessons and inspired hundreds of boys and girls to take up music and to continue enjoying it throughout their lives. As **Robert Agnew**, who was at the school in the 1980s,

Mrs Shefford taking an orchestra rehearsal in her last year at The Prep, 1995.

Senior school staff 1997   *gap year student
standing Mr J. Baines, Mr P. Oldroyd, Mr E. Oatley, Mr T. Dawson*, Mrs J. Oatley,
Mr B. Duncan*, Mrs W. Woolf, Mme J. Homer, Mr T. Bowen, Mr D. Smith, Mr P. Ratcliffe.
seated Mr M. Barnard, Miss L. Duncan, Mrs J. Wilkes, Mrs J. Low, Mrs S. Lewis.

remarked: 'her skill at pulling together a rabble of boys to create the sweetest angelic choir was quite remarkable'. Her other passions were drama and dance. She produced over 20 school plays with an average cast of 30 to 40 children.

She continued tap dancing lessons until she achieved her gold medal, and then passed on her expertise, not only to children but also to the mums who came to her evening tap dancing classes. Although she officially retired at the end of the summer term of 1996, she continued to take her tap dancing classes and be involved in drama. Her enthusiasm for music and drama was infectious and she never gave up on any child. She constantly encouraged them and gave up so much of her time to extract the best from everybody, even other members of staff – her Christmas pantomimes, which she wrote and produced, were brilliant, with all the staff who took part trying their hardest to make fools of themselves, much to the delight of all the children. There were other things – the Three Arts Festival, performing songs and dance routines for the elderly, training groups of boys in Morris dancing that was performed at The Stag Theatre, the drama club and folk dancing, as well as her sewing class 'Sew What' where she encouraged the boys to sew with great success. An ode was written to her when she left, which is in Appendix 4.

Mrs Janet Wilkes, the school's wonderful art teacher, decided to retire as a full-time teacher at the end of the 1997 summer term. A colourful personality in all senses of the word, with a wicked sense of humour, she was a tremendous source of inspiration to all the children she had taught over more than ten years.

Even children who were not naturally gifted enjoyed her lessons and produced some fine work. On Mrs Wilkes' retirement, **Mr Alan Chant** took on the senior art teaching with the help of **Mrs Sarah Harris** until 2000, when Mrs Harris and her family (her three boys **Oliver**, **Tim** and **Greg** were all at the school) moved to America for a few years. In 2001, **Mrs Jacquie Baldwin,** a teacher of both P.E. and art took over the department to enable Mr Chant to focus on the growing importance of IT in the school. Mrs Wilkes continued to help with the school's major artistic venture, notably designing, with **Mrs Lyn Witton**, the mosaic in the entrance to the sports hall which was opened in 2001.

In 1998, **Mr Michael Barnard**, who had been Bursar since 1984, retired. He had joined on an ad hoc basis to give **Mr Edward Oatley** some help with the administration but soon became full-time Bursar. He was very fond of his nickname, Mr B, by which he was known throughout the school by pupils and staff. Nothing had ever been too much trouble for him and very soon he became essential to the running of the school, a friend to all, and always willing to give time to any problem the children, parents, or staff may have. When he took on the role, he hadn't realised that one of his duties was to be Father Christmas at the school bazaar, one which he fulfilled for many years. Each November, all normal work ceased as his office and telephone were taken over by a group of mothers – the bazaar organising committee. Despite protesting that someone more responsible, perhaps, should be coerced – someone with a greater affinity for children, and less propensity to belt them round the ear when the elastic fixed beard was hauled six inches off their face, and then let go with the most satisfying results (as far as the child was concerned) – he was always asked to be Santa.

The senior boys always expected him to be Santa and would have been hurt if their pre-bazaar remarks of 'Getting the beard ready, Sir?' and 'Been practising your ho, ho, hos, Mr B.?' were found to have no value. Despite the chaos of the days leading up to the bazaar – with the realisation that nobody had arranged floats for the stalls or ordered the Christmas tree, that the Headmaster had lent the school bus to the scouts when it was needed to collect the tombola and other equipment, and that the piano teacher, who always had the hall for lessons on a Friday, hadn't been told about the event and was OUT TO CAUSE TROUBLE – everything worked out

Dressed for his annual ordeal as the man in red aka Mr B the Bursar.

in the end. Mr Barnard always found his wellingtons and his costume, a bit more tattered than last year and with the Velcro in its death throes and the beard a bit sparser, and the tree always was miraculously put up and decorated. The wide-eyed children came to see Santa with different degrees of confidence or lack thereof, some with cheekiness, some with shyness, occasionally some hysterical, some tongue tied, some giggling, but Mr Barnard always got through the ordeal, wondering if it was all worthwhile–which, of course, it was.

Earlier in 1998, a rumour had it that it was to be his 70th birthday in June but no one could believe it–he put his youthful appearance and attitude down to The Prep, Sunday tennis, and having to cope with the Headmaster for so long. Although he retired, he stayed involved with the school, specifically offering to organise an old boys' and girls' association, putting as much time as possible into completing and sorting the records. Nobody was better qualified to take on such an important job and the success of the 2000 reunion two years later was very much down to his hard work. His replacement was **Mr George Brand**, who joined the school in 1998 as a post-retirement position after a 40-year career elsewhere. When he started, he had no idea that he would stay 12 years and that The Prep would become such a defining part of his life and one of which he would be truly proud.

Mrs Barbara Adams, who had started the Little Oaks Club in 1992, left at the end of the 1998 summer term. The club had been a hit with the little ones from the word go, thanks to her wonderful way with children and her ability to inspire them to produce some superb and artistic work at the end of the school day, to mix the ages admirably, and to give them lots of structured entertainment. **Mrs Cheryl Ruprecht** also left in 1998, having taught in the Kindergarten for 15 years. She was a mum who moved into teaching and was always sympathetic to the needs of the very young children, encouraging and stimulating them with great care and affection. Another mum turned Kindergarten teacher who left in the same year was **Mrs Jane Murphy.** The school was saddened to hear that she died a year or two later. She had been a much loved member of the team. **Mrs Sue Lewis** left in 1999, having been a highly respected Form 3 teacher. She was active in both drama and music and her Form 3 plays were always a highlight for the children each year.

Mrs Barbara Adams on her last day with the Little Oaks Club.

KG with Mrs Lloyd, Mrs Ruprecht, Mrs Murphy, Mrs Spencer-Allen and Mrs Thomas circa 1995 – with visiting helicopter!

Mrs Sue Bullock retired in 2002 after nearly 20 years at the school. She had been an integral part of the Pre-Prep and a great support to **Mrs Marjorie Shea**. She showed outstanding professionalism and dedication to teaching, enriching the lives of many children in many different ways, bringing education to each individual, no matter what their educational needs. She was always most concerned about the personal needs of children, once saying 'Are we doing enough to serve the emotional needs of the children?' She would never be hurried: 'all in good time' was one of her many sayings; 'keeping the options open' and 'all part of life's rich tapestry' were others. She kept the other teachers' feet firmly on the ground and, never raising her voice, stayed reliably calm, cool and collected. Many a young teacher would remark, 'I wish I could be like Sue'.

Mr Brian Morrow decided to emigrate to Australia with his wife **Michelle** and children **Lauren** and **Michael**, who were pupils at The Prep, in 2002. Originally from South Africa, he had made his mark at The Prep, teaching senior history and geography, leading memorable Form 8 field trips to Bude, and achieving much success on the sports field with the teams he coached.

In 1995, when Mr and Mrs Heal retired from the Pre-Prep, **Mrs Chris Mason**, mother of **Ben** and **Jack**, took over as cook for the Pre-Prep. Mrs Mason's ebullient personality made her a natural with pupils and staff and she did so much more than just cook the lunches and help with match teas. She was always willing to help out in any way when needed.

Mr Nik Pears, who was later to be Head of the Pre-Prep, remembered with great fondness his initial interview in 2000. Having spent his summers as a student, working as a housemaster at Sevenoaks School looking after language school students, he had grown to love the area. Seeing a job advertisement in the Times Educational Supplement for a Form 3 teacher at The Prep, it all seemed perfect. He wasn't quite prepared for what would take place. He was greeted by Mr Oatley, who didn't really look like a typical Headmaster, dressed as he was in shorts and a singlet. The interview was basically a chat in the lounge, upstairs in the main school building. Mr Oatley didn't appear to have a desk, preferring to do everything standing up. Mr Pears was shown around the school, which at this stage was almost entirely made up of temporary classrooms, although the foundations for the new sports hall were underway. He was introduced to various teachers, including a young maths teacher called **Mr Philip Oldroyd**, who suggested to the Headmaster that he should sign up the applicant on the spot!

Mr Pears felt that it was rather a strange experience and recalled his then fiancé, **Emma** (who later taught music at the school), calling him to see how it had gone. He remembered sitting in the car park saying that it was all a bit quirky, wasn't what he was expecting, but there was something brilliant about it. Something intangible. At the time he couldn't quite put his finger on it, but he loved the school, the people that he met and really hoped he would be offered the job. Subsequently, he took up the post as Form 3 class teacher in September 2000 – not simply starting a new job, but becoming part of The Prep family, a most wonderful group of pupils, staff, and parents – he loved every minute of it.

2001 saw **Mr Luke Harrison** join the staff at The Prep. He had been at the school in the 1980s and, when he left Tonbridge, came back as a gap year student. He had visited the school in 2000 for the Millennium celebrations, which were held in the Pre-Prep as the new hall was being built on the senior side. Mr Oatley took him over to see the hall and said, 'I have a proposal for you'. He stood Mr Harrison in front of the shell of the hall and said, 'This is the theatre, how would you like to join the school to teach drama and English?' At the time Mr Harrison said 'no' as he was enjoying teaching A-level English and theatre studies at Kingston Grammar School. Eventually he was won round by Mr Oatley, but failed to understand that although Mr Oatley had sold him the idea of a theatre, he had also sold the hall to someone else as a sports hall and someone else as a music and dance studio! On his return to the school, he found that Mr Oatley hadn't changed a bit; he was still encouraging and supportive.

Mr Oatley's retirement
In July 2004, Mr Oatley had written to the parents telling them that he was going to retire at the end of the 2004-05 academic year and that Mr Oldroyd was to become Headmaster. In July 2005, there was a gathering to celebrate Mr Oatley's 28 years as Headmaster and to wish him and Janet well in their 'retirement'. Mr Barnard, who had worked with the Oatleys for 14 years from 1984 to 1998, spoke to the well-wishers. Extracts from what he said include:

'…The brew, however, is only as good as the man who prepares it, and men of the necessary calibre are few and far between. Edward is certainly one of these,

2015 The Oatleys' retirement celebration *left* Mr Oldroyd with Mrs and Mr Oatley enjoying the formalities.   *right* Mrs Oatley Senior chatting with Mrs Niki Oldroyd and Claire Oatley, Mrs Oatley's granddaughter.

and regrettably when he popped out of the furnace, the mould was broken, and can never be repaired or copied. Perhaps the most notable of Edward's gifts is his conviction that to lead from the front, both by example and by physical presence, is the only way that such leadership can be achieved. Not for him the delegation to subordinates given from behind a desk, and in Edward's case, what desk?'

'…His concern for the family, not just the child, is certainly paramount…this overall concern pervades every aspect of the school's life, treating pupils, parents, staff, and indeed the whole outside world, as one homogenous whole.'

'…You have taught [our children] to compete, in moderation, and to be proud, but not too proud, of success. They have learnt that the mastery of the 3Rs is not the be-all and end-all of education – but to do one's best in the classroom, on the sport's field and in the 101 other activities which are forever available at The Prep – that is an achievement. You have taught them respect for their friends and, perhaps above all, to wear adults comfortably, not as figures of perpetual authority but as companions on their way through the life of the school.'

Mr Barnard then added, referring to **Mrs Janet Oatley**:

'A Headmaster's wife can be many things, from being just a wife, uninvolved in any way in the affairs of the school, to that of someone deeply committed, almost to the point of total immersion. Such a one is Janet…Edward could not possibly have achieved what he has without Janet by his side, and frequently, it must be said, slightly in front!'

An editorial in *The Prep Post* that year said, 'School shop, match teas, parents' evenings, ski trips, class trips, chaperone, secretary, gardener, ambassador, stage manager, bus driver, nurse… the list goes on and on but would certainly be incomplete without *The Prep Post*. Janet has been central to the production of the school magazine for many years – coaxing material out of busy teachers, chasing photographs and articles, editing, censoring(!), deciphering and typing – and the worst job of all, proofreading, again and again – but always with her characteristic good humour and calm. *The Prep Post* says a huge, warm, heartfelt 'thank you', and looks forward to her help on the new annual *Prep Post* planned for next year – please!'

Mr Harrison, later to be Headmaster, recalled that the Oatleys were a tremendous, dynamic pairing and Mrs managed to rein in Mr beautifully. Her people skills are second to none, she was hugely popular with the parents, and she brought a huge amount to the school. Their marriage really strengthened the family bond of The Prep.

Mr Oatley's mother was present at the occasion for his retirement, and he acknowledged her support in his early days at The Prep. Reunions and bouncy castles, football and friends all took part in the celebration.

In an article in *The Sevenoaks Chronicle* on 1 February 2014, **Mr Bob Ogley** in his Chronicler column gave a history of the school (based pretty much on what is presently on the website) and reported that a meeting was to be held on Friday 7 March 2014, to which were invited past and present pupils, parents, and staff to hear about the future building plans. He quoted the then Headmaster (and former pupil of Mr Oatley) Mr Harrison, about Mr Oatley: 'He came to Sevenoaks Prep as Headmaster in 1978, where he worked for a year in tandem with Ken Ely. From the outset, it was clear that Edward was a dynamic, caring teacher with a huge passion for the education of the whole person. Academic success was always important, but so was the development of character, the role of family, the importance of trust and teamwork, and the success of Watford Football Club. Edward is closely involved with the Sevenoaks community on various bodies but is especially renowned for his charity cycle rides throughout the world which have raised thousands of pounds.'

Mr Oatley did not opt for an easy retirement. In 1989, while he was still Headmaster of The Prep, the founder of Steephill School, a small co-ed prep school for children up to age 11 in Fawkham, died and a group of the then parents of pupils asked him for help in continuing the school. He became, and still is, Chairman of the Governors. Immediately on his retirement he became Chairman of the Governors of The Prep, and changed the company which owned the school into a charity. He was Chairman for three years, is still a Governor and, as anyone who knows the school knows, is still, with his wife Janet, very much involved in its activities. He became a Governor at St John's Primary school in Sevenoaks in 2006; continues to help run the Three Arts Festival as Vice-Chairman, having been on the committee since 1980; and spent 20 years from 1996 to 2016 on Seal Parish Council.

He was involved with the Sevenoaks Triathlon from its beginning and still takes part every year. He had always encouraged children and parents to take part in charity bike rides and in 2000 he took part in his first overseas charity ride, in Egypt, to raise money for Mencap and the new hall building fund. Since then he has completed 10 others: the Great Wall of China, Brazil, Estonia/Russia, Rajasthan (India), Ecuador, North Vietnam, Death Valley California, South Africa, Panama/ Costa Rica/Nicaragua, and, most recently in 2018, South Vietnam/Cambodia, raising about £100,000 for various charities, both national and local, including the £12,000 raised in 2000 for the school hall. A lifetime of devotion to Watford FC continues, and he and Janet are now season ticket holders at Vicarage Road. In 2006, he was honoured to be awarded the MBE for services to education and the community of Kent and in 2017, the Sevenoaks District Council decided to present him with their Lifetime Achievement Award for his work on the Sevenoaks Sports Council and other voluntary organisations.

Press photo with Alex Perry *(Head Boy)*, Alexandra Minto, Toby May *(Form 6)* and Hannah Bramall *(Head Girl)* before Mr Oatley's charity Nile Bike Ride, 2000.

Dominic Low had always been grateful to Mr Oatley for giving him the chance in the 1990s, when he was at Tonbridge and university, of earning some cash and gaining valuable experience and responsibility at an early age. When he had children of his own, he and his wife sent them to The Prep. He wrote recently, 'I knew why Mr Oatley let me work at the school in so many roles, he trusted me and he knew I would do my best within my ability because he had educated me. He knew I would try my hardest. He created an ethos at The Prep which lasts today and subsequent Headmasters, Mr Oldroyd and Mr Harrison, have successfully carried forward that ethos and of course developed it further and tuned it with their own styles. Mr Oatley was interested in every single child who walked into the school, some very bright and sporty, some less so. Some had learning difficulties or even health problems. He saw every child as an equal. He encouraged each child to do the very best they can within their means. It worked. His success rate was incredible.

'Mr Oatley gave people a chance. He believed they could succeed, even with odds stacked against them. He created a totally open school environment where they discovered the ability to succeed. He provided the support network around them and they did the rest – buoyed by the confidence he gave them. The school was never shut – you could walk in and see him for advice on everything (which I often did) and he would be there to talk to you, to guide you. You could have walked straight through the unlocked front door on Christmas Day and he would probably have invited you to join the family for Christmas lunch!'

Dominic stayed in touch with both Mr and Mrs Oatley. He noted that the latter's role at The Prep should never be underestimated: 'Mr Oatley might have been the face of the school, but Mrs Oatley was the strength and support behind him.' So, when it came for him and his wife Joanna to choose a school for their daughter and son – **Megan** and **Oliver** – there was never a question. They never considered anywhere else and, of course, now they took girls. Dominic concluded, 'we didn't look around a single other school. There was no need. The Prep had served me well and I trusted it to do the same for my children'.

Inspectors' reports

The academic year 1996-97 got off to a controversial start when Mr Oatley was rung up by someone from the IAPS to warn him that *The Sevenoaks Chronicle* was going to publish a report headed, 'School criticised for unqualified staff' in their 26 September edition, together with a provocative editorial. The IAPS inspection, from which the paper had selectively taken extracts, had taken place some 15 months earlier in the summer of 1995. Many of the adverse points arising from the IAPS report were already being addressed at the time and most of the others were dealt with within a few months. The main point highlighted by the paper, that the parents had a right to know that unqualified staff were employed, was largely irrelevant, as the parents had always been aware that the school employed a relatively small number of experienced teachers, university graduates, and gap year students who did not have a formal teaching qualification.

Mr Oatley immediately wrote to the parents, emphasising that the IAPS recommendations had all been dealt with and noting that the Chronicle had declined his invitation for them to visit the school and see what actually went on there. He confirmed that practically every member of staff had been previously known to him personally and that most of the others had been recommended by existing staff. At the time of the publication of the newspaper's article, three members of the senior school staff, all university graduates, were undertaking or about to undertake their PGCE (Postgraduate Certificate in Education) course and every member of the Pre-Prep had a qualification relevant to the age group of the children they taught.

Mr Oatley had overwhelming support from the parents, many of whom wrote to the Chronicle extolling the virtues of the school, and from the IAPS. He also had support from Sevenoaks and Tonbridge schools, both of which had, in the past, employed teachers without formal teaching qualifications.

Fabric

During the summer holidays of 1995, portakabins to house Forms 4 and 5 and the art/DT and music rooms were brought in. The music room became the computer room and, 18 months later, **Mme Jacqueline Homer** and Mr Oldroyd moved into new premises for French and maths. The old French room became the library and the old maths room was remodelled as a much-improved school shop – there was even a carpet on the floor! The old school shop went to Stonepitts Farm, home of the **Clews** family, to become their strawberry shop. Previously, they had had the school's first ever hall, which they converted into stables. New French and maths classrooms arrived in the 1997 Easter holidays and were immediately useable, thanks to all the hard work of **Mr Graham Taylor**, the maintenance manager, and **Mr David Cochrane**, who had battled away with the foundations in the most appalling wet February half term – up to their waists in mud, sometimes.

In 1999, planning permission was finally granted for new permanent buildings and, in particular, the new brick-built hall, which was planned to provide a space for drama, music, and indoor sports as well as being an assembly hall. A demolition dance was announced for the end of term at which *The Old Boy Network* was to play, and shortly afterwards the school hall, which had been in the grounds since 1980, was demolished in April 2000 by a team led by **Mr Stroud** and **Mr Hart** supported by a number of staff and parents. Mr Taylor, who was supervising matters, was most impressed by their strength. Preparations for the new hall started the following month. The parents raised money for equipment for sports, music, drama, and dance and Mr Oatley took part in the Nile Bike Ride in February 2000 in aid of Mencap and the school hall fund. His diary of the ride (together with the others he took part in, in subsequent years) is included on the Memories CD.

Although the most important planning permission had been obtained, the application for a changing room block/pavilion was refused. It was therefore decided that the Stake Farm squash court should be turned into a two-storey changing room facility.

The construction of the new hall was the first major development at the school since the acquisition of Stake Farm, and was run by the school itself with **Mr Keith Robinson**, the school's accountant, Mr Brand, the Bursar, and the school's maintenance manager, Mr Taylor, overseeing and formulating the whole project. It was felt that, on completion, a special occasion to formally open the new hall was required. Mr Oatley, was, and remains, an avid football fan and still holds a season ticket at Watford FC where he has been a supporter since he was a boy. As a fan, he was a great admirer of the football manager **Graham Taylor**

above A typical demolition squad during the Oatley years.

left A Form 7 DT class with Mr Bowen in its new portakabin home in 1995. The view through the window was to change dramatically within a few years.

below The new hall, 2001.

left The choir, conducted by Mrs Ives, was a highlight of the hall opening ceremony.
right Mr Oatley pictured with both Graham Taylors!

who, by 2000, had had two spells of managing Watford, as well as having been manager of England between 1990 and 1993. Such was Mr Oatley's respect for him that it was often his practice to use the manager's Watford match programme notes as a basis for his morning school assembly addresses to the children.

Mr Brand wrote to Graham Taylor's P.A. to ask if the football legend would come to The Prep and formally open the hall on 10 October 2001, emphasising Mr Oatley's respect and admiration for Graham Taylor and his habit of plagiarising match programme notes for the guidance of the pupils. Suffice it to say Graham Taylor very kindly agreed to come down with his wife from his home near Watford and perform the opening ceremony. All these arrangements were kept a very close secret between Mr Brand, The Prep's Mr Taylor, and Mrs Oatley, who managed to keep her husband in the dark – something she had, over the years, raised to an art form.

Came the day and, with all preparations set, Graham Taylor duly arrived at the front of the school and was ushered into the school house whilst Mr Brand went to find Mr Oatley who, as ever, was to be found in the new hall attending to final details and arranging chairs – a favourite occupation. Mr Brand managed to get him away, telling him that 'Graham Taylor' needed to see him straight away, secure in the knowledge that he would naturally think Mr Brand was referring to the school's maintenance manager.

The secret held until Mr Oatley was ushered into the school house and came face to face with one of his idols, who had so kindly come along to meet him and declare the sports hall open. True to his reputation, Graham Taylor gave a superb address to the whole school and duly cut a ribbon, helped by 4-year-old **Jake Stanford**, which released a host of balloons in the school colours. Mr Oatley said

above Oliver Budd, the mosaic artist, Mrs Witton and Mrs Wilkes with the completed mosaic and *(below)* work in progress by a Pre-Prep and parent group, 2001.

that Graham Taylor 'stands up for all I believe in – teamwork, the youth of today, treating people correctly, and that "it's only a game"'.

The mosaic in the entrance to the sports hall was designed by Mrs Wilkes and Mrs Witton. It is a spectacular image, 4 metres by 1½ metres, in the entrance lobby and still stimulates endless talking points. An experienced mosaic artist, **Oliver Budd**, helped with the design, which includes school activities as well as featuring local architecture and landscapes. It was a whole school project with every child, parent, and teacher able to lay pieces, taking two days to put together and a further two to grout.

Other guests at the opening included **John Walker** from the Sevenoaks Sports Council and father of alumnus and Olympic medal winning sailor **Ian Walker**, and **Brian Kinsey**, an ex-professional footballer who had captained Charlton Athletic FC, playing 377 times for them between 1955 and 1971, and who became Sports Development Officer for the Sevenoaks district. In the 1980s he worked with Mr Oatley in organising local sports events for children; he later helped with football coaching at The Prep for three years, up to 2006. The school choir excelled itself with renditions of *One More Step Along the Road, Thank You Lord* (by the Pre-Prep), *The Rhythm of Life*, and finally *Happy Birthday to You*, as the day the hall opened was also Mr Oatley's birthday.

Happy Birthday to You was repeated later in the term when Mrs Oatley was certainly stunned by a surprise assembly involving the whole school to celebrate a significant milestone birthday, along with *Reeling and Rocking in Rhythm*. A story *Well Done Little Bear* read by **James Restall** reduced Mrs Oatley to tears on her special birthday and this was followed by the giving of presents from all the classes and the cutting of an enormous cake, cooked by Mr Oatley, in the shape of a tennis racket.

More building took place in the early years of the 21st century, with numbers reaching nearly 400 pupils. The new hall was followed by a new classroom block for Forms 3, 4, and 5.

The much-loved oak tree in the middle of the playing fields had to be felled in 2004; it was dying and the danger of falling branches made it unsafe. A set of benches, funded by the 2004 leavers, was made by **Mr Peter Gates-Fleming** and Mr Taylor using cast iron metal legs painted in the school colours. They have been positioned around the massive stump and provide welcome seating during matches and sports meetings.

Academic

The long tradition of sound, friendly teaching and learning remained the basis for the contemporary curriculum for the 320 pupils, whose ages ranged from 2½ to 13. All pupils between 4 and 7 could, if they wished, enjoy the Little Oaks Club, and all the older pupils could stay on at school to do supervised prep and society activities.

Six boys from the 1995's Form 6, **Stuart Cook, Oliver Everden, James O'Gorman, Alex Pay, Paul Kiley**, and **Simon Scotting**, had their poems accepted for publication in *All Aboard For Kent*, which was a collection of poems submitted by children from primary schools throughout the county.

In early 1997, each pupil in Forms 5 to 8 was given their own diary, open to their parents and their form teacher, to help them organise their own lives and to give their parents as much notice as possible of any matches, rehearsals, or the school activities in which they were involved, and the homework they had been set each evening. The diaries could also be used as a means of communication by the parents if they had a message for the form teacher.

Gabby Brunton left to go to Walthamstow Hall from Form 6 in July 1997. She was the first girl to have been with the school from the Kindergarten (where she won a form prize in 1990-91) all the way to Form 6, and on the way was one of the five girls who started in Form 1 when the school became co-educational. The other girls left before reaching Form 6 but the Brunton family stuck with the school, her sister **Danielle** following in Gabby's footsteps.

For the academic year 1998-99, The Prep took part in a teacher exchange organised through the Central Bureau for Educational Visits & Exchanges. **Miss Lauren Duncan**, the Form 3 teacher, spent the year at St Paul School in Westerville, Ohio, while **Miss Colby English**, a 30-year-old teacher of history and English to 9 and 10-year-olds and who had been a pupil at St Paul, came to The Prep for the year. Although the age range of the St Paul pupils was similar to The Prep's, it had about 800 boys and girls in classes which averaged 35 (The Prep

Mrs Lewis and Form 3 with Miss English *(right)* just before her return to the U.S.A. in 1999 after her year at The Prep as part of a teacher exchange programme.

at that time had about 300 pupils and the average class size was 16) and was a Catholic parish-centred school, so quite different from The Prep. According to *The Prep Post*, the exchange proved to be a great success for both participants and Colby has fond memories of the kindness and helpfulness shown to her by everyone at The Prep. One of her earliest memories was being asked at the beginning of the year, 'Why is your name English if you're an American?' She told the children, 'You may call me Miss America'. She was especially proud of teaching her Form 3E students to recite the American Presidents in order. Colby has continued to come to England with her mother every two or three years to meet up with her Prep friends and see more of Europe.

The new library was officially opened on 25 June 2004: a new room, new computers, hundreds of new books, and many, many hours of work by Mrs Biggs, **Mrs Bell** and an army of volunteers. The library was opened by the author **Neil Arksley** (his books include *Playing on the Edge*, *Result*, and *MacB*) who, afterwards, gave a lively talk and signed some of his books.

The Pre-Prep
By the mid-1990s, the numbers in the Pre-Prep were growing and it became possible to have two classes in each year group. In 1998, **Miss Anne Richardson** took over the older Kindergarten class from Mrs Ruprecht, conveniently allowing it to continue as KGR – classes in the same year were distinguished by having the first letter of the teacher's surname attached. A number of long-serving teachers many of whom are still at the Pre-Prep came during this period. **Mrs Gail Leathers** had joined in 1995 to teach one Reception class while Mrs Witton taught the other. **Miss Marina Grayston** taught a Form 1 class from 1992 to 1998 and then returned as **Mrs Routledge** in 2010 as a Reception

teacher, along with her two daughters, **Olivia** and **Sophia**. **Miss Karen Bleby** came in 1998 to take one of the Form 2 classes, became **Mrs Clark** in 2001 and then mother of **Ben** and **Abbie**. She now works as a teaching assistant but covers for class teachers if needed. **Miss Lindsey Leman** arrived in 2000 as a Reception teacher, changed to **Mrs Morris** on marrying and since returning from maternity leave with **Rosina** and **Franklin**, has been the learning support co-ordinator. In the same year, **Mrs Jane Riding** started as one-on-one support for a child with learning difficulties and stayed on after he left. **Miss Sarah Rudd** joined in 2002 as a Form 1 teacher and still returns, as **Mrs Andrews**, for emergency cover. When Miss Rudd stopped teaching full-time her mother, **Mrs Sheena Rudd**, took over and taught in Form 1 until she retired in 2017. Finally, **Mrs Beverley Buttery**, mother of **Harry,** joined as a Form 2 teacher in 2003 and is now Deputy Head of the Pre-Prep.

As the years progressed, outside influences of National Curriculum, SATS, Early Years Vouchers and inspections began to impose upon the daily life of the Pre-Prep. Paperwork became a necessary evil and **Mrs Lucy Wigley** became the part-time administrative secretary to keep abreast of this new problem. Even more demands came with compliance to a deluge of new rules and regulations which then required more time, but Mrs Shea successfully guided the Pre-Prep through IAPS inspections and OFSTED with flying colours. A fire drill was a regular occurrence. Is it sausages for lunch, was the question on everybody's lips when an unscheduled alarm sounded – and the answer was usually an affirmative!

The teachers and children in the Pre-Prep took as much advantage as possible of the wonderful natural facilities available on the doorstep. They spent a great deal of time outdoors digging, making camps, climbing trees, and exploring the beautiful school grounds and beyond. Spring brought them walks through

Springtime in the Pre-Prep: daffodils and an early adventure playground, 1990s.

Godden Wood to be greeted by a sea of wood anemones, then later bluebells, where they sang 'in and out the dusty bluebells'. In summer, the playing fields were filled with daisies and they would make (with difficulty) daisy chains. They would roll down the grassy banks and run and run. Autumn would find them jumping in puddles and making rainbows with bubble mixture, collecting piles of leaves to jump in, and later making leaf prints. In winter, they would make bird cake and hang it on the trees outside the classroom window, and would watch birds feeding using the binoculars they made with cardboard tubes. Later, they would take windmills and ribbons outside to be blown by the wind.

When the Pre-Prep teachers arrived at Stake Farm, they were often greeted by charming little pied wagtails, or even – on occasion – a cuckoo, umpteen wild rabbits who lived in huge warrens beneath the classrooms, and pesky harvestman spiders who had to be removed from the cloakroom before the children arrived. Quite often there were May bug invasions and, during the school holidays, mice would polish off any dried pasta which had been used for craftwork and left around.

Mrs Penny Spencer-Allen began putting on puppet shows for the Kindergarten classes. Others wanted to watch, so eventually she did puppet shows for the Nursery and Reception classes and, occasionally, to the whole school. It was such a surprise when, coincidentally on her 50th birthday, there was a whole school staff meeting followed by dinner at Stake Farm. During the dinner, Mr and Mrs Oatley came into the hall with a large walking puppet and a huge bottle of champagne for her. Mrs Shea's speciality was shadow puppet shows. She did an excellent *Three Little Pigs and the Big Bad Wolf.* Another highlight for the Pre-Prep was when **Mrs Alyson Thomas** did her party piece, dressing up in her Welsh national costume and waving her Welsh flag on St. David's Day. To the delight of the children, she would recite that very, very long Welsh village name – Llanfairpwllgwyngyllgogerychwyrndrobwllllantysiliogogogoch! She would also bring loads of delicious Welsh cakes for the staff to enjoy, and still does.

In addition to the everyday life of the school, an annual programme of wonderful events was developed, including the harvest festival, nativity and Reception Christmas shows, carols in Seal Church, maypole dancing, summer shows, music concerts, themed weeks, picnics in the park, and many educational outings. Several 'once in a lifetime' celebrations including the Millennium, the Golden Jubilee, and a royal wedding were all memorable occasions. The summer performances were a wonderful culmination of the year that set their own challenge of staging. These were performed outdoors on the playground, where the audience could be maximised. The fire escape at the front or the climbing frame at the rear lent themselves to being backdrops. On windy days, the Bursar, Mr Barnard (a keen dramatist) was known to sit behind scenery, hanging on for dear life. On wet days, they had to postpone.

The **Cloke** family from Shorehill Farm in Knatts Valley were instrumental in bringing visitors of the woolly, fur, and feather kind to the Pre-Prep. In the early

top A sea of red, white and blue when the whole school came together for a 'street party' to celebrate the Queen's Golden Jubilee in 2002.

above Maypole dance forming the 'spider's web', 1997.

left Christopher Columbus, a Pre-Prep concert using the adventure playground, 1999.

days, health and safety was not much of
an issue, so this allowed many kinds of
animals to be in the classroom. Sheep,
lambs, calves, chickens, ducks, ponies
(left outside), and numerous dogs and
puppies were all welcome and well-
behaved visitors. The Clokes invited
classes over to their farm, which was
always a fabulous treat. **Mr Howard
Cloke** brought lambs and sheep to
the school on family fun days. The
idea was for the children to walk the
sheep on leads! Watching Mr Cloke
and his helpers retrieve children and
sheep from all over the place was really
hilarious. All the Clokes' lambs that
came to the classrooms over the years

Mr Cloke's farm corner on family day
with Pre-Prep visitors, circa 1996.

appeared to be called Shaun. Once Mr Cloke brought a live turkey to the school
but did not have a suitable container for it. He eventually managed to find one,
but it is unlikely that the turkey was very pleased, as it turned out to be an old
cooker! The children went on trips to see other animals such as reptiles, and once
went for a special treat to visit meerkats on the way to Biggin Hill. Unfortunately,
the meerkats totally refused to come out and they had to make do with frogs,
snakes, and insects.

The Pre-Prep pupils included two young Romanian boys who had once been
among the small toddlers left in a cot all day in a Romanian orphanage and had
been adopted by British parents. One of Mrs Spencer-Allen's favourite memories
was the wonderful and touching day when her little Romanian pupil stood up and
sang all by himself (in English) to the social workers who had come to see how he
was getting on at his first school. There was not a dry eye in the house.

Drama and music

The 1996 play *Bertie's Genius* was the last one produced by Mrs Shefford, who
retired soon after it was staged. At the end of the summer term in 1997, Mrs Ives
was asked by Mr Oatley to explore the possibility of putting on a show the
following year where the whole school – children, parents, and staff – could come
together under one roof, something that was not, then, practicable at The Prep.
Mrs Ives set to work talking to people and asking them to come up with ideas as
to what form the show should take, and after much discussion and endless cups of
coffee, the decision was made to hire The Stag Theatre in Sevenoaks for a double
bill at the end of March 1998. It was decided to call the show *Curtain Up*; the
Pre-Prep would first stage *The Little Red Hen*, which needed at least a farmyard of

above
The 1996
reprise of Mary
Shefford's
Bertie's Genius.

right
Mrs Alison
Knapp with
her troupe
of 'dancing
monkeys' for
Yanomamo
in *Curtain Up*
at The Stag
Theatre, 1998.

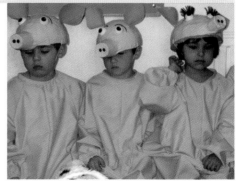

Year 2 characters, Kindergarten mice and
Reception class piglets waiting in rehearsal
for *The Little Red Hen*, the Pre-Prep
performance in *Curtain Up*, 1998.

animals, enough to involve every child, followed by the senior school's *Yanomamo*. Mrs Ives and Miss Duncan in the senior school and Mrs Shea in the Pre-Prep set the ball rolling, telling the children and teachers what was expected of them. Two parents, **Mrs Yvie Cloke** and **Mrs Pat McCann,** took on the massive task of organising costumes and makeup, and were soon overwhelmed by ideas and offers of help from all sides. Workshops were organised, materials ordered, and soon the most amazing array of costumes began to take shape. The children practised hard with the help of members of staff, and seemingly enjoyed themselves, although one child was heard to say, 'not another rehearsal!' (There were 82 after-school rehearsals.) The whole school took part, 281 children with the youngest aged 2 and the oldest 13, either on stage, doing makeup and costumes, or front of house.

There was an incident at one of the rehearsals at The Stag that no one who was there will ever forget. The choir was lining up at the top of the auditorium ready to come down to the stage, when one of the members accidentally leant on a red emergency glass box. This set off the fire alarm and the theatre's crew went completely berserk! The whole theatre plus all the cinemas had to be evacuated partway through the films. The fire engine arrived within three minutes of the alert to be met by bemused cinema customers outside and the children in the Plaza Suite, all having been accounted for within two minutes.

The Sevenoaks Chronicle published a review by Mr Barnard. The animals, sunbeams, and clouds of *The Little Red Hen* were, he said, beautifully costumed and wonderfully made up. The children sang and danced their hearts out. A highlight was when Mrs Thomas had the whole Kindergarten dressed as ducks, waddling around singing their song. Mr Barnard wrote that *Yanomamo*, a musical based on the lives and surroundings of a tribe of Indians in the Venezuelan jungle, was something different. From the impact of the first dance of the monkeys to the final number sung by the choir, people had to remind themselves that they were watching children, so accomplished were the energetic performers. It was a great achievement to produce a whole school play. Everyone had a part to play: crowd control backstage, teaching words, songs and movement. The staff, children, and parents all worked together to produce an outstanding, memorable occasion. A video of the performance was produced and 90 copies sold, while a special edition of *The Prep Post* was published in April 1998 that included some of the words, quotes from children, parents, and staff, lots of images, and Mr Barnard's review. In addition to creating a fabulous experience for all who took part, the school hoped to raise funds towards the building of the proposed new hall and in the end over £3,000 was contributed.

Because the hall had been demolished, there was no senior school play in the summer of 2000. Instead, two short comedies directed by **Mrs Jenny Whittaker**, *The Prince's Bride* and *The Two Brothers*, were performed in the temporary marquee which had been put up on the lawn. **James Ellis** was the lead performer in both plays with **Dominic Smith** as his brother in the second play.

Form 3 performing in the Millennium pageant in the marquee.

In the summer term of 2000, a Millennium pageant was performed by the Pre-Prep and Form 3. The highlight was probably the Nursery singing *Robin Hood*. It was amazing for 2 and 3-year-olds to be so accomplished. It also included performances from the Erpyngham Retinue, who give demonstrations to the public and schools on how life was during the period at the end of the 14th century. This was with a backdrop of a knights' campsite during the campaigns of the Hundred Years' War. During the demonstrations, examples of dance, arming-a-knight, and weapons skills, there were also practical examples of medieval cooking.

When Mr Harrison was being shown round the school at the reunion in July 2000 by Mr Oatley, he had been shown the foundations of the new school hall. 'It's not just a sports hall', Mr Oatley had said enthusiastically at the time, 'it's a theatre'. When he saw it next in September 2001 it had space, chairs, lots of coloured lines on the wooden floor and bars on the wall. It looked like a gym and Mr Harrison searched vainly for lighting, sound equipment, and staging. But Mr Oatley was true to his word, and by March 2002 everything needed for a theatre was in place. Mr Harrison's primary role when he came to teach at The Prep was to make drama an integral part of the school and Mr Oatley asked him to put on a spectacle to christen the new hall. It was decided to take two plays from C.S. Lewis' *The Chronicles of Narnia*, with the middle school performing *The Magician's Nephew* and the senior school *The Lion, the Witch and the Wardrobe*. The plays were performed over three nights with every pupil from Form 3 to Form 8 having a part. There were lots of ultraviolet lights and lots of pizazz. Mr Harrison had every pupil out at break time practising with wooden swords for the fight scenes, which Mr Oatley loved, but with every other member of staff looking very concerned.

With Mrs Cloke assisting Mr Harrison and mustering the help of the mums in the car park, 32 costumes were produced for the cast of *The Magician's Nephew*.

The Lion, the Witch and the Wardrobe (2002)

above In the art room with the hair and make-up team and then waiting calmly in the music-cum-green room before going on stage.

left In performance, the first drama production to be staged in the new hall.

Mr Barnard's review in *The Prep Post* gave credit to the volunteers: '…the production was quite brilliant, embellished by a variety of costumes produced by an army of parents, whose enthusiasm in some cases almost outweighed that of… the cast.' *The Lion, the Witch and the Wardrobe* had a cast of 54 children, with numerous others helping with the staging, refreshments, and front of house. Mr Barnard said that '…it would not be fair to single out any one particular portrayal for everyone involved was excellent.' He congratulated all the performers, those who helped behind the scenes and, of course, Mr Harrison. The maturity of the performers impressed and amazed the capacity audience on all three evenings. It was a wonderful first production for Mr Harrison and the first in the new hall.

The inaugural house drama competition was held in the summer term of 2002. Form 8 was given the responsibility of directing members of Forms 5, 6, and 7 so Mr Harrison could sit back. Rehearsals took place in the last three weeks of term, with the competition itself on 9 July with each house having a 20-minute slot to perform. Knole's play was *Rip Van Winkle*, Weald's *The Scarlet Pimpernel*, Vine's *Animal Farm* and Seal's *The Nun's Priest's Tale*. Mr Barnard adjudicated and was very impressed by the effort and imagination the pupils showed. He awarded the best cast to Vine and best direction to Knole, with 'Oscars' going to **Elliot Carter**, **Clare Hobern**, **Nick Berry**, and **Kathryn Dendias**.

Mr Harrison's adaptation of one of William Shakespeare's comedies, *A Midsummer Night's Karaoke (What a Dream!)*, was a great success. While sticking largely to the original plot, there were a number of innovations to make it more accessible to a younger audience including karaoke, comic figures called the Plums, and interaction with the audience.

Music at The Prep was going from strength to strength. The school choir had won the shield at the Three Arts Festival in 2002 and more and more children were learning a variety of musical instruments. **Mrs Emma Pears** joined as Head of Senior Music in 2002 with Mrs Sue Ives concentrating on music in the Pre-Prep. There were so many talented and enthusiastic musicians that in 2003 the summer concert had to be expanded to two nights, and renamed 'School Proms 2003'. The first night was for the school orchestra, while the second was for choral and individual/ensemble performances. After the school choir had opened the concert on the second evening, there were no fewer than 68 performances by pupils from Form 3 to Form 8. Mrs Pears had written a school song, *The Way of Life* (with some help from Form 7 on the words). While the song needed to be within the children's vocal range and simple enough to learn, it also had to be suitable for different occasions, such as church services and assemblies as well as concerts. Mrs Pears decided on a form of hymn, ignoring one of her colleague's advice that it should be a cross between *Land of Hope and Glory* and something by S Club 7, and its debut performance by the school choir was a fitting end to the two evenings.

In line with Mr Harrison's aim of doing something different each year for the senior play, the 2005 production was *A Play for Coarse Actors* by Michael Green, a production of five acts with each act seemingly being a separate play, each one being a skit on well-known plays or stories, as can be judged from the titles: *Streuth*; *All's Well That Ends As You Like It*; *Last Call for Breakfast*; *Pride at Southanger Park*; and *Stalag 69*. Mr Harrison was delighted with the tremendous acting, the reliable backstage technical crew, and the brilliant costume department.

School life

By 1996, after-school clubs included drama, cricket practice, athletics club, film club, computer club, tap dancing, and tennis, usually for an hour immediately after school, and these continued into the new Millennium. In 2003, a debating club was started by Mr Harrison and Mr Smith. Early topics included 'God does not exist'; 'There should be more violence on TV'; and 'Men are the superior sex'!

In 1998, a German publisher, Oldenbourg, developed a new textbook for the teaching of English in schools in Germany. The book was illustrated with pictures, which featured some taken at The Prep. The producer asked to take shots of an assembly, classrooms, sports, breaktime, lunch, pupils chatting, arts, computer studies, and of the Headmaster looking very stern, questioning two pupils about leaving school premises without permission.

Visits from Japanese teachers continued on a regular basis. There was a visit in October 1997 by 36 teachers plus an interpreter and they were amazed, according to the letter of thanks sent to Mr Oatley, at the small numbers in the classes and by the wide-open spaces and sports facilities. They even spent time in the school shop buying souvenirs for their children. Apparently, by this time, the Japanese Tourist Board was recommending The Prep as a school not to be missed on educational visits to the UK. When another Japanese visit of 16 teachers, an escort, and a translator from Osaka Prefecture took place in November 1999, to save time, Mr Oatley joined them at their hotel in London and took the opportunity to tell them about the school and its philosophy on the journey to Sevenoaks, something that was much appreciated by the visitors.

As the Millennium approached, the annual cycle of school life at The Prep was reasonably settled. In 1988, Mr Oatley had begun his second decade as Headmaster. The ambitious building programme initiated by him when he arrived had been completed. Over his second decade, from 1988 to 1997, numbers of pupils had remained in the 260-287 range, except for one year (1994 with 246), although this hid a steady decrease in the proportion of boys from 98% of the total in 1988 to 74% in 1998. Staff numbers had increased from 26 to 37 over that period, reflecting the need for more teaching assistants in the Pre-Prep, some more specialised teachers in the senior school, and an increase in administrative staff, both internal and external.

Regular school activities started in September with a week-long geography field trip to the west country for Form 8, followed by a parents' presentation evening for the senior school and a more informal parents' evening for the Pre-Prep, the harvest festivals for the Pre-Prep, the senior school concert, and carol services in Seal Church. There was a ski trip during the spring half-term and, at the end of term, the school play. The summer term saw the Three Arts Festival, the grand prix for the Pre-Prep, the senior music concert and, in most years, a family fun day. The school year ended, traditionally, with sports day and speech day.

In November 1999, Mr Oatley sent a letter to over 1,500 families linked to the school either as current or former pupils, parents, or staff. He was inviting them to come to a grand reunion at the school in the following July to celebrate the school's 80 years and the new Millennium. There was to be a barbeque, food and drinks, and classrooms full of old magazines, pictures, photographs, and videos of past events. It would also be an opportunity to look at the plans for the new school hall.

The reunion was a great success, with kind weather; over 600 people, mostly alumni and their families, came from all over the country as well as from France, with the oldest alumnus well into his 70s. The house in Vine Court Road where the old school had been was opened up by the owners, **Mr** and **Mrs Fleming**, whose sons were at The Prep, to enable visitors to reminisce. Pupils from Forms 7 and 8 showed visitors round, and souvenir mugs and caps as well as prints of the school were available. There were photographic albums to pore over, videos to watch, and the plans for the new hall and the reconstruction of the squash court were on display. A special edition of *The Prep Post, The Souvenir Post*, was published for the day and included many of the letters and emails which had been received by the school from alumni, former staff, and friends. A Millennium calendar was produced for the occasion with vivid and imaginative illustrations, which included every pupil's name, from each form.

When **Hannah Bramall** left The Prep in 2000 from Form 8, she had been the only girl in that class. Although there were over 90 girls in the school, almost 30% of the total, very few stayed on beyond the age of 11. Five of Hannah's class left after Form 6 and another had left the next year, leaving her on her own. But in the memories written by the class of 2000 for the souvenir edition of *The Prep Post* produced for the reunion, she says it wasn't all bad. In her words, 'There are more good points than bad points. The boys and I have a great laugh with each other, mucking around, but when it comes to organising our prefect jobs, we are quite sensible... altogether it has been a great year and I don't want to leave.' When her sister **Alice** left four years later, she was one of five girls in the top form. By this time, there were 123 girls on the school register and the proportion was creeping up gradually.

Transport in its various ways, be it bicycles, Maidstone & District or London Transport buses, school minibuses, or parents on school runs or helping transport children to activities away from the school, has always been a part of Prep school life. In the early days at Vine Court Road, many boys cycled to school or caught buses as few people had their own cars. The cycle shed at Vine Court Road was always full and often overflowing. Mr Oatley was and still is a cycling enthusiast and bicycles featured heavily in school activities under his headship from 1978. Memories of alumni, staff, and parents mention the hilarious slow bicycle races of family day, the BMX craze of the 1980s, taking part in the London to Brighton ride, cycling all round Kent during activity weeks, and up to London including Hyde Park Corner on one occasion.

One of the last cycling proficiency groups that The Prep was allowed to coach.

Mr Oatley encouraged children to take the cycling proficiency test and he coached scores of children successfully over the years. Mr Luke Harrison recalls that when he was at the school, the sight of a cemented-on radio on Mr Oatley's bike and his mangled ear from a cycling accident didn't fill one with great confidence that he would teach them to ride safely on the roads, but this lack of conviction was proved over and over again to be misplaced.

Sadly, coaching by non-officially qualified instructors has been outlawed, so this no longer happens. In any case, the roads around the school are now a nightmare compared to what they used to be. Once, you used to be able to cycle around Godden Green and see hardly any cars – but now it has become a rat run for people avoiding Sevenoaks, and often driving irresponsibly.

Mr Oatley is remembered for his daily, early morning rides into Sevenoaks for his swim, and for turning up on his bike in the most unusual places, such as the village of Lidstep in Pembrokeshire, some 300 miles from Godden Green, during one adventure camping holiday run by Mr Culley, just to see how the boys were getting on.

Towards the end of 2002, The Prep's staff and parents were becoming increasingly concerned over the increasing volume and speed of traffic in Park Lane, together with the inadequate signage about the presence of the school. In the following January, the pupils were encouraged to write letters to Kent Highways pointing out the dangers. Almost 200 letters were sent to **Mr Julian Cook**, an engineer in the Highways Transport Planning & Safety group. He replied to Mr Oatley saying that the historical level of accidents and the low density of housing in Park Lane did not justify any change in speed limits. However, he did promise to arrange for a traffic volume and speed survey to be carried out, and for the signage to be reviewed. Although the survey was carried out, the authorities did not consider that a speed limit was needed and the 60 mph one is still in place.

Mr Smith has one disastrous minibus memory during one of the Easter or summer fun outings in about 2001, when Mr Smith and Mr Morrow took two minibuses to Chessington and, at the end of a very successful day, they started to drive back, with Mr Morrow driving first out of the car park. Mr Smith followed, not realising that there was a big wooden sign ahead of them saying 'Thank you for coming to Chessington.' The first bus fitted underneath; the second didn't, and suddenly became a convertible. **Mrs Wendy Woolf**, mother of **Nick** and **Adam**, who was sitting next to Mr Smith, gave this enormous shriek – and there was the sky. Fortunately, it was a lovely day; if it had been raining, he would have been very unpopular. He just had to drive a little slower round the M25. What it did show up was just how flimsy the tops of buses were. Mrs Woolf had become school cook in the senior school in 1989 when **Mrs Liz Harrison** moved away, and remained until caterers were brought in on completion of the Oakery in 2009.

Another minibus memory for Mr Smith was getting stuck on rather soggy playing fields whilst taking equipment out for the Thomas Trophy, and giving rides to boys who were helping on the bonnet of an old blue bus, which **Mrs Alison Smith** remembers being used by everyone for anything, from party outings to moving furniture. The school now has a fleet of modern, fully safety-equipped minibuses, but minibus memories are being created still. When all the pupils were asked in December 2017 to record their best memory of The Prep, **Harry Morgan** from Form 5W said it was 'when **Mr Roberts** smashed the window of the bus'.

There was a successful visit from a group of Norwegian pupils, teachers, and parents from the Darbu school in March 2003, who spent a week at The Prep. For the previous two years, the pupils of Form 7 had been corresponding with the Norwegian children over the internet, so it was a great opportunity for them all to meet. One result of this visit was the gift of a toy bear called Wilfio that was then taken on every school trip abroad, as well as on one or two of Mr Oatley's charity cycle rides.

The transition from Pre-Prep to the senior school was a rite of passage for the children, and an emotional occasion for the parents and staff. Classroom teachers in the Pre-Prep get to know every member of a class and their families really well during a whole school year. In 2003, the Pre-Prep teachers devised a plan that Form 2 children would 'slide down the bannisters' and jump down into the hallway and then leave to go home for the summer holidays, never again climbing the stairs as a Form 2 pupil! It has become a noisy and light-hearted way to end the Pre-Prep years and everybody–pupils, parents, and teachers–all leave for the holidays laughing and happy. Leaving teachers had to slide down the banisters too!

In 2003-04, The Prep supported the 10/10 Challenge run by HOPEHIV, an AIDS charity working in Sub-Saharan Africa, and a challenge was set up by Mr Pears. All 26 members of Form 8 were given £10 by the Sevenoaks Amherst Rotary Club, of which Mr Oatley is a member, and challenged to turn it into £100. Collectively, the pupils turned their £260 into £5,000. A Young Enterprise shield was awarded to **Sam Joad**, who ran a tuck shop on the school ski trip to Barèges. Mr Pears travelled to South Africa and visited some of the centres supported by HOPEHIV and, on his return, gave a very moving presentation of the charity's work at the senior school end-of-term service. Later in 2004, the players of London Irish RFC heard about the efforts of The Prep and, as a thank you, three of their professionals came to the school and held a training session for the boys.

Some members of Form 8 decided to form a band named Limelite–and, helped by **Robin Collings** (then a gap year student), recorded a charity single with the proceeds going to the HOPEHIV charity. The band members, **Lucy Mote, Laura Ganis, Emily Smith, Lauren Kelly-Jones, Jordan Stanford,**

Stuart Underwood, Elliot Carter, and **Wayne Nussbaumer**, co-wrote the song *You Would Cry*. They raised £400 in 2005 for HOPEHIV as part of the Social Entrepreneurs Project, out of an astonishing total of £6,000 that went to two projects in Malawi.

In May 2004, four Form 8 boys, **Kieran Hayward**, **Kassim Ramji**, **William Ritchie**, and **Winston Surrey** wrote an open letter to about 40 local companies, organisations, and individuals, as well as to parents, asking for their help in trying to understand the increasing red tape, bureaucracy, and litigation in contemporary society. The inspiration for the project came from the weekly debating sessions run by Mr Harrison. They cited a number of examples: a teacher at the school tripped and fell down the stairs at a London railway station and was contacted by a solicitor the same day asking if he would like to sue British Rail; the Football Association had a (sensible) ruling that if players had a head injury they had to leave the field for treatment – but this did not apply to goalkeepers; a regulation that activity toys could not be more that 60 centimetres – a mere two foot – tall; an EU ruling imposing only one way of making yoghurt; the requirement for police officers to complete 77 questions on a form when they stop and search someone; and, finally, the need for school teachers to complete an onerous risk assessment form before any field trip.

The letter was printed, and the project reported on, in *The Sevenoaks Chronicle* and *Kent Messenger* newspapers. The replies were all supportive of the pupils' initiative and the boys were delighted to receive letters from several Heads of local secondary schools and an alumnus, **John London**, a Kent County Councillor. Some letters were provocative and put forward some of the reasons for the apparently illogical and unnecessary regulations.

For 10 years from 1991, The Prep had supported the Worldwide Fund for Nature through its participation in the Walk for Wildlife every October. The Prep's contribution over the years was recognised by the sponsors, Canon, who gave The Prep two printers. In 2002 alone, The Prep raised over £2,700 (the most raised in any one year was around £3,000). The walks were organised all over the country; for The Prep, there were three walks of 3, 7, and 10 miles, with the latter including Knole Park, Ightham Mote, and Stone Street.

Alex Bell was an eager member of the countdown club and of the general knowledge teams that **Mr Donald Smith** arranged for both internal inter-house quizzes and for competing against other schools. He appreciated The Prep's ability to foster young minds, noting that all four members of the school general knowledge team of 2004 – in descending order of age, Kassim Ramji, Emily Smith, himself and **Celia Dyson** later found their way to Cambridge University. Alex had little doubt that they all benefited from being inspired about learning and taught to be curious during their time in the portakabins.

In 2004-05, Mr Oatley appointed Emily Smith, who won a scholarship to Walthamstow Hall, joint head girl with Laura Ganis, who went on to Sevenoaks

School. At prize-giving in July 2005, he commented that her father (Mr Donald Smith) had been one of his first head boys and Emily one of his first head girls (and his last).

A regular visitor to the school was a local policeman, PC Wenham, who used to give a child friendly

PC Wenham was a regular visitor. KG always enjoyed trying on his array of hats – but he brought serious messages, too. This photo is of a 1999 visit to KG.

chat to the Pre-Prep about the policemen's job, bullying and respect, right and wrong and, later, internet safety. He was terrific with the children and they had great fun trying on a selection of police hats and even being allowed to give the very brave PC a friendly tap on the backside with his truncheon. In June 2000, he came and spoke to the Form 6 and 8 leavers about drugs. He showed the pupils examples of different drugs, explained how they were taken, and the dreadful things that happened to your mind and body if you did take drugs. He was a regular visitor to other local preparatory and primary schools. He continued to visit schools after his retirement from the police force.

Other visitors who used to come to the Pre-Prep included mothers who were, or had been, nurses and told the children all about their work and showed them how to apply bandages, use stethoscopes, etc. Other parents were willing to bring their babies to be bathed, changed, and dressed by the children. There were numerous wonderful mums and dads with interesting jobs or items to show the children, for which the teachers were most grateful.

Sport and recreation
On Sunday 24 March 1996, twelve boys from Form 4 took part in a celebratory children's dance at Wembley before the League Cup Final, a match between Leeds and Aston Villa, in front of over 77,000 spectators (Aston Villa won 3-0).

The proposed athletics programme for the 1997 summer term was severely disrupted by weather. The day of the Kent Prep Schools Championships and the days assigned to sports day saw torrential rain, and the school had to rearrange the track and field events onto separate afternoons. However, in between the showers, **Adam Ruffells** won the U14 long and triple jumps at the Kent championships and went on to win a silver medal in the long jump at the national championships in Stoke. It was fortuitous that the SEC had financed the installation of an artificial cricket wicket for the 1997 season as reportedly it was a good one – just wet.

The Under 9s football squad, wearing Aston Villa and Leeds United kits, performed at Wembley in 1996 – a memorable day for the boys and Mr Oatley.

Over these years, the boys' games coaches reported 'balanced' seasons, 'see-saw' seasons and a few 'outstanding' or 'tremendous' ones but Mr Smith's phrase 'more graft than glory' captures this decade best – but at The Prep graft is applauded, too. Teams did reach tournament finals and played in various 'plate' competitions, even winning one (an U9 Rugby Regional Tournament, 1999) but the most consistent 'glory' moments came in cricket. Colts A teams brought home the Julian Parker Trophy from Rose Hill three times between 1999 and 2002, and the 1st XI won the Aberdour Tournament in 2003. The Under 9 footballers had a moment, too, in 1999, by winning the Yardley Court Sevens.

As more girls joined The Prep and moved through to the senior school **Mrs Linda Underwood**'s coaching skills were integral to the development of girls' sport at the school. Spring 1996 saw the girls competing in a cross country meeting and by the autumn term they fielded both U9 and U11 teams at a Derwent Lodge meeting, where they finished third overall out of the five schools competing. In later seasons **Mattie Govan** would win individual gold and silver medals.

Autumn 1996 saw the first inter-school netball matches in which the two age groups experienced wins and losses, but above all they continually improved and by the following term both teams were reported as having successful seasons. The girls in Form 2 were introduced to pop lacrosse in 1995-96 and by 1998 the U10 and U11 girls played their first matches. After a number of close defeats the U11s were first to secure an uplifting win, against Merton Court. With the arrival of Mrs Baldwin in 1999, a senior county level lacrosse coach, enthusiasm for the game grew.

Mixed hockey was also introduced and by spring 1997 The Prep was able to field its first U11 team, which recorded a win and a draw in its first season. Unfortunately the rounders team waited another year for its first win when the Under 10s played Derwent Lodge in 1998 – but they had had six of their seven 1997 fixtures cancelled! By 1999 there was a small group of girls in Form 7 but

above The first Under 8 netball team fielded by The Prep (1998-99) drew with Derwent Lodge and lost to Hazelwood but showed great potential.

right The first Pop Lacrosse squad with girls from Years 6, 7 and 8 in 1999.

too few to field a full team in any sport and so on occasions they joined with Sackville School's Years 7 and 8 to form U13 teams.

On the athletics track, and in the field, girls regularly contributed to The Prep's success at all levels – for instance in 2004 five of the seven athletes qualifying for the IAPS National Finals were girls. On that occasion **Helen Rennardson** (100m) joined **James Simmons** (800m) in returning with a silver medal. Eventually more coaches were helping Mrs Underwood and by 2003 a full time PE teacher was appointed. **Miss Danielle Agius** had responsibility for girls' games as well as athletics and cross country across the senior school.

Mr Ken Smart died on 24 January 2004 at the age of 93. A very talented amateur cricketer and footballer, as an all-rounder he played for Sevenoaks Vine 1st XI from before the Second World War up to the early 1970s, when he was over 60, taking over 1,800 wickets and scoring several centuries. He taught games at The Prep from 1969 until 1987 and many alumni greatly benefitted from his cricket and football coaching and refereeing. A school choir sang at the memorial service in his honour at The United Reform Church in Sevenoaks.

In May 2004, there was a special football match in memory of Mr Smart between the team of 1969 and the 2003 school 1st XI. This came about when **Mr Richard Bennett**, who had left The Prep in 1970, visited the school for the first time since he had left. He saw the photograph of the 1969 team in the hall and was told that two of the featured players, **Mr Tim Dickinson** and **Mr Will Stewart**, had children currently at the school. Mr Dickinson, son of Mrs Madeleine Dickinson, alumnus, parent and current (2018) Governor, came to the school to meet Mr Bennett where they spent a morning reminiscing. A germ of an idea came into their heads and, within a week of returning home to Felixstowe, Mr Bennett had telephoned the entire 1969 team and arranged for all but one of them, **Mr Keith Blackmore**, to come to the school for a reunion match.

The referee was **Mr Frank 'Scoop' Baldwin**, the editor of *The Sevenoaks Chronicle*, while Mr Oatley and Mr Oldroyd acted as super subs. The game was played in front of a large crowd and, after going behind 4-0, the 'oldies' rallied and pulled the scoreline back to a more respectable 4-3 by the final whistle. At the get-together afterwards, Mr Dickinson presented Mr Oatley with a trophy

Ken Smart's memorial football match
1969 and officials: *(standing)* Mr Harrison, Mr Smith, Mr Frank Baldwin, Mr Richard Styles, (standing in for Mr C. Blackmore), Mr Tony Wheeler, Mr Oatley, Ms Eleanor Griffiths, Mr Tim Dickinson, Mr Lauder Stewart, Mr Mark Griffiths *(hidden)*, Mr Richard Bennett, Mr Martin Andrews, Mr Chris Alcock, Mr Jonny Burcham, Mr Oldroyd. *Team members not pictured:* Rev. Paul McVeagh and Mr Richard Jenkins. 2004 *(kneeling)* Ben Regan, Will Harris, William Ritchie, Wayne Nussbaumer, Kassim Ramji, Jonny Barber, Ed Cloke, Stuart Underwood, Will Simmons, Tom Gilman, Sean Rush.

in memory of Mr Smart on behalf of the alumni. Initially, this was presented to the team of the year – not necessarily for just sport, as it was won one year by the general knowledge quiz champions and in 2008 by boys who played Buddy Holly and the Crickets in *The Buddy Holly Story*. Later, it was sometimes awarded for an outstanding achievement by an individual.

Outings and holidays

The first ski trip in the spring half-term was to Italy in 1982, organised by **Mr Tim Baldock**, father of **Christian, Luke** and **Piers**, and Mr Rogers, followed by trips to Switzerland and France. The success of these trips was largely based on the dynamics of the trip appealing to both the older children who went on their own, and entire family groups. An added bonus was the reassurance of the Baldocks' superb organisation, a Prep family experienced in the ski holiday business. When the Baldocks moved on in the early 1990s, another Prep family versed in running travel holidays, **Mr** and **Mrs John Tangney**, whose sons **Nicholas** and **William** were both pupils, stepped into their shoes. After a few initial trips to Würmlach in Austria, they settled on taking the school to Barèges, in the Pyrenees, an area well known to them through their core business: Tangney Tours of Borough Green, which specialised in organising pilgrimages to Lourdes. Their contacts meant that the school established strong relationships in the town and on the slopes, and many successful and enjoyable years were spent with the local ski school and in restaurants and bars. An undoubted highlight of every trip was an evening staying up in the mountains when the ski lift closed, at the Chez Louisette restaurant, for an evening of tobogganing in the moonlight on the empty slopes, eating delicious local food in front of the log fires, singing songs with the hosts, and then a torch-lit trek back through the pine trees, organised by the ski instructors, to the Hotel Europe either on foot or on skis for the more adventurous. Tangney Tours organised many other trips for the school, including a staff outing on a canal boat one year, which was a huge success.

The trips to Barèges continued up to 2006, led by Mr Oldroyd and **Mr Tom Bowen**, following the familiar pattern of trips by bus through France, with parents helping to make up the numbers of adults needed, or just coming along for the holiday. Younger pupils had to be accompanied by a parent. There were ski lessons, lunch – food, especially frites, seemed to play a big part in all the trips – then free flow skiing in groups, snow sculpting, or sledging in the afternoon, followed by the hat ceremony where the wally of the day was nominated for and voted on by all present at dinner, and more food. After dinner, various activities such as table tennis, pool, quizzes, and word games occupied the time. Mr Bowen always enjoyed these trips and was especially excited when he visited a local disco for the first time. A poem by 'The Bard of Barèges' (aka **Peter Fitzgerald**) from *The Prep Post* of autumn 1998 sums up the atmosphere of these trips. It is included in Appendix 4. The 2006 trip was probably the largest with 93 participants, the

above Barèges, 1990s.

left An evening on the mountain was always a trip highlight, 2002.

below left Apres-ski entertainment! At the hotel in Barèges, 2000.

below right Würmlach, 1990s.

largest age range (from Year 1 to 'over 29'), the greatest number of parents and the widest range of skiing skills. By this time, Mr Oldroyd and Mr Bowen had led the trip for 12 years and were ready to hand over the reins to the next generation.

The first geography field trip to Bude in September 1997, led by Mr Morrow and Mr Smith and written up in *The Prep Post* by **John Ratcliffe**, was a good example of the variety of activities that were arranged to develop the children in their last year at the school. It not only covered work for their Common Entrance

2001 Form 8 geography field trip to Bude.

geography project, but also helped to establish leadership qualities for the head boy (and later the head girl) and prefects for the coming academic year. The activities included surfing, abseiling, outdoor geography exercises, swimming, kayaking, and orienteering. They also learnt about the history, geography, and geology of the area around Bude, including visiting the Eden Project after it opened in 2001.

Alumni

In September 1999, a special recital of organ music was held in Yalding church to celebrate **Julian Collings**' appointment as an organ scholar at Christ's College, Cambridge. Julian had started playing keyboard instruments at The Prep at the age of 7 and took up the organ aged 10. He left The Prep from Form 8 as joint head boy in 1994 to take up a music scholarship at Tonbridge School. After graduating, he has established a high reputation as a professional organist and musical director.

Julian's elder brother **Daniel Collings**, who left in 1992 with an academic scholarship to Tonbridge, went on to the University of Oxford where he had his first book published in his final year. He co-authored *Britain Under Thatcher* with **Mr Anthony Seldon**, then Headmaster of Brighton College. He went on to be a writer, journalist, and TV producer specialising in Anglo-American relationships. He has worked on landmark biographies of John Major and Tony Blair with Anthony Seldon and others. There were two more Collings boys at The Prep: Robin returned to teach after university and **George** was in the Pre-Prep, before leaving from Form 3.

In 2000, the school heard the sad news that **Tom Butlin** from the class of 1989 had died earlier that year. At the age of 8, while he was at The Prep, Tom suffered from an inoperable brain tumour but, after extensive radiotherapy, appeared to have been cured. He was remembered at The Prep, not only for his courage and fortitude in the battle against his illness, but also for his impression of Margaret Thatcher in the school play, a role he was to perform again when he was at Sackville School. After leaving Sackville, he had eight adventurous weeks in Australia travelling on his own, which according to his parents was 'a heroic achievement'. On his return, he worked in a care home in Langton Green and continued with his love of amateur dramatics. Sadly, in May 1999 illness struck again, this time fatally.

One of the most notable of The Prep's alumni is Ian Walker, although he was only ever in the junior school. He is one of Britain's most successful sailors, with two Olympic silver medals to his name, at the 1996 summer Olympics in Atlanta and at Sydney in 2000. He also coached **Shirley Robertson** and her Yngling Team to gold at the 2004 Athens Olympics. When Britain launched its first bid for the America's Cup for 14 years in 2000, Ian was named as the skipper. In the 2002 Louis Vuitton races (the winner of which then challenged the holders for the America's Cup), Ian as skipper was joined by fellow alumnus **Mark Sheffield**. The Prep signed up as official support of the GBR Challenge and their progress was followed closely by the staff and pupils until they were eliminated by a USA yacht in a quarter-final. In the 2007 America's Cup, Ian joined fellow Olympic medallist **Iain Percy** as the tactician of the Italian team +39 Challenge. In 2015, he won the Yachtsman of the Year Award following his success in skippering the winning boat in the Volvo Ocean Race, a 40,000-mile round-the-world highly competitive event.

The Prep noted its 90th birthday with the establishment of Sevenoaks Prep Alumni (SPA), the school's first official former pupils' association.

Alumnus **Martin Purdy** was awarded his rugby blue when he represented Cambridge against Oxford in December 2000. In 2005, by which time he was playing professional rugby for London Wasps, he spoke at the school's annual rugby dinner held at Edwards Brasserie in Sevenoaks Weald.

Other schools and organisations

In June 1999, The Prep hosted a reunion for Alumni of Winchester House, which had closed in 1985, and gave Solefield School use of the grounds to put up a marquee and hold a party.

The premises continued to be used by external organisations. October was a regular date for the Sevenoaks AKCC 6-a-side cricket tournament, for which The Prep sometimes entered a team, but with limited success—except for 1995, when they beat the Orbilians, the teachers' side from Sevenoaks School, in the final. There was (and still is) a good relationship with Sevenoaks Rugby Club, who used The Prep's grounds on a Sunday for training and matches when pitches at Knole Paddock were unavailable or all being used. The rugby club's veterans' side, *The Acorns*, enjoyed playing on the small pitches at The Prep when there were too many senior games at the Paddock on a Saturday.

Parental involvement

The social events committee (SEC) was well established by 1998 when the chairmanship passed from **Mrs Wendy Higgs** to **Mrs Kate de Angeli**. It ran a regular programme of well-supported activities, which contributed to the family feel of the school while often raising money for 'extras'. The autumn term started with a murder mystery evening or some other social occasion and was followed by bonfire night, often shared with Solefield School, and the Christmas bazaar. The spring term saw regular quiz nights. A summer ball took place at different venues including the Foulston Centre, Brands Hatch and the Wildernesse Golf Club, while there were occasional tennis tournaments for parents and the annual family fun day.

The most ambitious parents' and friends' ball to date was planned by the SEC for the Millennium. After a year of planning, worrying about the size of the marquee, agonising over the choice of bands, and endless discussions about the menu, table size, and choice of wines, it finally took place in July 2000.

It was a huge relief to **Mrs Kate de Angeli, Mrs Karen Parrett**, and **Mrs Clare Minto**, the principal organisers of the ball, that everyone seemed to have a good time and that everyone appreciated being 'at home' rather than celebrating at a golf club or other commercial venue. The marquee looked splendid, thanks in no small part to the foliage donated by **Mr Martin** and **Mrs Suzy Brookman**, and Mrs Minto's newly acquired floristry expertise that was developed by working with Mrs de Angeli, a professional florist and teacher of flower-arranging classes. In true Prep tradition, the splendid catering was by former parent **Mrs Sara Hester**, mother of **Tom**, with her company *Tandem Catering*. The band, *Careless Talk*, was excellent and managed to get even the most incalcitrant fathers on to the dance floor.

Nearly £30,000 was raised in 1999-2000 towards the building of the new hall, including almost £12,000 from Mr Oatley's Nile bike ride and over £5,000 from the Christmas bazaar.

A festively transformed cloakroom pre-2000 – in the old hall the bazaar filled every available corner.

--- 10 ---

The Way of Life (2005-18)

When Mr Edward Oatley took over in 1978, there had been 147 boys with an age range of 5 to 13 and 13 staff. When he retired in 2005 and Mr Philip Oldroyd became Headmaster, there were 360 pupils (225 boys and 135 girls), with some in the Nursery as young as 2½, and 45 staff. This increase had been accommodated in a series of building works, starting in 1978 with the temporary wooden buildings in the gardens of Fawke Cottage being gradually replaced by slightly more permanent portakabins, then these being replaced in turn by more enduring structures. The final replacement of temporary buildings and portakabins was part of the 10-year plan for the school, which it hoped to complete by 2019. The period of Mr Oldroyd's tenure saw the opening in 2009 of the Oakery, which included new premises for drama and music; the inauguration of now traditional events, such as Prep Idol; and some outstanding academic and sports results. His last full year was 2010-11, the same year that Mrs Shea, who had been the Head of the Pre-Prep since 1992, retired. During her time, Stake Farm had been turned into a true family home for the Pre-Prep, girls had been fully integrated into every year, and she had been responsible for the development of some outstanding teachers. When Mr Luke Harrison took over as Headmaster of The Prep in January 2012, pupil numbers had hardly changed (370), although there had been an increase in staff to 54. Of the pupils, about 57% were boys and 43% girls. The total number of pupils went up to 386 at the start of the 2018-19 academic year, but the split has remained fairly consistent throughout Mr Harrison's headship (54%/46% in 2018-19). This period saw the further development of Stake Farm and, in 2019, the beginning of the replacement of the last senior school portakabins by a magnificent centenary block housing classrooms and a social area for the senior school pupils.

Heads and staff

In his July 2004 newsletter to parents, **Mr Edward Oatley** had written:

'This is to inform those of you who were not present at prize-giving that I will be standing down as Headmaster from July 2005. I am sure most of you are aware that Mr Philip Oldroyd will become Headmaster of Sevenoaks Prep in my place at the end of the next school year and it gives me great pleasure to announce this formally.

'Philip has been Head of Year 7 and 8 maths and PE for the past ten years, is Deputy Head and holds the respect of children, staff and parents alike. I have the utmost confidence in him carrying the school forward while keeping the ethos and philosophy of the school intact. We will be working together as the pendulum swings and he visits senior heads and brings his own thoughts and ideas into the way forward for the school. He is a Prep boy through and through, educated here from the age of 7 and moving on to Judd at 13. Following a successful career at Judd he went on to Trinity and All Saints College, the teacher training college for Leeds University, to take a sports and business studies degree. After teaching for six years at Sackville he came back to The Prep and has been here ever since. He is now a member of IAPS.'

In 1994, Mr Oldroyd had married **Miss Nicola Ash** and their two sons were educated at The Prep; **Tom** started in 2000 and **Dan** in 2002. As with the wives of previous Heads, Mrs Oldroyd (known as Niki) was a massive support to the Headmaster. She took a lead in the layout and quality of the food in the

Staff on Mr Oatley's retirement in 2005

back row Mr G. Brand, Mr D. Sayer*, Mr F. Russell-Flint*, Mr S. Andrews*
third row Mrs S. Ramji, Mrs S. Wells, Mrs J. Lucas, Mrs S. Young,
Miss S Perks, Mrs J. Baldwin.
second row Mrs K. Stewart, Mrs M. Peirce, Miss F. Stephen, Mrs J. Riding, Mme J. Homer,
Mrs R. Copeland, Mrs V. Reynolds, Mr D. Smith, Mrs A. Smith,
Mrs A. Darton-Bigg, Mrs L. Underwood.
front (seated) Mrs S. Thompson, Mrs B. Guy, Mrs W. Woolf, Mr K. Robinson,
Mr T. Bowen, Mr P. Ratcliffe, Mr L. Harrison, Miss K. Briggs.

Oakery, in managing the improvement in the appearance of the school, with the prospectus, publicity and smartening up the grounds, and working on the website. Tom remembers having had a unique experience during the 11 years he spent at The Prep, as throughout his entire time at the school the Headmaster happened to be a close member of his family, from Nursery to Year 2 under Mr Oatley and from Year 3 until Year 8 under his father. It was impossible for him to play off parents and school as most children do!

Mrs Penny Spencer-Allen, Mrs Jackie Low, and **Mrs Cathy Sharman** retired in July 2006, all three having been involved with The Prep for at least 20 years. Mr Oatley had taught Mrs Spencer-Allen's brothers at Winchester House in the 1970s, her sons transferred from Winchester House to The Prep in 1985, and she joined the staff in 1991, initially in the Nursery and then with her own Kindergarten class. Both Mrs Low and Mrs Sharman had also had boys (**Dominic** and **Adam**, respectively) at the school. Mrs Low had taught English and maths to Years 5 and 6 and ended as a Year 5 class teacher, while Mrs Sharman had taught and coached swimming.

Mr Tom Bowen retired in 2007 after 15 years, just in time to head off to the rugby world cup in France. As well as being a Year 4 teacher, he had coached just about every sport over the years, but rugby remained his favourite. Well-known for wearing a variety of rugby shirts through the years, when he gave his farewell speech he was wearing several rugby shirts which he took off one by one with the last being a Prep shirt. It was all quite emotional.

back row Mr N. Pears, Mr A. Chant, Mr J. Baynes, Mrs S. Ives, Mrs E. Pears.
third / second row Miss L. Harrison*, Mrs C. Mason, Miss J.Walther*, Miss L. Leman, Miss S. Rudd, Miss V. Stevens, Mrs L.Wigley, Mrs K.Topliss, Mrs J. Lewis, Mrs A.Thomas, Mrs B. Buttery, Mrs G. Leathers, Miss A. Richardson, Mrs S. Binnie.
front (seated) Mrs J. Oatley, Mr E. Oatley, Mrs M. Shea, Mr P. Oldroyd, Mrs J. Low, Mrs P. Spencer-Allen, Mrs S. Boulter, Mr D. Cochrane.

*All staff (excluding *gap year students) continued into 2006*

In 2008, **Mr David Cochrane** retired after 24 years at the school. On his first day, he had planted a Dutch Elm tree with **Mrs Beth Sadler** and her class and was proud that it was still standing tall on his retirement. Over the years he had been celebrated for the quality and size of the bonfires he constructed for the school's bonfire nights, which he always lit with a single match; as **Alex Bell** recalled, 'cold firework nights were turned into spring by David's efforts with the bonfire'. While he is remembered for going steadily and meticulously about his work, tending the beds, cutting all the hedges by hand and mowing with a small mower, he often seemed to be in the way when the classes needed to be outside!

Mrs Alison Smith took the gardening on board when the Oatleys moved away. **Mrs Janet Oatley** couldn't believe that, after her years of going round the school with watering cans, a watering system was installed just after she left; unfortunately, it never worked, so she didn't miss out. On Mrs Smith's first morning, when Mrs Oatley was still living in the school, she remembered being nervous because she wanted to make sure she didn't let the side down, as the garden looked so wonderful. She was weeding and from behind her came Mr Cochrane's voice, saying to her, you will never ever get the ground elder out of that – there is no point in even trying. Mrs Smith thought to herself, this is a challenge! Unfortunately, he was absolutely right.

Mr Cochrane was notorious for the number and variety of bonfires he lit around the grounds, often just as Mr Oldroyd or one of the other coaches was about to take football or rugby training. Mrs Smith used to help Mrs Oatley with the cricket teas, and they would be setting out the tea on the lawn when Mrs Oatley's face would suddenly fall and she would rush off to 'sort out David'. **Mrs Marjorie Shea** remembered that fires and smoke were a daily complication for outdoor activities, and that every aerial photograph of the school in that period featured smoke. His enthusiasm sometimes got the better of him. Imagine Mrs Shea's horror on the day of the Pre-Prep's circus-themed concert when she found that her props had disappeared. Mr Cochrane the bonfire enthusiast had only taken them all and burnt them. She and the children spent the morning remaking them, and the concert on the lawn happened without incident. Another time, he was collecting the rubbish after sports day and accidentally burnt all the results, which had been written out by **Mr Michael Barnard**. As a fond farewell to Mr Cochrane, the Pre-Prep 2008 summer performance included *Gardener's World,* a show with a garden theme. Although he retired from school, he still comes for lunch in the Oakery on Wednesdays and proudly builds the bonfire for firework night each year.

Mrs Lucy Wigley retired in 2009 after a 17-year association with the school and, in particular, the Pre-Prep. Her son **Thomas** had started in 1992, with his older sister **Keira** joining later, and in 1994 Mrs Wigley joined as a classroom assistant and the 'computer person' before becoming Mrs Shea's assistant.

Mrs Shea commented that her professionalism, quiet counsel, versatility, and common sense would be sorely missed.

Mr George Brand, the Bursar, had been at the school for 12 years when he retired in 2010. Although known affectionately to most people as the car park monitor, he had been involved in many other activities for the school. He recalled that, as Bursar, he had met many other independent school bursars, but never found one who was not only allowed to coach the 1st XI football team but also, for a number of years, had organised the pyrotechnics for the school bonfire night and in the company of others, notably Mr Cochrane, yearly spent 20 thrill-packed minutes wandering through the school field actually lighting the fireworks and dodging the sparks. Eventually health and safety decreed that a slightly less perilous approach should be taken and they had to use outside 'experts'.

The end of the summer term of 2011 saw the retirement of several long-standing members of staff and The Prep family. Mrs Marjorie Shea had been an inspirational teacher and Head of the Pre-Prep since 1992, delighting in the

Pre-Prep staff autumn 2009
back rows 1 Mrs S. Andrews, *2* Mrs L. Morris, *3* Mrs A. Bellwood, *4* Mrs M. Shea, *5* Mrs A. Haselden *6* Mrs L. Wigley, *7* Mrs T. Leeds, *8* Mrs K. Topliss, *9* Miss S. Perks, *10* Mrs K. Johnson, *11* Mrs B. Calver, *12* Mrs L. Hamer, *13* Mrs D. Bell, *14* Mrs K. Stewart, *15* Mrs V. Dussek, *16* Mrs C. Bourne, *17* Mrs K. Hougham.
front row standing Mrs J. Roubicek, Mrs G. Leathers, Mrs J. Riding, Mrs S. Rudd, Mrs B. Buttery, Mrs S. Shaw, Miss S. Hyman, Mrs K. Clark, Mrs A. Thomas.
kneeling Mrs S. Binnie, Mrs M. Greening, Mrs J. Lewis, Mrs L. Witton, Miss A. Coad.

vagaries and eccentricities exclusive to early childhood. She always maintained that the education of young children was more far-reaching than just developing the intellect, and that enhancing heart and soul and ensuring that every child had the wherewithal to be their best selves was paramount. Her staff were provided with a safe and supportive environment in which they flourished. As well as Mrs Shea, **Miss Anne Richardson** and **Mrs Kay Topliss** left the Pre-Prep after 13 and 9 years respectively. Miss Richardson had a passion for the natural world and made her classroom a rich and stimulating place in which to learn; she was succeeded by **Mrs Lorna Belither.** Mrs Topliss looked after the children in Year 2 and was always able to bring out the best in her charges. Her love of the outdoors is best illustrated by the fun 'camp days' for pupils and parents that became an annual fixture in Year 2's calendar.

   Mme Jacqueline Homer also retired in 2011, having come from Winchester House as long ago as 1985. When paying tribute to her, Mr Oldroyd commented that all The Prep's destination schools complimented the school on the exceptional linguistic ability of the pupils, and that many alumni had gone on to take languages in the sixth form and at university. Mrs Smith recalled talking to her girls, **Emily** and **Lizzie**, about Mme Homer retiring and how much they had enjoyed her teaching. They decided that she would be the ideal person to be their Granny since Mrs Smith's mother had recently died, and they asked their father, **Mr Donald Smith**, to ask Mme Homer if she would be when she retired. He did and she was very moved. Emily still revises five minutes of French vocabulary every evening even though it is 13 years since Mme Homer taught her.

   Mrs Linda Underwood ended her long association with the school in 2011 when she left to become registrar at Woldingham School. Another who first became involved as a mum, she began as a teaching assistant in the Pre-Prep in the early 1990s and went on to become school secretary, first aider, and then, with co-education, Head of Girls' Games. As she was often the first person to be contacted by prospective parents, she became skilled at 'selling' the school and then continued to build close relationships with the families throughout their time there. She was replaced by **Mrs Louise Enderby** as PA to first Mr Oldroyd and then **Mr Luke Harrison**.

   In 2011, after a very successful tenure as Headmaster, Mr and Mrs Oldroyd decided for personal reasons to move from Sevenoaks to Norfolk, where Mrs Oldroyd's parents lived. Mr Oldroyd was succeeded by Mr Harrison, another alumnus who had gone to Tonbridge in 1986 and, after university, qualified as a teacher. He had joined The Prep's staff in 2001, concentrating on drama and English as well as coaching various sports teams. Mr Oldroyd and Mr Harrison had one term, the autumn of 2011, to work together before Mr Harrison took over as Headmaster in January 2012. Mr Oldroyd had taken over as Headmaster in 2005, but as an alumnus his links with the school went back far longer than anyone remembered. When he first returned in 1994 as a maths and class teacher, the school would have been recognisable from his own school days. By 2011, he had witnessed a vast transformation and had directly overseen the development of the splendid new block that houses the Oakery and the drama and music departments. The move to Norfolk was good timing for their boys, Tom and Dan, aged 13 and 11 respectively, who were at a natural age to change schools. Within a couple of years, Mr Oldroyd was Headmaster of a prep school in Norwich.

Mr Harrison inherited several members of staff who are still teaching in the school as it enters its centenary year. In addition to those recorded on pages 197-8, the Pre-Prep's teachers include **Mrs Merrhis Lemmon** who came in 2006 as a Kindergarten assistant and Little Oaks supervisor; and **Mrs Bridget Calver**, who since 2007 has been another Kindergarten assistant. In the senior school is **Mr Robin Collings**, an alumnus, who returned in 2005 for a gap year after university and never left! As well as teaching English, after Mr Harrison became Headmaster he took over as Head of Drama; **Mrs Wendy Culley** came in 2007 as a Key Stage 2 teacher; **Mrs Madeleine Matthews**, who is Head of English, came in 2008, also as a Key Stage 2 teacher; **Miss Dee Ablett** had joined in 2008 and has been a senior games and history teacher; while in 2009 **Mr Stephen Lemmon** joined his wife at the school and teaches Year 5. On administration, Mr Harrison inherited **Mrs Wendy Kent** who had been appointed Bursar after Mr Brand's retirement in 2010 and **Mrs Michelle Peirce** who has been the Bursar's assistant since 2001. When **Mr Peter Gates-Fleming**'s sons joined the school, Mr. Oatley discovered he had carpentry skills and asked him to help with some shelf assembling. By 1988 he found he was working full time in the maintenance department and after twenty years is still there along with **Mr Matt Tye** who has been groundsman for the same length of time, initially on a casual arrangement but on the full-time staff from 2006.

Mr Peter Ratcliffe had, apart from a 'gap' year in France, been teaching at The Prep since 1998. Hundreds of pupils benefitted from having him as their class, geography, history, or games teacher. His dry sense of humour was a wonderful thing to behold, but this did not get in the way of him ensuring that every one of his pupils received the most insightful and helpful feedback on their work. Mr Smith remembers 'Ratty' always making the same joke when everyone was warming up with leg stretches for cross country: 'now, over onto your left leg, change legs – not with anyone else'. On his retirement in 2012, Mr Harrison paid tribute to Mr Ratcliffe, describing him as one of the most humble and caring people it had ever been his privilege to meet. Mr Ratcliffe, for his part, said that he had always found The Prep to be a warm community in which to work and be. **Mrs Gail Leathers** retired in 2012 after nearly 20 years as an exceptional Reception teacher; she had also taught swimming alongside Mrs Sharman and continued with this when Mrs Sharman left.

Mrs Lyn Witton had been a part of The Prep family for over 23 years when she retired in 2013. She made an enormous contribution to the school over this period; she was the mastermind behind countless stage sets over the years, produced most of the artwork on the walls of the Pre-Prep and, with **Mrs Janet Wilkes**, designed the mosaic in the lobby of the main hall.

The year after Mrs Shea became Head of the Pre-Prep in 1992, she had recruited **Mrs Sue Binnie** to establish a nursery for children rising 3 which allowed the Pre-Prep to separate what had been two Kindergarten classes into three early year classes: Nursery, Kindergarten, and Reception. (The Pre-Prep also included Years 1 and 2 – rising 6 and 7 (see Appendix 2).) Mrs Binnie's personal and professional qualities were soon recognised and for 23 years she embodied the essence of a superb nursery teacher, oozing warmth, sincerity, intuition, wisdom, and calm as a fount of knowledge, experience, and a vast understanding of her subject. So as to develop the youngsters in her care, learning was based on play and a holistic approach. Hundreds of children and parents will remain forever in Mrs Binnie's debt for the start their boys and girls were given in the Pre-Prep Nursery. Mrs Shea's concluding words when she was paying tribute to her on her retirement in 2015 were, 'Sue Binnie, not just outstanding but a legend'.

Mr Stefan Purdy had been a pupil at The Prep in the early 1960s and had gone to Sevenoaks School, where he had excelled at rugby and athletics and later played first class rugby for Harlequins and Wasps. His children **Martin**, who also played rugby at a high level, **Graham**, and **Stephanie** are also alumni. After teaching for many years, mainly to disadvantaged children, he joined The Prep staff in 2005 as Head of Maths and as a sports coach. He set up, and for many years ran, the archery club as an after-school activity. He retired in 2015.

Mrs Shea and Mr Pears at the Pre-Prep's sports day in 2011 during their handover term.

Mr Nik Pears had left The Prep in 2008 to pursue an opportunity to work in the music industry and was thoroughly enjoying this new venture. One day, in 2011, he received a message from Mr Oldroyd asking him to come and see him at the school. Mr Pears' first thought turned to his son **Josiah**, who was in Nursery at the Pre-Prep. Surely he couldn't have done anything so terrible that he was already being called in to see the Headmaster – after all, Josiah was only three years old! Fortunately, what transpired was that Mr Oldroyd wanted to have a conversation with Mr Pears as he was beginning the search for someone to take over from Mrs Marjorie Shea as Head of the Pre-Prep. Not unnaturally, Mr Pears was daunted by the prospect of following in Mrs Shea's footsteps – for not only was she was the most brilliant Head and would certainly be a hard act to follow, but he would be the only man in the Pre-Prep!

In due course, Mr Pears – in his own words – 'had a fantastic time in the junior school and thoroughly enjoyed developing [his] understanding and appreciation for these most critical years in child development. It was also a lot of fun!' One of his best memories was of a staff outing to the Globe Theatre to watch Shakespeare's *A Midsummer Night's Dream*. The group was gathered at Sevenoaks station ready to purchase tickets for the train journey to London Bridge – about 20 staff and about 35 different opinions on the best tickets to buy – group rates, OAP fares, 'buy one get one free' offers, everything being discussed, at once, loudly… it was chaos! Clearly having come to the end of his tether, the gentleman in the ticket office shouted, 'Would you all please just stop! All I can hear is what sounds like medieval music!' Mr Pears responded by laughing out loud and replying, 'You should count yourself lucky, I have to work with this lot!' The staff fell about laughing and from that day on, whenever he needed to call things to order in staff meetings, without fail those immortal words would be used!

At the end of the summer term 2016, Mr Pears moved from his post as Head of the Pre-Prep to become Head of Kent College Preparatory School in Pembury. During his time at the school, in addition to being Head of the Pre-Prep, Mr Pears had also established the Social Entrepreneurs Project for Year 8, had been one of the founders of Prep Idol, and had also been Head of Music and a 1st XV rugby coach. He was also a compliance inspector. When Mr Harrison paid tribute to Mr Pears at speech day, he said that Mr Pears was the true master of The Prep's *Way of Life* and had demonstrated all its qualities throughout his time at The Prep. Mr Harrison also paid tribute to **Mrs Emma Pears**, who had contributed enormously as a support for Mr Pears and in her own right as a superlative teacher of music.

Mr Alan Chant had arrived at The Prep in 1997 to teach information technology and retired at the end of the 2016-17 academic year. Over these 20 plus years, his subject changed more dramatically than any other. He guided the pupils (and staff) carefully and without ever losing his enthusiasm in the minefield of confusion and uncertainty that IT became, from BBC B machines, through Windows PCs and CRT monitors, to widescreen displays, the Raspberry Pi, Apple Macs, and iPads. He did this with patience and good humour and every single pupil whom he taught benefitted from his guidance and support. In addition to this, he found time to teach some maths and to run the chess club and organise table tennis. He filmed dozens of plays and the DVDs of the productions were sold to parents and friends, with the proceeds going to charities.

Mrs Jan Lucas also retired in 2017, having joined The Prep family in 1995 when her elder son **Mark** joined the school, to be followed by his brother, **Chris**.

When Mr Oldroyd became the Headmaster, he identified Mrs Lucas, with her bubbly, friendly personality, as the ideal person to be the first point of contact for the school in the Reception Office of Fawke Cottage, a role which she made her own with a smile and comforting presence for children, staff, and parents, especially prospective ones. She also took over the school shop from Mrs Oatley, helped by Mrs Alison Smith.

At the end of the summer term of 2018, a number of long-serving staff retired or moved on. **Mrs Alison Bellwood** had joined as long ago as 1992 as a Reception teacher, and over those 26 years hundreds of children had benefited from her kind nature and her wisdom. She navigated every change in the Early Years Curriculum with calm and a steady hand–always knowing that the most important thing to remember was the child sitting in front of her. One colleague said that Mrs Bellwood intuitively knew when to help, when to sit back and when to listen, and when to give a child a hug, which is the mark of a great teacher.

Mrs Karen Jeremy first arrived at The Prep in 1984 as **Mrs Karen Wilmot**. Her son, **Daniel**, was a pupil, leaving in 1992. She quickly involved herself in school life, becoming a form rep, Treasurer of the Friends of Sevenoaks Prep, and helping to organise school events. It wasn't long before the calling into the classroom beckoned, and between 1990 and 1993 she worked in the Kindergarten and Reception before embarking on a teacher training course, gaining her BEd degree in 1997 before returning to The Prep in 1999 as **Miss Briggs**, reverting to her maiden name. She then took on a variety of roles, from a Year 3 class teacher, to Year 6 English, maths, geography and history and some Pre-Prep French as well as being very involved in the ski trips in the Easter holidays. As Director of Studies, she helped shape the curriculum and has guided the school through numerous inspections. She oversaw the 11+ process, guided training and newly qualified staff through their first years of teaching, recruited many teachers and led numerous educational trips. One colleague said of Mrs Jeremy, 'She is plain-speaking, deeply caring, and always has the courage to speak her mind for the benefit of pupils'.

Mr Ian Culley first taught at The Prep from 1981-88, then for two years from 1990-92, before returning in 2006. During those years away he had taught at Ashdown House, Querns in Cirencester for two years, and was then Head of Claremont School for six years. He returned to The Prep in 2006 and from then on was a strong right hand man for the Headmasters, Mr Oldroyd and Mr Harrison. He taught maths and geography as well as all sports, introducing rugby as a major sport, and showed a real talent for directing and often writing plays that were all extremely successful and hugely enjoyed by the cast and audience. His organisational skills were second to none, which were invaluable for sports days, timetabling, school trips, camping holidays and many other activities. He was always a natural, warm, and popular person to have around the school, making everyone feel it was a great day and, although retiring from full-time teaching in 2018, continues to help out with maths. One of his colleagues summed up his contribution to the school with, 'Mr Culley epitomises the right combination of authority, care, love and wisdom. He is firm, yet gentle; agreeable but not gullible; strict, but not negative; fun but not flippant. You would want him around both at a party and in a crisis'.

Mrs Cathy Chandler-Bourne, mum of **Georgia** and **Megan**, had been the Pre-Prep secretary since 2008, but was not your average school secretary. She took on any job that needed doing and found time to produce shows and teach music box in the Pre-Prep, as well as taking the lead (and being the only one to learn her lines properly) in the staff pantomime. She left in 2018 to pursue her interest in interior design. **Mrs Kate Stewart**, whose sons **Anthony** and **Jamie** had been Prep pupils, was another stalwart of the Pre-Prep who retired in 2018 after 15 years at the school. After many years working in the Nursery, where she helped all the children in her care with patience and kindness, she decided she needed to sit down more and changed her role to work in the office for her last few years.

For much of his professional career, Mr Harrison had worked closely with his wife, **Mrs Clare Harrison**, who is also a qualified teacher. Once their daughters, **Lucy** and **Esme**, were settled in the Pre-Prep, Mrs Harrison joined the staff officially in 2012 as Assistant Head, Director of Admissions, and a senior history teacher. She had been Head of History at Kent College. Other senior staff who came to the school in this period included **Mme Amanda Clark** who was appointed Head of French in 2011; **Dr Joanna Rolls** was appointed Head of Science in 2013, and was joined by **Mrs Felicity Mayrs** in 2015; the new Director of Music in 2014 was **Miss Izzy Piper**; and **Ms Carol Juxon** came as Head of Mathematics in 2015. In the Pre-Prep, **Mrs Helen Cook** was appointed Head in 2016 after Mr Pears left, and **Mrs Louisa Rowland** became Head of the Nursery in the same year. In 2018, **Mr James Ashcroft** joined as Deputy Head and **Mrs Sarah Howe** came as the Pre-Prep secretary and receptionist. **Mrs Sarah Johns** joined the senior Reception Office team in 2017 to work alongside **Ms Val Chalmers-Stevens**.

Governance

The school is a charitable company, Sevenoaks Preparatory School Limited, whose Directors are also Governors of the school. The Governors normally meet once a term while the Chairman and Vice-Chairman meet monthly with the senior members of the school's staff. The day-to-day running of the school is delegated to Mr Harrison and Mrs Kent, who work in co-operation with the senior management team of the school.

In the 1960s, under **Mr Kenneth Ely,** the school had been a limited company with him, **Mrs Betty Ely**, and **Mr** and **Mrs Ronnie Webb** as shareholders. Mr Oatley acquired the company from the shareholders when he became Headmaster in 1977. In 1999, the company was turned into a charity, SPS

Charitable Trust, and registered with the Charity Commission. Initially, the charity had three directors, who were also trustees. Mr Oatley was Chairman, with Mr Brand, the Bursar, and **Mr Keith Robinson**, the school accountant, as fellow Directors. Mr Robinson was also the secretary. In 2015, the name was changed to the present one. **Mrs Jan Berry** succeeded Mr Oatley as Chair in 2012. Her two children, **Matthew** and **Hannah**, had been pupils at the school in the 1990s.

Inspectors' reports

At the beginning of the 2008-09 academic year, there was a joint inspection of the school by Ofsted and ISI (the Independent Schools Inspectorate), joint because of the government's indecision between the two inspection processes. Although this made the whole process even more gruelling than usual, the school was delighted with the results, which praised both the academic and pastoral life of the school, the obvious success of the Oakery, and the excellent exam results gained by both girls and boys in the 11+ and 13+ exams. One Inspector commented that it had been a pleasure to have been in such a wonderful, happy, and industrious environment. Another was almost in tears as she fed back her findings on how content the children were, both inside and outside the classroom, and how well the staff judged the balance between supervision and independence.

In May 2013, there was a further inspection by ISI. The first lines of the report said, 'The school is successful in meeting its aims and accords strongly with its ethos for the individual child and their family. A good quality educational experience is offered to all pupils', and then went on, 'Throughout the school, pupils' development is excellent'. This praise continued throughout the report and there were only five areas where further improvement was recommended; most of these were relatively minor, and several were already being progressed by the school.

An ISI regulatory compliance inspection took place in 2017, which was a more limited review, concentrating on the school's performance set against laid-down standards covering such matters as quality of education, children's development, their welfare, the quality of leadership, staff, and premises, and parental complaints. All standards were met.

Fabric

In 2006, Mr Culley had returned to The Prep. The biggest change he noticed when he came back after 14 years was the buildings. He remembered coming to the opening of the sports hall in 2001 and walking round the corner, seeing the brick-built hall, and thinking, how on earth did Mr Oatley pull that one off, because up until then it had always been set in stone that the school couldn't have any permanent new buildings. When he had heard about the hall, he thought it was going to be another all-singing, all-dancing portakabin.

Opening of the Oakery with Gary Rhodes, the celebrity chef in 2009.

Further building took place during Mr Oldroyd's period as Headmaster, under the guidance of Mr Brand. The Oakery, a brand-new kitchen and dining room, first opened for business in the Easter break when everyone, including parents, was invited to a free lunch. This dry run enabled the kitchen staff to produce a real lunch and iron out any potential problems with the brand-new equipment. The building was formally opened by chef **Gary Rhodes** in June 2009. He spoke about his philosophy towards food – local, simple, and above all, tasty. With the opening of the Oakery, the school decided to outsource its catering, so the cooks and kitchen staff were no longer directly employed. The same building housed a state-of-the-art performance studio for drama and music, with practice rooms, on the floor above. It had always been Mr Brand's ambition to eventually replace the portakabins with more permanent buildings, but it wasn't managed before he retired in 2010.

Over the years, the school had built up an excellent relationship with its landlord, the Knole Estate, to such an extent that they could plan for permanent buildings to replace the older buildings and portakabins, while the success of the school provided the Knole Estate with a regular and sustainable income. In 2010, the initial 10-year development plan was shared with Sevenoaks District Council so that this would not be a surprise to the planners when permission for permanent buildings was sought. A development committee comprising parents, alumni, and staff was established in 2012 under the chairmanship of **Mr Kevin Rush,** whose three children, **Andrew**, **Sean**, and **Kelsey** had been pupils, and **Mrs Liz Reading** was appointed as Development Manager. Mrs Reading managed the development fund as well as the school marketing strategies, and was responsible for the website, the newsletter, advertising, and the school media. In 2016, she

Phase 1 of the development plan: four new junior classrooms were completed in 2015. All of the rooms open onto an enclosed garden shared by KG and Reception, some of whom are seen here listening to a story read by Mrs Hougham *(Form RH)*.

was joined in the Development Office by **Mrs T.J. Richards**. Some of the most successful fund-raising events in recent years have been the golf days at Knole Park GC organised by **Mr Alan Bumstead**, a grandparent of current pupils and a member of Knole. The fifth such day in 2018 was the largest to date, with 21 teams taking part and over £16,000 being raised towards the Centenary Centre.

In 2013, the school set out a new 10-year plan for capital development with a total projected cost of nearly £4.5mn; the first phases of the plan were to be funded by the school, but there was the need for a considerable fund-raising effort. After three years as Chair of the Development Committee, Mr Rush stepped down in May 2015; his period of office ended with him officially opening the

A much-loved guest of honour, Mrs Sue Binnie, at the annual ball in 2015 – retiring after 22 years as The Prep's first and formative Nursery teacher.

The ball and two golf days raised a record amount towards the development fund that year.

The Pre-Prep hall extension was officially opened in January 2017 but before that the children's first glimpse of their newly completed hall was at a fun 'reveal' ceremony. A group of children from all forms burst through a wall of paper into the new space!

new Kindergarten and Reception classrooms, which had been phase 1 of the plan. He was succeeded by **Mr Rob Burgess** with **Mrs Marianne Ismail** as Vice-Chair, and the committee continued with its philosophy of setting a proper tone for fundraising by making it as personal as possible. Thanks to the committee's work and the generous support of its community, the school was able to make significant progress in the years leading up to its centenary with phase 2, a dining room with a kitchen and hall extension in the Pre-Prep, achieved in 2016, despite some issues with bats accessing the overhanging tiles in the old Stake Farm building. A development ball had been held in summer 2015, with Mrs Binnie as guest of honour to celebrate her 23 years heading the Nursery. Held in the school grounds, 285 guests enjoyed dinner, games, auctions, and dancing until the small hours. That year, with the ball, two golf days, and other regular events, over £53,000 was raised towards the development fund.

The Pre-Prep hall extension was opened in January 2017 by Mrs Shea, who was joined by staff and parents in celebrating the opening, with songs and poems performed by the children of the Pre-Prep. For this special occasion, the wonderful chef **Mrs Michelle Watson** created a gingerbread house replication of the new hall, and a new song was specially composed for the occasion by **Mrs Elizabeth Billingham,** the Pre-Prep music teacher.

During the early part of 2016, the school submitted plans to Sevenoaks District Council for a new sports pavilion, and launched a specific fund-raising initiative to raise £40,000 towards its realisation. Thanks to the generosity of some private donors and fund-raising from another successful golf day, family

Computer generated image of the new Centenary Centre due to open in 2019.

day, and the summer party, the target was reached just as planning permission was received. Specific donors' gifts included the fantastic digital scoreboard from the **Clarke** family and the clock from the **Poole** family. The grand opening was in the summer term of 2017, and it was fitting that the ribbon was cut jointly by **Miss Hazel Lovegrove** and **Mr Aaron Bailey** in recognition of all they had done, and continued to do, to promote sport at The Prep.

In October 2016, a Centenary Campaign was launched by the school and the Development Committee with the aim of being able to open in 2019 a new state-of-the-art building, the Centenary Centre, at the heart of the campus, combining classrooms, a science lab, an IT suite, an art studio and, at its core, a library, a café, and a social area for the senior school. This new building was to replace the portakabins in the senior school, which in 2017-18 had housed Years 6, 7, and 8. By 2017, when the plans were finalised by the architects Hazle McCormack Young, the estimated cost had almost doubled to £3.8mn; most of this was to come from the school's resources, and the campaign's aim was to raise the balance of £600,000. In March 2018, planning permission was received; by the end of the summer term 2018, the campaign's target was reached and building started in the summer of 2018 with the removal of the last of the senior school portakabins to a temporary location, as they were still needed as classrooms while the new building went up. Further plans for the early years of the next decade from 2020 include an atrium linking the old and new buildings in the Pre-Prep, a refurbishment of the older parts of Stake Farm, and an all-weather sports pitch.

Academic

Mr Oldroyd continued with Mr Oatley's vision for development. This included investment in technology, not only in the classrooms with interactive screens and the use of computers, but also the development of a website and using technology for better communication with parents. The academic results in 2011, Mr Oldroyd's last full year, were outstanding. From Year 6, **Thomas van Issum** was awarded a major music scholarship and **Lucy Eifion-Jones** a sports scholarship to Sevenoaks School; **Ellie Watts** received two scholarships, academic and sport from Kent College, and **Kate Dow** one for drama from the same school. Among the Year 8 leavers, **Oscar Gilbert** was awarded an academic scholarship from Sevenoaks, having already received one from Caterham; **Max Paillard** received an academic scholarship from Lingfield Notre Dame, but also chose to go to Sevenoaks; and **Maaike Veldhuizen** and **Isabel Turnbull** were awarded academic scholarships by Kent College. The academic results continued to improve. In the five years from 2014 to 2018, an average of 12 pupils per year left to go to Sevenoaks School, with many being awarded academic and other scholarships. In 2016-17, the school was awarded two academic, a drama, and a sports scholarship by senior schools at age 13 and three academic, two sports, and a drama scholarship at age 11. Six pupils were awarded 11+ places at local grammar schools. The results in 2018 were similar, with two academic scholarships to Sevenoaks together with an academic and a music scholarship to Sutton Valence from Year 8, and two exhibitions to Walthamstow Hall. Seven boys went on to Tonbridge that year from Year 8, the most since 2004, and six from Year 6 to local grammar schools.

In 2011-12, the Oak Award was introduced for Years 7 and 8 by Mrs Harrison to encourage pupils to get involved in their community, take on a new challenge, or do something creative. Many volunteered in their local community and took part in fund-raising.

Mme Clark organised the inaugural French exchange for pupils in Year 6. The exercise was an outstanding success, thanks in no small part to the hospitality and trust provided by the parents, topped with them organising a barbeque for the departing French students. By 2016, this had grown to such an extent that Year 6 spent a week in February at their exchange school, Ecole St Pierre in Lille, accompanied by Mme Clark and Mrs Jeremy, before hosting 42 pupils and teachers from Lille for a week in April. Trips for The Prep pupils in Lille included

left The gold, silver and bronze oak award badges.
right Year 6 at tea with French exchange friends in April 2016.

a visit to the Lille LAM art gallery and an evening tenpin bowling. While in England, as well as a busy week of activities at The Prep, the French group found time for excursions to Hampton Court Palace and Dickens World.

The dyslexia unit, which had been established by **Mrs Judy Bailey** in the 1980s, had broadened its scope over the years to incorporate helping children with other special educational needs. In 2001, **Mrs Sue Barton** retired as the Head of the Dyslexia Unit and Special Needs Co-ordinator to be replaced by **Mrs Rachel Copeland**, who headed the unit as Director of Learning and Development, overseeing the progress of pupils under her care right across the school. She was an extremely hardworking and diligent teacher, with an encyclopaedic knowledge of her field, who gave great support to the parents and was fully committed to the children. Mrs Copeland was succeeded by **Mrs Therese Wickham** in 2012, and the department is now run by **Mrs Helen Shere** and **Mrs Esther Beugeling**.

At the end of June 2016, there was a new initiative: a creative arts week bringing together art, dance, and music through inspirational artistic and cultural activities, displays, performances, and workshops, many of which were run by visiting professionals. All pupils from Nursery to Year 8, as well as other children from local primary schools, had a chance to enjoy the activities, which included: iPad orchestras, carnival dance workshops, puppetry demonstrations, circus skills classes, mask making, printing, drumming classes, and a large choral workshop. The artist-in-residence for the week, **Will Jordan**, worked with all classes on a sculpture of a large tree made from wire, which was displayed in the Oakery to commemorate the week and is now permanently placed in the garden outside the Oakery. There was also an exhibition of pupils' work for all to visit and enjoy.

Creative Arts Week exhibition, 2016. Year 5 fish and Year 7 figures in the foreground.

In 2017-18, the school's general knowledge team won the IAPS regional competition, the Year 6 scientists enjoyed success by coming home victorious from the prep school science competition at Tonbridge School, and a team reached the finals of the Greenwich University Robot Wars competition. iPads were rolled out across Pre-Prep and Prep classrooms, with the children making use of technology to enhance their learning, from researching topics to designing 3D houses.

For many years, the school had taken part in the UK Mathematics Trust Junior Maths Challenge, with up to 250,000 students across the UK sitting the challenge run by the trust. 2018 was the best year yet with 8 gold, 9 silver, and 19 bronze certificates awarded to Prep pupils. The challenge is aimed at Years 7 and 8, so the ten Prep pupils from Year 6 who achieved awards performed exceptionally well.

The Pre-Prep
When Mrs Shea retired in 2011, the Pre-Prep was fully co-educational, with 180 children in nine classes and a waiting list which, if they had chosen to, could have filled another class. There had been three sets of architects plans since 2001 to give the Pre-Prep the facilities it sorely needed; however, the emphasis was, not unnaturally, on improving facilities in the senior school. Mrs Shea's successor, Mr Pears, was lucky enough to see the first phase of the building completed in 2015.

The Pre-Prep celebrated the Queen's diamond jubilee with a garden party in the summer of 2012, complete with a picnic on the lawn, some wonderful music from the senior school musicians led by **Mrs Elizabeth Dwinell** and **Mr Jozik**

Pre-Prep's garden party at Stake Farm for the Queen's Diamond Jubilee, 2012.

Kindergarten nativity, 2007.

Twilight Nativity in the Pre-Prep, 2013.

Kotz, a 1960s routemaster bus, an appearance from an Irish guardsman, and a guest appearance from the Queen and Prince Philip – Mr Oatley and Mrs Shea in disguise! It was a fabulous day and a lovely time together for The Prep family. By a happy coincidence this was also the 25th anniversary of the Pre-Prep's move to Stake Farm, a further cause for celebration.

Christmas 2013 saw the first twilight nativity for the Pre-Prep with a procession of shepherds, kings, and angels who visited Mary, Joseph, and baby Jesus in the stable. It was wonderfully atmospheric and culminated in a nativity story from **Rev. Anne Le Bas**, vicar of Seal, and carols round the stable scene.

In June 2016, the school celebrated the Queen's 90th birthday and this was used as an opportunity to open the fantastic play fort in the Pre-Prep. The fort has a series of easy and not-so-easy challenges for the young children, who can amuse themselves with simple slides or challenge themselves with climbing on rope ladders. For many years, the teachers in the Pre-Prep have taken advantage of the school's beautiful setting and encourage the children to explore the fields and wood surrounding the school. In 2015 a dedicated nature trail was created, which included a pond and 'mini-beast hotel'. By 2017 an outdoor learning area, Forest School, was established on the senior side but is used by the whole school. The Go Wild club, as well as Kindergarten and Years 1 and 2, spend many happy hours under the supervision of **Mrs Sarah Woodgate** (KG teacher) and **Miss Cheryl Cashin** (Year 3 teacher) building camp fires and cooking, and practising outdoor skills and crafts. They observe the wild life and imitate the building of homes by birds and woodland animals from natural materials by constructing their own dens and shelters.

April 2018 saw a Pre-Prep staff reunion, some 80 current and former teachers and other staff from the past 30 years gathered for a celebratory lunch and entertaining speeches by Mrs Shea, Mr Pears, Mrs Cook, Mr Oatley, and others.

Year 2 in the Forest School. This outdoor learning area is sited on the senior side of the school and used regularly by all year groups. This and the Pre-Prep's nature trail were constructed by Mr Matt Tye of the ground maintenance team.

Drama and music

The senior school play in March 2006 was an ambitious production directed by Mr Harrison using the original text of Shakespeare's *Henry V*, but staged in modern times and based around the upcoming 2007 rugby world cup. The result was entertaining and enjoyable. **George Cloke** was a superb Henry V and all the actors created performances that reached acts of dramatic tension and fell to the depths of comic bawdiness. It was also the first school play to be staged in the round and the cast coped with this challenging staging with aplomb. **Mrs Yvie Cloke** and her team worked superbly in sourcing, creating and managing all the costumes.

Private Peaceful by Michael Morpurgo was another challenging production in the spring 2007 term, but helped by the fact that the novel on which it is based

left Private Peaceful, 2007, with a very effective projected back drop. *above* The Buddy Holly Story, 2008. All the music was performed live, including a unique performance by Mr Harrison on guitar.

was being studied for Common Entrance that year. **Joshua Chant** recalls having the difficult role of being on stage for the bulk of the production without speaking any lines. For the academic year 2007-08, a more expansive programme for school plays was introduced, with a senior play in December, a middle school play in March, and Year 3 plays in July, with the summer term to be rounded off with Year 8 directing Years 5, 6, and 7 in the house plays. The first senior production in December 2007 consisted of two performances, a comedy called *Half an Idea* and a farce called *Black Comedy*. In December 2008, *Buddy – The Buddy Holly Story* was an ambitious and extremely successful production by Years 7 and 8 with all the music performed live – quite an achievement! Mr Harrison had decided to stage this play when **Jack Ferguson** showed him how well he could mimic Buddy Holly. His subsequent performance in the title role and that of **Fred Roberts** as The Big Bopper were exceptional. Mr Culley revived his production of *Island* from some years previously for the middle school production in March 2009.

The plays put on by the school in 2010-11 were varied and challenging, too. The seniors produced a compelling production of *Frankenstein*, a frightening prospect – and not just because of the horror. The middle school's offering was a musical and a regular favourite, *Oliver*, and it was a great credit to the Year 6 pupils who took on the difficult roles of characters such as Fagin, Bill Sykes, and Nancy, and presented them with aplomb and no shortage of acting skills. Year 3's play was *Little Red Riding Hood*, while the Pre-Prep's productions were *The Toybox* and *The Fairy Tale Show*. The senior play in 2012 was unusual in that it was specially written for the cast, as well as being produced, by Mr Collings. *The Mariner* was a tale of love, murder, and vengeance, with everyone in Years 7 and 8 taking part. Years 5 and 6 had an extremely talented group of actors, and the opportunity was taken to put on two separate plays, *Faith, Hope, Charity and Cream Cakes*, written by Mr Culley, and *The Emperor's New Clothes*, produced with a modern twist and filled with laughs.

The 2009-10 issue of *The Prep Post* featured an article on the senior school's peripatetic music teachers who supported Mr Kotz, who had joined that year as Head of Music. These included Mrs Dwinell, who had been teaching mainly violin but also cello and recorder at The Prep since 1986, **Mr Dan Clews** (guitar), **Mr Michael Grant** (clarinet), **Mr Ben Grove** (guitar), **Mrs Jane Hanna** (brass), **Mr Anthony Roberts** (singing), **Mrs Kathy Sheldrick** (piano), **Mrs Jane Tandy** (flute), **Mr Mark Thompson** (drums), and **Mr Alan Tower** (piano). In the Pre-Prep, a long-serving peripatetic teacher is **Miss Kathy Johnson** (piano and recorder). Always willing to help out whenever an extra pair of hands is needed, she is still involved in music at the school – as are a number of the other teachers.

Drama and music continued to go from strength to strength, from the delightful Pre-Prep nativities to the senior drama productions, from smaller intimate musical performances in the Oakery to larger concerts in the Hall, Seal Church, and the Three Arts Festival, with the pupils never failing to impress

above The senior production of *Frankenstein* in 2010 was staged in the round and used projected images.   *below* In 2011 the middle school performed *Oliver*.

through their ability to get up on stage and demonstrate their talents. A particular highlight of 2017-18 was welcoming the pupils from Seal St Lawrence Primary School to two afternoon workshops at The Prep, where the orchestras collaborated and performed for parents at the end of these sessions.

School life

Two new events were introduced in Mr Oldroyd's first year, Prep Idol and Prepchef, both of which went on to be regular features in the school calendar. The first Prep Idol concert, organised by Mr Pears and Mr Collings, was a highlight early in the 2006 summer term. It was open to local rock groups with members aged 13 or younger and the winning band, *Optimism*, came from Judd, TWIGGS, and

Prep Idol 2015 winners *Walk Away*, a four piece band of Year 7 pupils from The Prep.

Bethany schools, and included some Prep alumni. Proceeds from the evening were in aid of HOPEHIV (now called, from 2015, WeSeeHope). Meanwhile, Prep Proms–the school's own talent show–continued to draw an appreciative audience and unearth previously unknown talents.

Later in that summer term, Prepchef took place, which was an inter-house competition for Year 8 pupils. Each team was given a £20 budget to spend in Sevenoaks and was required to produce a Kentish meal for a panel of three judges: **Mrs Pat McCann**, ex-mum and professional cookery demonstrator, **Mr Andre Woodward** from the *House on the Hill* restaurant, and **Mrs Wendy Woolf**, the senior school cook. The first winner of the competition was Seal with a meal of roast chicken and a summer fruit mille feuille. By 2008, the competition had been renamed House Masterchef.

The design of *The Prep Post* evolved over the years as technologies changed. The first full colour magazine was published in 2008, a marked development from the simple paste-up pages of text with a line drawing or black and white photograph of the early 1990s. It is no coincidence that Mr Chant with his knowledge of IT was initially part of the production team and another computer specialist, **Mrs Helen Hamilton-Brown**, mother of **Natasha**, **Oliver** and **Ben**, was enlisted to help. She also worked on the editorial side with Mrs Oatley who was

For 2009-10 *The Prep Post* adopted the landscape orientation of the new prospectus.

first acknowledged as an assistant editor of *The Acorn* in 1987 and continued to gather, edit and proofread all the magazines until she retired, when she swapped the three jobs for just one, proofreading.

Mrs Sarah Harris joined the team in 2004 taking over the layout and design of the regular issues (25 and 26) to enable Mrs Hamilton-Brown and Mrs Oatley to concentrate on their last magazine, *The Souvenir Post* in 2005 for Mr and Mrs Oatley's retirement. Mrs Harris continued for the next 12 years, over which time the magazine became an annual publication and saw a number of changes in its content and design. In particular it offered each class in the Pre-Prep a double page spread to fill with whatever they wanted. Inspired by the Pre-Prep teachers' endeavour to include every child on their pages, for issue number 35 it extended the same format and principle to every year group in the school, making *The Prep Post* unique amongst school magazines (as far as we know). Throughout this period various members of staff helped with different aspects of the task, most notably Mrs Underwood, Mrs Thomas, Mr Harrison and Mr Collings. An invaluable volunteer, **Mrs Jayne Hoare**, mother of **Dominic** and **Natasha**, did the bulk of the typing (handwriting deciphering!) and shared the proofreading. Another volunteer, **Mrs Katherine Bright**, mother of **Oliver**, **Toby** and **Phoebe**, joined the team in 2012 on the gathering and editorial side.

Issue number 40 for 2015-16 was Mrs Harris' last one as a member of the production team and the last one designed and prepared for print in-house. For issue number 41, the editorial team was **Mrs Sarah Hillman** and **Mrs Antonia Gawn**, with special thanks to Mr Collings, Mrs Richards, and Mrs Reading in the Development Office, and Mrs Oatley, still proofreading the school magazine after 30 years.

The Social Entrepreneurs Project (SEP) was a ground-breaking initiative co-ordinated at the school by Mr Pears. It combined enterprise education with social responsibility by encouraging pupils to set up and develop their own small businesses, with profits going to support the HOPEHIV charity. Each pupil in

SEP 2013
One of two initiatives devised by the most successful group that year involved working with a company, *'Phil' the Bag*, which collected clothing and textiles for recycling. Their mass school-wide collection alone raised over £530.

Year 8 was given a £10 seed capital with the challenge of turning it into £100 or more. Working in much the same way as traditional business entrepreneurs using initiative, creativity and all resources at their disposal, they set about exploiting a target market with the intent of making as much profit as possible. In small groups, pairs or as individuals, pupils were encouraged to put together simple business plans, keep accounts and document their progress. They were given advice from visiting speakers and took part in workshops organised by the local Amherst Rotary Club, who also generously provided the seed capital.

OFSTED commented in a report, 'Pupils make an outstanding contribution, both to the community and their own future economic well-being, through their involvement in the [SEP]'. The project spread beyond The Prep to other schools and was supported by people in the world of business and entertainment, with two notable patrons in the England cricket captain **Claire Connor** and the rugby international **Lewis Moody**. In 2007-08, the SEP pupils showed great creativity and resourcefulness. There were so many different events vying for time that the school had to publish an SEP calendar. This advance notice for parents and pupils made the whole exercise more efficient, while further integrating the SEP into the life of the school. The shield awarded annually for the most innovative, independent, and committed entrepreneur (not the one who made the most money) went to **Adam Bennett** for his Sevenoaks Prep teddy bear. Together with the proceeds from Prep Idol, £5,000 was raised for HOPEHIV that year.

In 2007, when the Scout Association held their centenary celebrations, Mrs Topliss, who was involved in the movement, took a whole school assembly in campfire style. Mr Oldroyd was rather alarmed when Mrs Topliss built a campfire inside the sports hall. She did not, of course, light it, but she encouraged the children to sing some songs and talked about being members of the scout or

Year 2's camp day 2010
above Mrs Topliss leading the campfire singing.
right Tents pitched, wood collected, fire lit, lunch soon.

left Healthy Living Week in 2009 included a themed fun run for The Haller Foundation, one of The Prep's favourite charities.   *right* Circus Week, summer 2010.

guide movement. She did say, 'if you ever see a little plume of smoke from the Pre-Prep grounds you will know that Year 2 are cooking their own sausages for lunch'. Out of this arose the idea for an annual camp day, which has happened ever since. Many, many parents have come to enjoy these days, which have seen tents go up, wood collected, camp fires built, potatoes peeled, lunch cooked and washed up, and wonderful campfire sing-songs enjoyed before taking down tents and going home to get in the shower! Since 2012, Kindergarten have also enjoyed their own annual camping day and Year 6's overnight 'Leavers' camp has become a tradition – but is definitely more barbecue and party than campcraft!

The boxer **Chris Eubank** visited the school during the 2009 healthy living/ healthy eating awareness week organised by Mrs Oldroyd. He spoke at length to the assembly about the need to have personal moral qualities and standards to guide one's life. He then quoted from three poems that encourage dignity, conscience, and determination. These were *If* by Rudyard Kipling; *The Guy in the Glass* by Dale Wimbrow; and the anonymous *Don't Quit*. He recommended the three poems as ones that children might print out, stick on their wall, and repeatedly read until the philosophy in them is appreciated.

After Common Entrance was over, Year 8 welcomed 45 American students from Ohio, Pennsylvania, and Florida to the school for a day of activities and an exchange of views. The activities jointly followed by the two groups included drama, art, ICT, and cricket! It was a good opportunity for the students to appreciate that, although separated by an ocean, students are students wherever they live. All the participants learnt a little about how the other country's educational systems worked and how they differed from each other.

There was a distinct circus theme to the 2010 summer term. The Pre-Prep production of *Ffinlo*, a short musical play by **Mary Gentry** that was aimed at infants and lower juniors, provided immense enjoyment to performers and audiences alike. The plot involved Santa bringing his helpers to the circus, but as the performance is set to begin, Ffinlo the clown has lost his red nose, but the show must go on! The SEC circus-themed summer ball was held in a beautifully decorated big top with dodgem rides to add to the excitement.

The school handwriting competition and Year 7's poetry challenge both involved a circus theme. The poems were required to demonstrate the use of techniques such as alliteration, assonance, internal rhyme, sibilance, and similes. At the end of the summer term, circus week included two days of interactive workshops with Kent Circus School. All the children from Nursery to Year 8 were entertained by the performers and had the opportunity to try a variety of skills, from juggling and plate spinning to tightrope walking. At the end of the week, family day included tightrope walking, circus tricks, and displays by Kent Circus School, as well as the usual bouncy castle, rounders and cricket matches, tea and barbeque.

The school fashion show in 2013 achieved new levels of excellence. Each year group took to the catwalk to strut their stuff. Every performance was entertaining and the energy of the crowd truly electric. As well as hearing a collection of old and new songs and seeing some excellent dance moves and actions, the audience was treated to a special performance by Prep Idol winners *The Enlisted* who performed *Hysteria* by *The Muse*. As ever, each class and their teachers deserved tremendous credit for the inventive and entertaining show they put on.

In January 2014, a new venture was started with the creation of the School Council. This was chaired by the joint heads of school with two class representatives

The newly formed School Council in 2014. Note Years 7 and 8 in their dark blazers: these were introduced in 2012 to signify being the senior pupils of the school.

from Year 2 and above, who were asked to bring ideas from their peer groups for ways in which the day-to-day life of the school could be improved. These ranged from forming a cookery club, having a tuck shop on site, more skinny fries on the lunch menu, and chocolate digestives for the Pre-Prep! This was followed in 2016 by the establishment of a Staff Council.

A new innovation in January 2016 was the introduction of a breakfast club, welcoming pupils from 7:30am each day to enjoy a delicious and healthy breakfast and provide early activities.

The school had, for many years, supported local and international charities. In the official accounts of the Charitable Trust that runs the school, one of the aims stated by the Governors in their report is to develop the school's involvement with local, national, and international charities. In 2015-16, the different events and the range of charities supported showed the school's commitment. The autumn term began with pupils 'rowing' an impressive 119 miles in ten days as part of Dandelion Time's virtual 'rowathon' from Marden to Madagascar, and adding over £2,000 to their project supporting local families with emotional issues. This was closely followed by the Pre-Prep's harvest festival supporting Age UK and a local foodbank. The Christmas bazaar, the children's Christmas cards, and angel boxes all supported The Salvation Army. In the spring term, over a hundred children braved the four-seasons-in-one-day weather of the spring walk in aid of Demelza Children's Hospice. It was the turn of international charities in the summer term, with Prep Idol attracting a sell-out crowd of over 500 who were entertained by 13 acts from the school competing in the battle of the bands. The eventual winners were Year 8's *Social Media Sins* with considerable sums being raised for the charities HOPEHIV and The Haller Foundation, both of which support children in schools in Africa. The same charities were supported by Year 8's Social Entrepreneurs Project. Finally, at the end of term, a collection was organised for the Loaves and Fishes Foodbank. Overall, more than £10,000 was raised in a single year for charity.

There was an individual piece of charity fund-raising as part of Children in Need in November 2013. **Joe Hayward**, one of the head boys and hooker for Sevenoaks RFC U13s, had his head completely shaved at assembly, with Mr Collings in charge of the clippers. His target of £1,500 was easily exceeded, with a final total of almost £2,100 going to two charities, Children in Need itself and the Brain Tumour Charity (his great uncle had been diagnosed in 2011 with an incurable brain tumour).

Sport and recreation

There was continued development in girls' sport with the appointment of Miss Lovegrove as Head of PE in 2005. Miss Lovegrove is a talented sportswoman herself and has, in the last few years, played cricket for Kent and the MCC and hockey for Sevenoaks Hockey Club. Inevitably, in 2009

U13 mixed hockey team with Mr Smith and Miss Lovegrove, 2010.

cricket was added to the girls' repertoire of games for the summer term. Netball was played in the autumn term from under 8s upwards with the 2011 season reported by Miss Lovegrove to be the best she had seen since she had arrived – the U9 and U11 teams reached five tournament finals between them. In the spring term, hockey was played by both girls and boys and the girls played pop lacrosse. In 2018, some girls played tag rugby for the first time. The summer term saw the girls playing rounders and cricket, and taking part in athletics events. In March 2016, girls from Years 5 to 8 participated in their first football tournament at Hazelwood School and in that summer, girls joined the after-school cricket club for coaching and net practice with visiting Kent coach, **Mr Phil Pass**.

The Prep's Thomas Trophy cross-country event continued to attract over 600 children from schools across south-east England each autumn to take part in six events for boys and girls across different age categories. The event in October 2005 was especially successful for The Prep, as **James Simmons** won the U13 boys race (out of 120 runners), leading the school to second place. In December, he went on to win the Knole run, an event organised by Sevenoaks School for teams across the south-east and beyond, this time leading 170 other runners home. In recognition of these performances, he received the Ken Smart Trophy. Throughout these years there were other notable runners and teams. The Thomas Trophy yielded individual gold medals for **Declan Sinclair** (U9 in 2007), **Benjamin Harvey** (U9 in 2013), **Olivia Breed**, (U9 in 2013 and 14, U11 in 2015 and 16), **Vita de Munck** (U13 in 2012 and 13), and a team gold for the U9 boys in 2013.

The 2006 rugby season was successful throughout the school, the highlights being four wins out of five for the colts A, including an epic win against The New Beacon. There was a thrilling draw 36-36 for the 1st XV against Yardley Court

Cross country team for the 2015 *Brenchley Relays* when the girls' fours ensured an overall silver for the squad. At their next event The Prep's *Thomas Trophy*, the girls' teams won another team silver.

and a very creditable second place in the annual Solefield 10s tournament. **Sam Maynard** scored a staggering 38 tries in the season, easily a school record.

The 1st XI cricket had a successful 2006 season with several hard-fought matches and a second place in the Bethany 6-a-side tournament. The individual highlight of the season was an unbeaten century by **Ben Richardson** against Vinehall.

Fencing was introduced as an after-school option in 2006-07. **Fenella McLuskie**, who was in Year 5, had been fencing outside school and was climbing through the grading system. Her success, that of another pupil, and finding out that there were others who were already participating in the sport, convinced Mr Oldroyd to contact **Mr Alex Brentall**, a fencing international and passionate fencing coach. Within a few weeks, 50 pupils were attending the after-school sessions under Mr Brentall's tuition. That year, Fenella was runner-up in her class in the SE regional championships. Ten pupils took part in the national prep schools' tournament, which involved over 250 fencers from 49 different IAPS schools. The Prep girls came sixth equal and the boys seventh equal; Fenella won her class, while **Rob Hudson** and Oscar Gilbert got through to the last 12. Overall, this was a fantastic achievement.

If you gauge any football season by the results achieved, then 2009 was a hugely successful one for the school as a whole and the 1st XI in particular. The firsts began well enough in their first two games with impressive wins, but the first real indication of their potential was shown at The New Beacon 7-a-side tournament in late September. They reached the final of this competition for the first time in many a long year, coolly defeating the hosts on penalties in the last group game. The final itself was disappointing as a very strong Dulwich Prep side were too good, but it set the tone for the season. The 1st, 2nd, and 3rd teams only lost a handful of games and played magnificently in the process, a fitting send-off for Mr Brand, who had coached the senior boys for several years and retired at the

above The successful 2009 First XI football team with their coach, Mr Brand, in his retiring year—but only as the school bursar—his coaching continues!

below First XI cricket team with Mr Lemmon, 2010.

end of the 2009-10 academic year, although he was asked to come back to coach the 1st XI the next year and is still doing so today. The U13 netball squad also had a fantastic season, winning the St Michael's tournament without losing a game. Senior boys' football had a good term in 2015 when, for the second year in a row, three teams were fielded with the 1st XI having an unbeaten season.

The 1st XI cricket team of 2010 was the most successful for a long time and in **Leo Cammish** and **Jamie Richardson** had two outstanding prospects. Leo scored

550 runs at an average of 137.5 and played for Sussex U13 as a wicketkeeper, while Jamie averaged 24.3 with the bat and 10.8 with the ball. In the colts side, **Rhys Joseph** had the unusual distinction at that level of scoring an undefeated century. He went on to Sevenoaks School where he captained the cricket 1st XI in 2018. In other sports, **Paul Wood** came second in the national U14 long jump and Isabel Turnbull was the national sabre champion and represented Great Britain at U17 level, a remarkable achievement.

If there had been a cricket honours board at The Prep, **Max Denniff** in 2013 would have had his name up there for batting after a quick-fire 107 against Rose Hill. With an 82 not out and several half centuries, his devastating batting contributed to one of the better seasons in terms of results. He was also a star of the rugby 1st XV and on the athletics track, winning the county hurdles race for his age group. Unsurprisingly, Max was awarded a sports scholarship to his senior school, Bethany. Now at Durham University, he has taken up hockey seriously and plays for England U18s.

By 2013, tennis was enjoying a higher profile again at The Prep with after-school clubs for all age groups under the guidance of KG teacher **Mrs Lorna Belither,** an LTA coach. The school competed in some inter-school competitions and eight lucky students had a day at the Wimbledon championships that year.

2017-18 was an outstanding year across all sports. The U13 girls' hockey team had an excellent season and there were great strides made by the girls in both football and cricket, with the latter replacing rounders in the games curriculum. This development allowed the house cricket tournament, for the first time ever, to combine both the boys' and girls' results, as they all played the same summer sport, regardless of gender. The boys 1st XI football team recorded five wins out of seven while the 3rd XI was unbeaten. It was an excellent rugby season with an undefeated second team and excellent results for the colts. Although the 1st cricket XI had a mixed season in terms of results, there were some sparkling performances as the season progressed, one of the highlights being an outstanding 110 not

2017 girls' house hockey competition.

above Bude field trips: a kayaking exercise in 2005 and with Mr Baynes in 2008.
below Bushcraft outdoor adventure and team-building weeks, 2013 and 2017.

Years 7 and 8 trip to the First World War battlefields and monuments, 2014.

out from **Max Lindsay** against Kings Rochester. This was not only his maiden century but the first ever in the school history made by a Year 7 pupil. The third of July 2018 was an amazing day for **Esme Harrison**, **Oliver Bartlett**, **Olivia Breed**, and **Sam Breed** who represented Kent at the IAPS National Athletics Finals in Birmingham. Their outstanding performances in long jump, 100m, and 1500m events earned them two silver medals and a bronze medal between them. Their performance was just reward for their hard work and dedication throughout the year. In the same year, the school's Year 6 gymnasts were the U11 IAPS national gymnastics champions, a superb achievement.

Outings and holidays

The Year 8 geography field trips to Bude in September continued. Mr Oldroyd, in his end-of-year speech in 2006, commented that not only did these trips allow the children to collect the necessary data for their geography Common Entrance work, but they also gave the chance for the senior pupils to bond and form a cohesive leadership team for the forthcoming year. He emphasised the opportunity that The Prep, in the form of the prefect system, gave the children to play constructive and guiding roles in helping the school run as efficiently as possible. Having been run by Mr Ratcliffe for several years, in 2006 he had handed over to Mr John Baynes, so it became a science trip rather than a geography field trip. It made little difference to the leisure activities such as swimming and kayaking as he, the children, and the staff still got very wet every day.

However, although these trips had been very successful, it was felt by 2010 that a move to somewhere closer to home, thus cutting out two days of travelling, was called for. The last Bude trip, in 2009, had been a resounding winner with a coastal study, canoeing, abseiling, surfing, and a visit to the Eden Project where the pupils took part in an excellent workshop on biomes. As Year 8 pupil **Matthew Moore** wrote, 'Even though Bude was hard work I thoroughly enjoyed it and would love to go again'. The new location was the JCA Adventure Centre at Pestalozzi village, about ten miles north of Hastings. The geography fieldwork was completed in the nearby River Cuckmere and ended on a windswept Beachy Head. The week continued with a series of activities including pond dipping, fencing, archery, zipwire, abseiling, and wall climbing. One evening included a night walk and campfire, and another a disco.

In the following years, the Year 8 field trip went to different places in the south-east, but all followed a similar pattern. In 2012, the trip was to Ashburnham Place, a Christian centre near Battle, and included a trip to Bodiam Castle. Since 2013, the field trip has been in Oxfordshire with the Bushcraft Company, where the pupils live in the woods for a week at the start of the autumn term. Since 2006, there has been a bi-annual trip for Years 7 and 8 to the First World War battlefields and memorials in Normandy and more recently a combined history and French language trip to Bayeux for Year 7.

All year groups enjoy a variety of field trips and outings throughout the year.
above left Year 5 surveying the River Darent in Horton Kirby for a geography project, 2015.
above Year 4 at Penshurst Place, 2016.
left Year 2 at The National Gallery, 2014.

After many years of the annual ski trips going to Barèges in the Pyrenees in the spring half-term holiday, in 2007 Mr and Mrs Pears, along with Miss Briggs (later Mrs Jeremy) decided to take the trip back to Austria. Miss Briggs had discovered the resort of Alpendorf close to the town of St Johann im Pongau and the resort allowed for Easter skiing rather than February half term, and thus a more relaxed holiday. This also brought the dynamic of April Fools' Day occurring regularly during the holiday. This became synonymous with **Mr Howard Cloke** (a regular attendee of the trip for many years, having four boys at the school) and his very willing child helpers. It is amazing how many different uses he found for eggs – Mr Pears was the first to suffer with his hard-boiled egg being swapped for a soft one when he wasn't looking – and the adults definitely didn't want an early fall on the slopes, as eggs were slipped into the pockets of salopettes and jackets!

This new destination proved a great success, with a combination of superb instruction on the slopes and après ski entertainment at its heart. Mr Oldroyd's and Mr Bowen's après ski games and competitions from the trips to Barèges were replaced with trips to bowling arcades, spa baths, and ice cream parlours. There was no doubt that The Prep ski trip had found a new home; however, there was to be one change for subsequent years, as the accommodation was upgraded to a super luxury hotel in the resort, saving the bus journey to and from the town every day. How the owners of the magnificent Hotel Sonnhof agreed to accommodate the trip is a mystery, but everyone loved being able to ski out of and back to the hotel's door, and the wonderful indoor/outdoor swimming pool – allowing for the children to roll around in the snow and jump back into the warming waters! The adults also thoroughly enjoyed the new surroundings – the food, spa facilities, and accommodation were superb and great value. The only major drawback experienced on the 2008 trip was with the opening of Terminal 5 at Heathrow. The Prep party was very 'lucky' to be some of the first passengers to fly out of the new terminal. Everyone was safely and efficiently delivered to Salzburg airport, and the coach was waiting to take them on the short transfer to the resort. However, half the bags did not arrive and people had to wait until their return to the UK to be reunited with them as they arrived, one by one, at The Prep in the weeks that followed! Fortunately, Mr Oldroyd had the school's credit card and organised a trip to C&A to clothe those who arrived bagless – even though some of the children rarely changed from the clothes they travelled in, thus putting the pong into Pongau!

With Mr and Mrs Pears moving on, Mrs Jeremy continued to run the trips with the help of Miss Lovegrove and Mr Collings; however, the introduction of a summer water sports trip saw this and the ski trip run on alternate years. The final trip to Alpendorf was in 2013.

In 2016, Years 6, 7, and 8 had a trip to Jersey with the pupils trying their hand at all manner of adventurous activities ranging from coasteering to abseiling, from banana boating to stand up paddle boarding. All pupils rose to the challenge before them and conquered various fears along the way.

Alumni

Having just driven to championship victory in the 2006 Lloyds TSB Insurance British Formula 3 International Series, **Mike Conway** chose his old prep school as the venue for the BBC South-East News coverage of his success. In a specially extended school assembly, Mike was interviewed for the cameras by Mr Oatley, who had been Headmaster during Mike's years at The Prep. He was showered with endless questions from an excited audience who wanted to know everything from what motivated him to what he ate before a race. Mike also kindly took the time to sign many autographs – mainly in contact books and pupil planners! Mr Oatley produced a rediscovered article by Mike from a 1997 *Prep Post* where Mike had been asked to explain his passion for racing, which was presented to Mike to his great delight. Some of Mike's teachers were interviewed by the BBC; Mr Ratcliffe summed it up perfectly in saying, 'His success lies in that he knew what he wanted and has whole-heartedly gone for it'.

James Graham-Brown, who had left The Prep in the 1960s, became a schoolteacher after a successful period as a professional cricketer. He was Head of Truro High School for eight years before taking up the position of Head of the independent girls' school, The Royal High School, Bath. He retired in December 2009 after 11 years in the position, and has since written more than 20 plays under his pseudonym of Dougie Blaxland. His one-man play *When* *the Eye Has Gone*, about the life and death of the cricketer Colin Milburn, was performed around England in late 2016, including performances at all 18 county championship cricket grounds and at Sevenoaks School.

In 2013, **Kieran Hayward** (2004) became another alumnus to become an international sailor when he took part in the round-the-world Clipper Race as a crew member of the Great Britain. The team won the second leg of the race from Rio de Janeiro to Cape Town and came second overall. In 2014, recorder player **Sophie Westbrooke**, who had left in 2010 to take up a music scholarship at Sevenoaks School, was a finalist in the BBC's Young Musician of the Year competition, playing Gordon Jacob's *Suite for Treble Recorder and Strings*. Also in 2014, Isabel Turnbull (2011) was selected for the Great Britain U17 fencing team to take part in the European championships. In 2013, she had been the GB Cadet Women's sabre champion.

The first alumni drinks get-together was held in November 2017 at the Antelope pub in Sloane Square, attended by some 30 alumni, staff, and friends. It is planned to make this a regular event.

Other schools and organisations

When Mr and Mrs Oatley retired in 2005, one of the presents they received was a cheque towards a round-the-world trip. As part of this they visited the area worst affected by the 2004 tsunami in Sri Lanka in January 2006 to see for themselves how the £35,000 raised by schools in Sevenoaks under the offices of the Senahasa Trust had been spent. This trust was a local one set up by a 77-year old grandmother from Columbo, **Mrs Carmen Ratnatunga**. The Oatleys met her and her family, who showed them the devastation and how the trust was spending the money raised wisely and efficiently. When he returned, Mr Oatley was able to come back to Sevenoaks and, with pictures and film, show the school how much had been achieved.

In 2009, The Prep announced plans to build a relationship with St John's primary school in Sevenoaks, where Mr Oatley had recently become a Governor, as part of their charitable obligations – this is a worthwhile link for both schools, as resources and expertise can be shared.

Years 5, 6, 7, and 8 were fortunate to be able to attend the annual Sevenoaks School Innovation Week in March 2016. This event had been running since 2009 and enabled thousands of local Kent schoolchildren to enjoy a variety of scientific shows and activities. In 2016, over 12,000 students took part in over 50 shows during the week. Of The Prep pupils, Year 5 attended an exciting *Music to Our Ears* lecture on the basics of sound and the latest developments in music technology; Year 6 took part in a coding workshop, in which they wrote their own version of a computer game, *Flappy Birds*; and Years 7 and 8 found out how science and technology was used to fight crime, as well as being an opening into a future career in engineering. Years 5 and 6 also had the opportunity to participate in a *BBC micro:bit* workshop, which included designing racing cars. The week ended with an amazing science show on the Friday evening, which many pupils and parents attended and greatly enjoyed.

The school continued to foster and expand its links with local communities. As it approached its 100th anniversary, it was still supporting a range of charities including the Salvation Army, Demelza, the Dandelion Trust, HOPEHIV (WeSeeHope), The Haller Foundation, Help for Heroes, and Seal Church. The school's facilities were used by a diverse group of local sporting organisations, many of which ran sporting and summer camps open to children from other schools. These included ones run by Charlton Athletic FC, Activate (for cricket), Otford Netball Club and a fencing training school. Clubs such as Sevenoaks Town FC and Tonbridge Knights Basketball used the facilities for training, and groups such as the Three Arts Festival committee held its meetings at the school.

For the last few years, The Prep has been host to the annual Sevenoaks Amherst Rotary Club Cyclo Sportive annual challenge cycle ride for charity. In September 2017, 550 cyclists set off on a 130k, 80k, or family 40k ride into mid-Kent. On their return, there was a lunch of soup, baguettes, fruit, and cake waiting for them at the school. Over £10,000 was raised for Hospice in the Weald and Macmillan Nurses. The 2018 event saw the youngest ever participant when **Johannes Bleeker**, aged 7 and a pupil at The Prep, cycled the 40k course with his father **Derek**.

Parental involvement

The Social Events Committee (SEC) continued to go from strength to strength under the chairmanship of Mrs Yvie Cloke. In addition to the long-standing events such as bonfire night, the Christmas bazaar, quiz night, the Pre-Prep grand prix and, at the end of the school year, the ball and family day, by 2007 **Mrs Louisa Makepeace** was leading walks in London and locally, and **Mrs Rebecca Eifion-Jones** was organising visits to London theatres. All these activities had tremendous support from the parents and staff, and the ones aimed at the children were thoroughly enjoyed by all who took part.

In 2008, the need for an updated summer uniform for girls in Years 3 to 6 was identified by Mrs Oldroyd. With the help of **Mrs Karen Stanford**, mother of **Joshua**, **Jordan** and **Jake**, who under her maiden name **Karen Millen** was a renowned fashion designer a blouse and skirt were designed to flatter and fit the girls, who were thrilled with the new uniform. Through The Prep's links with The Haller Foundation, a UK charity working in Kenya for which Mrs Eifion-Jones was a fundraiser, the old school shop stock of dresses was sent to a school in Mombasa along with some football kit.

A Masked and Moustached May Ball was held at the Spa Hotel in Tunbridge Wells in the summer of 2009, which was a special occasion with a delicious dinner and a wonderful band, *The Spring Feathers*. The parents, friends, and staff who attended got into the spirit of the theme, producing several extremely embarrassing photographs when looked at in the cold light of day. That year, now under the chairmanship of **Mrs Jane Rigney**, the fund-raising efforts of the SEC provided an audio-visual system for the Oakery, four visualisers, a data harvest logging kit, a video-microscope, and an outdoor table tennis table.

Embarrassing? Some guests wore the look rather well!

Following the change of chair from **Mrs Anneli Nix** to **Mrs Kathryn MacPherson** in 2015, the SEC, which largely looked after social events, evolved into a Parents' Forum and a separate Events Group. While still working together, the two separate bodies had specific roles. The forum took responsibility for effective two-way communication between parents and the school through the year reps. The reps enthused people to attend events, arranged rotas to man stalls, organised coffee mornings and nights out while, at the same time and perhaps most importantly, welcoming new parents to the school. Concerns raised by the forum during its first year, 2015-16, included the perennial subjects of uniform, lunches and, inevitably, the car park, but also covered opportunities for girls to play cricket and the communication process. The events group did not get off to a good start as bonfire night was rained off, but the traditional events of the Christmas bazaar, quiz night, a golf day, family day, and the summer party all went well, and the funds raised funded a new minibus for three years and a cricket bowling machine, while also contributing to the pavilion fund.

A new event organised by the school in September 2015 was Grandparents Day, when many of the pupils invited their grandparents to the school for a morning. In 2017 it was held in May, when the itinerary included an enjoyable

tour of the senior school given by Years 7 and 8, refreshments in the Oakery, spending time in the new outdoor learning area, and attending a Pre-Prep assembly where all 120 visitors joined in a rousing rendition of the school song. It is now an annual event.

The first Grandparents Day held in 2015 included a session of classroom activities in the Pre-Prep.

Looking Backwards and Forwards

The four quarters of a century

Sevenoaks Prep has done remarkably well in its first hundred years, growing from a small add-on for little boys in Sevenoaks School to a vibrant, independent, co-educational school providing an education, both academic and in life, for nearly 400 girls and boys. At first glance, its history divides conveniently into four quarters of about 25 years each: the first from the foundation of the school in 1919 up to the end of the Second World War; the second a quarter century of recovery and establishment of a traditional boys' preparatory school, culminating in the move to Godden Green in 1969; 25 years when the school expanded into its wonderful site with new and refurbished buildings, the Stake Farm lease, a dynamic Headmaster and his wife, the addition of a nursery, co-education, and a strong commitment to family and the community; while the last 25 years have been a period of both consolidation and advance, latterly under two heads who had also been pupils, seeing the replacement of temporary buildings with innovative, permanent ones and the reinforcement of the family ethos with the school's *Way of Life* and *Golden Rules*.

Visionaries

This, however, masks those moments when someone of vision, usually the Head at the time, took a decision which changed the direction of the school. In 1922, **Rev. C.G.** and **Mrs Mary Holland** bought 4 Vine Court Road and moved the school from The Cottage in Sevenoaks School to its own premises. Just after the Second World War, **Mr Miles Jukes** suffered the double blow of his co-Head, **Mr Frank Morgan**, leaving, followed closely by a debilitating accident which left him bed-ridden. He had the foresight to ask

Mrs Agnes Lang to take over as Headmistress, a move which led to a period of consolidation but, above all, survival.

In about 1967, **Mr Kenneth Ely**, the then Headmaster, began to look for new premises for the school, realising that the cramped site in Vine Court Road had ceased to be suitable. He had the vision to take a lease on Fawke Cottage and its grounds in nearby Godden Green, and move the school there in January 1969. When he handed the school on to **Mr Edward Oatley** some ten years later, there had been little development on the site, but Mr Oatley soon got to work with an ambitious refurbishment and building programme which, because planning and other constraints restricted the school's ability to build permanent structures, resulted in a series of wooden buildings and, later, portakabins.

Mr Oatley recognised that the demands of parents were changing and that the school needed to change. From the start, he took a hands-on approach to running the school and his wife **Janet** was a massive support over the years, taking on many roles. Mr Oatley was ahead of the trend in lowering the school's joining age, going co-educational, and in establishing a separate Pre-Prep with its own Head. In 1981, he invited **Mrs Rosemary Cooke** to join with her nursery, thus bringing in much younger children, including some girls. In 1987, the opportunity to acquire the lease of Stake Farm gave the school the chance to have a permanent site for its burgeoning Pre-Prep, including the Nursery; in 1991, he announced that the school would become fully co-educational by 1998; and in 1992, **Mrs Marjorie Shea** re-joined the staff as Head of the Pre-Prep.

Mr Oatley made use of parents and parents' contacts in developing the fabric of the school and involved the parents, through various groups, in its running. Parents took the lead in organising bazaars, summer balls, and family days, and assisted in the production of plays and taking children on annual ski trips. While it is invidious to name some and leave out many others, two deserve a special mention. **Mr David Fry** was a massive help to Mr Oatley during the first building phases of the 1980s and 1990s, and **Mrs Christa Dando** was the inspiration behind many of the early social and fund-raising activities, including the school shop.

In 2001, one of Mr Oatley's long-standing aims, to have a permanent brick-built, multi-purpose school hall, was achieved. After his retirement in 2005, **Mr Philip Oldroyd**, who followed him as Headmaster, and **Mr Luke Harrison**, who has been Headmaster since 2012, continued with the vision of housing the school in permanent buildings. Under these Headmasters and the Governors, the school, in co-operation with its landlord the Knole Estate and the local planning officers, developed a ten-year plan in 2010, which was revised in 2013. The building housing the Oakery dining room and music and drama studios had already been opened in 2009. Stake Farm was expanded to provide an enhanced home for the Pre-Prep and the Centenary Centre, at the heart of the campus and combining classrooms, a science lab, an IT suite, and art studio, is planned to open in 2019. Soon, the days of wooden buildings and portakabins will have ended.

The school's ethos

The school's prospectus from the mid-1920s had concluded, 'The general aim of the school is to provide a real home school under ideal conditions, with only a limited number of boys, thus ensuring individual care and attention in every case. The boys are taught to learn and *think*, not merely to acquire a certain number of facts, while it is recognised that the true aim of education during these important years of a boy's life is the development of moral character'. Apart from expanding from 'a limited number of boys' and going co-educational, this conclusion still underlies the school's ethos.

This ethos is summed up in an extract from the latest accounts for the charitable company that owns the school, which says that the school's principal aim is to provide an education for life and to achieve this through the Pre-Prep *Golden Rules* and the *Way of Life* in the senior school, together with an academic approach that focuses on the need of the individual. In addition, the school sets out to encourage every pupil to be the best they can be, both inside and outside the classroom. Its ethos emphasises strong pastoral care of pupils, nurturing each one and supporting parents and children alike.

For **Mr Donald Smith**, the philosophy of The Prep was summed up with his story from the 1990s about a very quiet boy who didn't shine academically and wasn't sporty; he was not too sure of himself, someone who just quietly went through life. Mr Oatley found out that outside school he was learning to tap dance, and with **Mrs Mary Shefford**'s help and Mr Oatley's arm-twisting – 'come on, you can do it' – the young boy got up in front of the school and performed this amazing tap dance that Mr Smith thinks probably changed his life. Mr Smith tells this story to every child, probably several times. From then on, in assemblies, the school regularly asks children to talk about what they are doing outside school and bring in medals and certificates they have been awarded, or just talk about what they have taken part in.

Mr Ian Culley, who retired in 2018 after a long association with the school, wrote, 'I don't think the school will ever lose its atmosphere, it's engrained in the school's DNA. I do think there is a shift in the parents' attitude but by and large they still want their children to be at The Prep because they do like the family atmosphere and this is certainly not going to change overnight. It is also interesting how many ex-pupils and staff still have connections with the school, with their children or grandchildren as pupils. The school is still doing well.'

Robert Agnew, an alumnus who left in 1987, summed up the ethos of The Prep when he wrote, 'for me, the strongest memory through all my years was softer, social skills, an abundant sense of friendship and community. The Prep was a special place which marked it out from any other school. It always felt that we were a unique, close knit family – among teachers, pupils and parents – school was a way of life, an extension of home which brought so much pleasure to me and my immediate family. There was always a genuine warmth of encouragement for all pupils, a sense of identifying the good in everyone and celebrating the willingness to 'have a go' at anything – not least inspired by Edward's leadership in his myriad of sporting and charitable endeavours. There was an undertone (not an edict) through my time at The Prep of strong values – to be competitive, to do one's best, but most importantly to 'have a go' at everything, explore, stretch ourselves – with humility, while respecting all around you. And when things went wrong, we had to face failure and understand that others were inevitably better than us, but our direction was to go on and find our own strengths – which Edward was always so quick to call out – at an assembly, end-of-term service and prize-giving – in one of his many inspirational speeches. The Prep was a way of life for us, not just in our formative years. Uniquely, the school was successful at nurturing, while promoting the skills necessary to advance us all in preparation for later life. I have many other fond memories of The Prep, which I believe maintains a unique bond between fellow pupils, parents and staff with whom we were fortunate to have shared precious time at this most special of schools.'

The pupils

In December 2017, all pupils aged from 6 to 13 were asked to write down, 'What do you like best about The Prep?' and 'What is your best memory of The Prep?' The answers were recorded with only the minimum of editing and are included on the CD that accompanies this book. The most common words used by the children were: play or playing, 61; friends or friendly, 46; kind, 32; nice, 27; help and helpful, 26; food including lunch, 18; drama and plays, 17; art, 12; music, 12; and songs or singing, 10. In this book, it has been impossible to record the many achievements of the pupils, all of whom do amazing things every day, whether it is solving their first maths question, writing a poem, learning their part for a play, passing a music grade exam, scoring a goal, or just making friends. These have all been recorded in the school's magazines – *The Acorn* from the 1960s to 1992, and *The Prep Post* since then.

Inspiration

'Inspire' or 'inspiration' are words which have cropped up frequently in this book and in the memories of alumni and staff. The references range from the love of learning coming from **Mr Colin Pugh** in the 1960s and of enjoying writing with **Mrs June Biggs** in the 1980s, to **Mrs Angela Lucas**' English teaching over many years.

Mrs Shefford inspired hundreds of children with her music and drama teaching, many of the children entering and starring in the Three Arts Festival. There have been other long-serving staff such as Mrs Lang who took over as Headmistress in the very difficult post-World War Two period, **Mr Peter Larcombe** taught boys about history, art, and religion, as well as about life both inside and outside the classroom, and Mrs Shea inspired both children and teachers as Head of the Pre-Prep. Pupils are still having their minds stretched with Mr Smith's general knowledge quizzes and Mr Harrison's weekly debates.

Sport, and especially cricket, was taught by the long-serving and excellent cricketers in their time, **Mr Ronnie Marchant** and **Mr Ken Smart**, over several decades. The achievements of sporting alumni continue to inspire: the international sailors **Ian Walker**, **Mark Sheffield**, and **Kieran Hayward**, the international cricketer **Paul Downton**, the racing driver **Mike Conway**, **Jon Clarke** for challenging himself to compete in wheelchair marathons despite his spina bifida, and many, many others.

The future

By its nature, a history always looks back, but it is worth looking at where The Prep is at the end of its first century and what its prospects are going forward. In an article in *The Sevenoaks Chronicle* in 2014, **Mr Bob Ogley** had written about the school and his words are still true today: 'The present head of The Prep is Mr Luke Harrison. Mr Harrison is one of four former pupils of the school who are currently members of the teaching staff. The school's ethos remains the same – education at The Prep is for life, not just the classroom. The school's teaching is based on the understanding that children are individuals who mature at different times in different ways. An ethos of strong pastoral care and constant two-way communication with children and their parents results in a reputation for producing happy, well balanced, high achievers'.

In detail, the aims of the school, as recorded in its formal accounts, are to:
- ensure the safeguarding of all pupils;
- afford all pupils opportunities to succeed both inside and outside the classroom;
- recruit and retain the highest calibre of teaching and support staff who embody the *Way of Life*;
- provide excellent pastoral care and nurture outstanding relationships between staff, pupils, and parents;
- be a warm, friendly, family school; provide individualised learning, which is best provided in small class sizes;
- utilise technology to aid student learning and to ensure that information and communications technology provision complements existing and future teaching strategies;
- progress the school's commitment to bursaries; develop the school's involvement with local, national and international charities;
- maintain and enhance the school's environment and facilities; and
- maintain a balanced budget approach to managing the financial resources and expenditures.

In 2019, the school finds itself with modern permanent buildings set in beautiful grounds, an established senior management team, caring teachers and staff, nearly 400 energetic, happy children, a vibrant partnership with the parents, strong links with the local community, and an enviable reputation for its academic, sporting, and extra-curricular activities. It looks forward optimistically to the next hundred years.

above Way of Life tree

Mr Luke Harrison
Headmaster, 2011–

Mrs Helen Cook
Head of Pre-Prep, 2016 –

opposite: top 1870 map showing both buildings and an aerial photo pre 2001.
     middle Aerial photo of Senior School, 1990s.
     bottom Computer generated aerial image of the Centenary Centre.
overleaf 'Look back and compare'

Look back and compare

Scenes from earlier decades alongside photographs taken in the last two years.

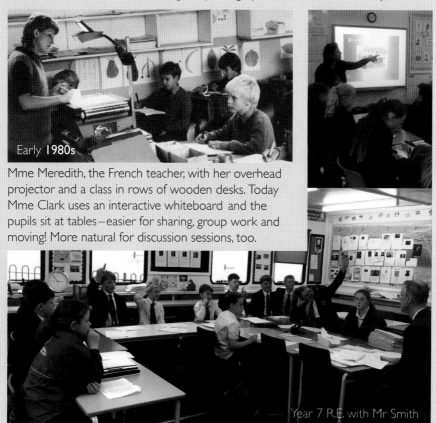

Early 1980s

Mme Meredith, the French teacher, with her overhead projector and a class in rows of wooden desks. Today Mme Clark uses an interactive whiteboard and the pupils sit at tables—easier for sharing, group work and moving! More natural for discussion sessions, too.

Year 7 R.E. with Mr Smith

Science without safety glasses! Early 1980s

Early 1980s

This photo of the old senior school kitchen caused much consternation because the view from the serving hatch is wrong. The reason? There is no serving hatch, the boys used to go into the kitchen itself to collect their meals – unimaginable today. The hatch was installed a short while later behind where Mrs Burden *(centre)* and her assistants are standing. Today this room is the Development Office.

The cafeteria style Oakery opened in 2009 offering a choice of hot meals, daily salads and fruit, with space for many more to eat lunch at the same time.

Lunch in the Pre-Prep is just one of many activities enjoying the spaciousness of the newly extended hall.

Christmas 1990s

1966 sports day at Knole Paddock: teacher attire included jacket, bow tie and pipe.

1965 at Knole Paddock

Sports day on the school field in sight of the 2017 sports pavillion, with an array of gazebos and staff attired in their blue games kit–baseball cap optional!

1994 Reception

Kindergarten

Having been on duty at all the Kindergarten and Reception nativities for at least the last 25 years, the trusty manger is still going strong.

circa 1990

The stage may be bigger and there are girls but the orchestra still has staff and pupils performing and the uniform is still a white shirt. Now, however, mobile phones recording the event punctuate the darkened ranks of the audience.

Senior summer concert in the hall

Appendix 1 Pupil and staff numbers 1963-2018

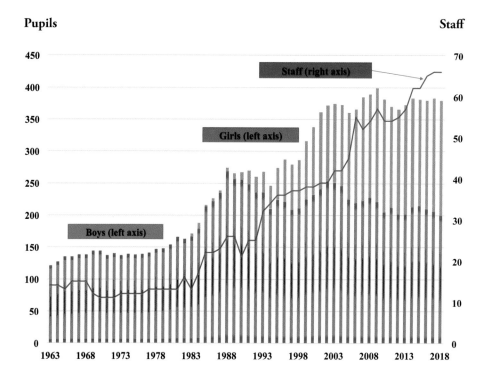

Appendix 2 **Class structure and names**

	Mrs Garrod	(b) 1920s	Mr Jukes/ Mr Ely	Mr Oatley (to 1992)	1993 onwards (e)
Rising 13			(c) U6	8	8
Rising 12			L6	7	7
Rising 11			5	6	6
Rising 10		3	4	5	5
Rising 9			3	4	4
Rising 8		2	2	3	3 (g)
Rising 7	(a) KG		1	2	2
Rising 6		1(KG)	KG	1	1
Rising 5				(d)KG2	Reception
Rising 4				(d)KG1	KG
Rising 3					(f)Nursery

(a) KG – Kindergarten. When Mrs Garrod started the school, it was described as a 'Kindergarten for boys aged 5-9'.

(b) A prospectus from the 1920s says the school was for 'little boys age 5-10'.

(c) Under Mr Jukes some boys stayed to 13 or even older.

(d) Mrs Rosemary Cooke joined with her Kindergarten in September 1981, which included girls.

(e) Up to 2005 each year group was called 'Form 8' etc. From 2005, in conformity with national curriculum nomenclature, the year groups were called 'Year 8' etc.

(f) Mrs Sue Binnie joined in September 1993 to start a formal nursery.

(g) In September 1992 Mrs Marjorie Shea re-joined the staff to be Head of the Junior School and renamed it the Pre-Prep. The dark line shows division between senior school and junior school (Pre-Prep).

Appendix 3 The Way of Life and The Golden Rules

The Prep's *Way of Life* started as a school song written by Mrs Emma Pears before the Millennium celebrations, and this was then augmented by a list of values and principles pupils should adhere to in the course of their life within and outside the school, which is sometimes depicted as a tree with key words as foliage (see page 266). There was a similar list for the Pre-Prep, *The Golden Rules*.

Song

Boys and girls from around the world
Are welcome in this school
Each has their own gift to bring
To teach us one and all

To think of each other and not just of ourselves
Looking out for a friend in need
To encourage each other with honesty and love
Makes a better world for you and me

I make choices every day
On how I will behave
True and helpful things I'll say
Being kind always

To think of each other and not just of ourselves
Looking out for a friend in need
To encourage each other with honesty and love
Makes a better world for you and me

After school or out at play
When no-one's there to see
I just want to be someone
That I am proud to be

To think of each other and not just of ourselves
Looking out for a friend in need
To encourage each other with honesty and love
Makes a better world for you and me

The Way of Life

I ought to think at all times how my every action will affect others in my life: parents, friends, relations, teachers and everyone younger than myself.

I ought to treat all others as I would want to be treated myself, and take a personal interest in how other people feel.

I ought not to touch anything that is not mine, unless with permission or unless I am being helpful.

I ought to be polite to everybody at all times and be positive in my actions.

I ought to take responsibility for my own maturity by ensuring I assist in the smooth running of the school and my home.

I ought to take ownership of my studies, concentrating and applying myself to achieve to the best of my ability.

I ought to obey in the right spirit the instructions of my teachers and parents.

I ought to report immediately any damage or unfortunate behaviour to my teachers and/or my parents.

I ought to remember that in life my aim should be to solve problems not cause them, to build bridges rather than knock them down, to trust others and to be trusted, to put the needs of others first and mine last, to improve and make better whatever or whoever I am involved with.

I ought, at all times, to be totally honest to myself and to others.

The Way of Life Tree

Words from the tree: brave, positive, caring, resilient, inspirational, friendly, mature, interested, thoughtful, helpful, responsible, trustworthy, respectful, selfless, polite, kind, considerate.

The Golden Rules

1. Be gentle
2. Be kind and helpful
3. Be honest
4. Listen
5. Work hard
6. Look after property

Appendix 4 **Songs and poems**

Over the years, a number of songs and poems were written, or existing ones adapted, specially for school events. A selection of these is set out below.

Mr Oatley's efforts from a boy's perspective by Jeremy Hill (1981)

Mr Oatley's our head
He's really jolly nice,
When he asks for help
We'll be there in a trice.
He built a new building.

With the help of dads and mums,
They pushed and pulled and dragged and banged
Until they had sore thumbs.
Mr Oatley's very brave.

He stayed up day and night,
Painting with his little brush
To make the hall just right.
Spooks and ghouls are not his scene.

He never takes a fright,
He'd hit them with his paint tin
If they attacked him in the night.

Now the work is finished
It is a superb hall.
We can fit everybody in it
And there is room for us all.

Mrs Bryony House's limericks on her retirement (1984)

At first all the lessons were taught,
By Ely and staff at Vine Court,
But times since have changed,
The school's re-arranged,
It's on other folk now I report.

There is a young lady called Perks,
Teaches class 1 their physical jerks,
'Up straight' she will call,
When addressing them all,
Tap dancing is one of her quirks.

An elegant lady we see,
(Her name being Madeleine D.),
Teaching class 1 and 2,
Their handwork to do,
And all the fine art that you see.

Sue Bullock's replaced dear old Chris,
(A teacher all of us miss),
Sue's gentle and kind,
But knows her own mind,
What more can you ask for than this?

Beth Sadler is everyone's pet,
From her you know what you'll get,
A sparkle, a smile,
A lady of style,
But watch out if she gets upset.

There's Madame Laidlaw you must meet,
'Mon Dieu', to see her's a treat,
She's pretty and fair,
Teaches French with a flair,
And the boys worship her, at her feet.

Peter Larcombe comes here day by day,
He teaches us all how to pray,
He sings with loud voice
'Come on and rejoice',
Before we go on our way.

The under nine team made its name,
By beating New Beacon – what fame!
For loud the calls rang,
From Culley and Crang,
'Play up, play up – play the game!'

Pretty Mary is playing a tune,
For the choir to perform here in June,
She produces a play,
Almost every day,
The practices take place at noon.

Mrs Lucas has been here for years,
She's watched boys throughout their careers,
Her English is swell,
Her Latin as well,
But cricket's her forte, one hears.

Mr Pegg we have recently found,
To teach science lessons all round,
The children all learn,
Their bunsens to burn,
And the physics of light waves and sound.

If you're hungry you know where to look,
Janet Oldroyd's a beautiful cook,
She's secretary too,
And between me and you,
Does all the odd jobs in the book.

We now come to Mrs Biggs, June,
Whose services here are a boon,
She's been here a while,
And teaches with style,
She'll do all the English quite soon.

James Cooke is really retired,
But when the Headmaster enquired,
If the boys he would teach,
With a toffee for each,
He came back, and they were inspired.

We've other kind helpers here too,
The gardeners, the cleaners – too few,
The cooks that we need,
David Clark to help read,
Music teachers, and jolly Andrew.

But Edward's the boss of it all,
Looks after us well, large or small,
He's done such a lot,
See what we have got,
A music room, art room and hall.

Dear colleagues, boys, friends of this school,
I now must stop playing the fool,
My job here is done,
It has been such FUN,
Good luck and God bless you all.

'Sounds' by Luke Harrison (1986)

Silence,
My world's aslcep, The moment before the dawn.
Suddenly,
The birds awake,
And silence is gone.
Noise!
My world's awake,
A milkman clatters by.
Tunefully,
A postman whistles his song,
And car radios switch on.
Cacophony!
The noise is at its peak,
Voices, engines, whirring wheels,
Dusk,
At last silence has come!
I welcome my world of sleep.

To Ronnie, Mike and Janet with love and thanks from Mary (1992)

Two 'property ladies', viz Janet and Ronnie,
When working backstage found the least thing so funny,
That helpless with giggles they snorted and hooted
(Their infectious mirth sounds so genteelly muted)
Wrestled with table and fences, a bike,
Given a hand by the dear, stalwart, Mike;
What great fun was had and, oh, how well things went
But long they'll remember that stripy tea-tent!

Dan and Martin Clews' song about The Prep (1993)
(to be sung to the tune of *Wild Rover*)

The school is set in the jewel of Knole Park
and the buildings they vary from manor to ark
But the spirit is willing and the flesh is strong
Eat your heart out New Beacon, we're the best all along!

And it's one year later
We're all sat here again
But Form 8 they are leaving
All ready for victory and fame.

We've all sorts of masters from English to Art
They're all keen as mustard and playing their part
Messrs Pegg, Smith, Bowen and Hankey to boot
Anderson, Ratcliffe, Valentino for sport.

The ladies are charming as one might expect
Mesdames Homer and Wilkes teach their art to effect
Eloquent grammar from Jeffers and Low
And musical seeds Mrs Shefford does sow.

Bursar Barnard, he's banker and whips in the cash
and keeps us in line all the time at the dash
Without him we're told the school fees would be free
But his organised boss, Ready Teddy, disagrees.

The Senior Concert is swinging along
The boys are all queuing to give us their song
The orchestra's playing all bent to their task
Just you get in tune, Mrs Shefford does ask.

For Janet and Edward it's the end of a term
One more chapter of boyhood is written in stone
Form 8 now they're ready to take on the best
And it's thanks to The Prep that they'll all pass the test.

Ode to Mrs Mary Shefford, unknown author (1996)

On the first term at Sevenoaks
Our school head gave to me:
A long-suffering pia-no

On my second anniversary
My husband gave to me:
Two woolly dogs
and a long-suffering pia-no

On the third year at Sevenoaks
We all learnt to our cost:
Three Fine Arts
Two woolly dogs
and a long-suffering pia-no

In her life here at Sevenoaks
Mrs Shefford gave to us:
One hundred and forty-four detentions

Three Fine Arts
Two woolly dogs
and a long-suffering pia-no.

In 1986
The yearly play was shown:
Twenty-six long years
One hundred and forty-four detentions
Three Fine Arts
Two woolly dogs
and a long-suffering pia-no

In her last year at Sevenoaks
Her last play was performed:
Old Father Time
Twenty-six long years
One hundred and forty-four detentions
Three Fine Arts
Two woolly dogs
and a long-suffering pia-no

Over the many years groups
Have been formed:
Choirs and orchestra
Old Father Time
Twenty-six long years
One hundred and forty-four detentions
Three Fine Arts
Two woolly dogs
and a long-suffering pia-no

In her ninth year at Sevenoaks
An accompanist was found:
Gwen Bowen
Choirs and orchestra
Old Father Time
Twenty-six long years
One hundred and forty-four detentions
Three Fine Arts
Two woolly dogs
and a long-suffering pia-no

In the hall one evening
A sound could be heard:
Ten tappers dancing
Gwen Bowen
Choirs and orchestra
Old Father Time
Twenty-six long years
One hundred and forty-four detentions
Three Fine Arts
Two woolly dogs
and a long-suffering pia-no

Now there's one person missing
Who helped Mary's life along:
Maureen Perks
Ten tappers dancing
Gwen Bowen
Choirs and orchestra
Old Father Time
Twenty-six long years
One hundred and forty-four detentions
Three Fine Arts
Two woolly dogs
and a long-suffering pia-no

And this is the last verse
I do promise you:
Goodbye Mrs Shefford (hankies)
Maureen Perks
Ten tappers dancing
Gwen Bowen
Choirs and orchestra
Old Father Time
Twenty-six long years
One hundred and forty-four detentions
Three Fine Arts
Two woolly dogs
and a long-suffering pia-no

Things Go Better with PrepSki Solar – The Bard of Barèges (1999)

It is that time of year again,
When Sevenoaks Prep board that Tunnel train,
To seek the sun and the snow of France's hills,
Anticipating all the thrills and spills
Of a ski trip to Barèges.
It seems to be the holiday of our dreams.

Calais. Paris. The route unravelled.
It doesn't seem that far we've travelled.
We arrive quite early – well what do you know,
The whole place is covered with lovely deep white snow!

So off we trot; skis and poles at the ready,
To find out if our ski-legs are still steady,
The snow is great, the kids are good,
Après-ski is excellent, that's understood.
The week flashes by, each day an event.
The company, scenery, it's all heaven sent.

But come to an end as all good things must,
We pack up our cases which have been gathering dust.
Back on the bus for the long journey home,
We came, saw and conquered like they once did in Rome.

With a smile and a laugh and a hint of a tear,
Just try and stop me from coming back next year!!!!

On Mr Oatley's retirement (2005)
New words by an unknown author to *Just Like Eddie* by Heinz and
My Teddy Bear by Elvis Presley

Ooooooh Ohhhh OOOOOOOOO etc.

Wherever we go, whatever we do
Oatley's made us ready
We read what he said, we went where he led
Just like Eddie
Ooooooh etc.

We go on a bike, we go where we like
Oatley's made us ready
We go for a swim, and we follow him
Just like Eddie
Ooooooh etc.

We watch football, play for the school
Oatley's made us ready
We tackle and fall, we miss the ball
Just like Eddie
Ooooooh etc

[change to My Teddy Bear *tune]*

Edward we have placed our children in your care
You have took 'em by the hand, and led them everywhere
Oh can they be, Your Eddie Bears?

Janet wants to stay, your ever loving wife
Spend her time around you, and be there all your life
Oh she can be, Your Eddie Bear

We don't want to play for Watford
Watford play too rough
We don't want to play for Man U
Cos Man U's got a team that's good enough
We wanna be, Your Eddie Bears
You have led us by the hand, and took us everywhere
Oh let us be, Your Eddie Bears

[change back to tune of Just Like Eddy *after Ooooooh etc.]*

Ooooooh Ohhhh OOOOOOOOO etc.

We travelled around, some foreign land
Oatley's made us ready
We went around, and hit the ground
Just like Eddie
Ooooooh etc.

Wherever we go, whatever we do
Oatley's made us ready
When leaving school, won't obey the rules
Just like Eddie
Ooooooh etc.

We're ending this song, it's much too long
Oatley's probably ready
We'll sit and laze, in the sunny haze
Unlike Eddie
Ooooooh etc.

Appendix 5 **Memories CD**

Included with the book is a CD of memories of the school from alumni, staff and friends. These have been sourced from: the original text of *The Half & Half's*; memories written for the commemorative magazines published for the reunion in July 2000 and for Mr Oatley's retirement in 2005; responses to requests for memories sent to alumni and staff in 2017; tributes to leaving staff in editions of The Acorn and The Prep Post; and anything else available! These memories and tributes have been reproduced mostly as written, with only minimal editing of obvious typos and spelling errors.

The CD also includes responses to two questions asked of every pupil from Forms 2 to 8 in December 2017–what he or she thought was the best thing about The Prep and what their favourite memory (to date) was. The answers have not been edited!

Lastly, the CD includes transcripts of Mr Oatley's diaries from his overseas cycle rides between 2001 and 2018 that raised funds for the school and various charities.

As the CD is in PDF format, it is possible to find topics by using the search text function.

If you do not have access to a CD reader, the contents of the CD are available on the school website http://www.theprep.org.uk/homc. For the password please contact the school's Development Office on development@theprep.org.uk using Centenary Memories in the subject line.

Index of people